Multinationals and European Integration

Regional Policy and Development Series

Series Editor: Ron Martin, Department of Geography, University of Cambridge

Throughout the industrialised world, widespread economic restructuring, rapid technological change, the reconfiguration of State intervention, and increasing globalisation are giving greater prominence to the nature and performance of individual regional and local economies within nations. The old patterns and processes of regional development that characterised the post-war period are being fundamentally redrawn, creating new problems of uneven development and new theoretical and policy challenges. Whatever interpretation of this contemporary transformation is adopted, regions and localities are back on the academic and political agenda. *Regional Policy and Development* is an international series which aims to provide authoritative analyses of this new regional political economy. It seeks to combine fresh theoretical insights with detailed empirical enquiry and constructive policy debate to produce a comprehensive set of conceptual, practical and topical studies in this field. The series is not intended as a collection of synthetic reviews, but rather as original contributions to understanding the processes, problems and policies of regional and local economic development in today's changing world.

Multinationals and European Integration

Trade, Investment and Regional Development

N.A. Phelps

Regional Policy and Development Series 14

Jessica Kingsley Publishers
London and Bristol, Pennsylvania

Regional Studies Association
London

First published in the United Kingdom in 1997 by
Jessica Kingsley Publishers Ltd
116 Pentonville Road
London N1 9JB, England
and
1900 Frost Road, Suite 101
Bristol, PA 19007, U S A

with
The Regional Studies Association
Registered Charity 252269

Copyright © 1997 N.A. Phelps

Library of Congress Cataloging in Publication Data
A CIP catalogue record for this book is available from the Library of Congress

British Library Cataloguing in Publication Data
Phelps, N.A.
Multinationals and European integration: trade, investment and regional development. – (Regional policy and development; 14)
1. International business enterprises – Europe 2. Europe – Economic integration 3. Europe – Economic Conditions – 1945 –
I. Title
338. 8'884

ISBN 1 85302 353 1

Printed and Bound in Great Britain by
Biddles Ltd, Guildford and King's Lynn

Contents

List of Tables

List of Figures

Acknowledgements

I am grateful to the department of City and Regional Planning at Cardiff for funding the research upon which this book is based. I must also thank staff at the many companies who responded to the postal survey and took part in interviews.

A number of people deserve thanks, but none of the blame, for their various inputs to this book. Thanks to Jeremy Alden and Kevin Morgan for their interest in, and encouragement with, the research. I am grateful to Jeremy Howells, John Lovering and Max Munday for commenting on chapter drafts and providing advice. Janice Cole and Pat Rees prepared the diagrams and typed parts of the manuscript. Thanks to Alison Simmonds for typing the bulk of the initial chapter drafts and for keeping me amused with some novel terminological concoctions!

Several friends must also be thanked for their support for the researching and writing of this book. Thanks to Mark and Jutta Hepworth, Graham Sadler and Teresa Connolly, and Rob Imrie and Sarah Fielder for providing me with accommodation from which to carry out research in London. Cheers to Gary Higgs, Mark Tewdwr-Jones, Patrick McVeigh and Sean White, among others, for many beers and much tolerance.

Finally, I am grateful to the following organisations for granting permission to use and reproduce copyright material: Office for Official Publications of the European Communities for the material in Figures 3.1, 4.1, 4.2 and 4.3; Oxford University Press for the material in Figure 3.1; and the Welsh Office for the material in Table 5.4.

Foreword

This book represents my first venture on the subjects of multinational corporations and European integration. The empirical material contained in this book was intended as an initial and modest exploration of the impact of European integration on the restructuring of multinational manufacturing companies.

My interest in the role of multinationals in processes of economic integration in Europe developed hand in hand with my teaching a postgraduate option course on European integration and industrial Restructuring in the Department of City and Regional Planning at Cardiff. The research was conceived during the first two years of that course (sessions 1992/93 and 1993/94) and carried out in the subsequent two years (sessions 1994/95 and 1995/96).

During this time, and despite the intense academic interest in the impact of the Single European Market, it seemed to me as though there was very little detailed empirical work on the contribution of multinationals to European integration. There seemed little to bridge the gap between, on the one hand, econometric studies and aggregate analyses of trade and investment statistics and, on the other hand, retrospective and generalised interpretations of industry or company patterns of restructuring. Very few studies appeared to be asking detailed questions about the organisation of multinationals operating in Europe and how and why they make decisions regarding the reorganisation of production on a European-wide basis. A number of specific research interests are therefore brought together in this book. First, I was intrigued by the lack of studies concerned with the extent of inter-plant rivalries and decision-making regarding rationalisation and sourcing within multinationals despite the prevalence of multiplant operations in Europe. Second, my teaching on the subject had alerted me to the existence of sub-European market clusters and the misnomer of the Single European Market. Finally, my own existing research interest in issues of the embeddedness of multilocational firms suggested that the process of corporate restructuring accompanying European integration was one likely to be characterised by considerable inertia.

Quite apart from the usual revealed inadequacies with the research design, there are a number of more general limitations with this study. For instance, the research concentrates mainly on production issues and has less to say about the non-production activities of multinationals. The research also adopts an essentially economistic outlook on the process of economic integration in Europe and is much less disposed to considering the cultural, social and political bases to such economic processes. Finally, the book does not address itself to the recent impacts of the latest enlargement and relations with Eastern European countries.

This book is intended primarily as an academic contribution to the debate about the role of multinationals in European integration and regional development. As such I hope it will be of interest to students and scholars interested in the organisation of multinationals and/or European issues.

N.A. Phelps
May 1996, Cardiff

CHAPTER 1

Introduction

Coincident with the rhetorical arrival of the Single European Market (SEM) at the start of 1993, Maytag's Hoover subsidiary announced a relocation of production from Dijon in France to Cambuslang in Scotland (Taylor, R., 1993a). The relocation provided a vivid example of the dynamic effects of European integration on the activities of a multinational company – the sorts of effects that are supposed ultimately to benefit EU consumers and promote industry competitiveness.[1] However, Hoover's decision also prompted fierce criticism in France and began a debate regarding the influence of regional, national and EU policy on the location and quality of multinational investment.

Cases like Hoover's relocation periodically make a spectacle of processes of regional economic integration; processes which are altogether more insidious. The Hoover case focused attention on a quite limited set of issues regarding choice of location and regional, national and supranational policy affecting the competitive-ness and mobility of multinational investment (Goodhart, 1993; Ramsay, 1995).[2] On the face of things, the Hoover case appeared to be a prime example of 'social dumping' in the context of national variations in direct and indirect labour costs and in attitudes towards the social chapter of the 'Maastricht Treaty' – at least this was how it was widely interpreted at the time. Yet other contingent factors clearly played some part in the decision to relocate and, in particular, to relocate to an area of lower overall labour costs. Virtually at the same time as Hoover's decision

---

1 Although the term European Union (EU) is used in the text, this book does not consider the implications of fiscal and monetary union implied in the term. The book concentrates on the implications of European integration culminating in the effort to complete the common market. The expression EU(6) is used to refer to the original six members of the EEC and EU(9), EU(10) EU(12) etc. to refer to successive enlargements.
2 The term multinational is used in this book instead of the term transnational. The latter is certainly more precise than the former in terms of defining the possible range of multinationals in terms of the geographical spread of their operations. However, the term multinational is perhaps more accurate than the term transnational as a description of the current nature and structure of most firms with international operations which rarely transcend or are independent of national economies in the way implied in the term transnational (see Hirst and Thompson, 1992).

to relocate, Nestlé made a decision to relocate in the opposite direction from Scotland to Dijon, France (Taylor, R., 1993b). Nestlé's decision appears to have been based on issues of market access rather than labour costs and serves as a reminder of the potential diversity of motives for shifts in production including, for instance, access to markets, skilled labour and certain material inputs. Hoover and Nestlé are just two in a steady, if small, stream of such international shifts most of which receive much less publicity and the motives for which may be less clear.

Furthermore, the impression left by the spectacular shifts of production exemplified by Hoover and Nestlé should not obscure the fact that the majority of multinationals remain attached to existing production locations. For example, there are a large number of intra-national shifts in production which have some connection with processes of European integration. These also receive little attention but constitute an important element in the restructuring of EU industry. Such intra-national relocations and transfers of production highlight the extent to which firms, multinationals included, remain tied to particular locations as centres of consumption. The largest number of relocations are, of course, intra-regional. Whilst few of these may have an explicit connection with European integration, they nevertheless highlight the fact that firms are tied to locations as centres of production; one of the main reasons being to retain skilled labour and avoid re-incurring the non-recoverable sunk costs associated with training.

The integration of national markets within the EU brings with it both pressures, and opportunities to reorganise production within multinationals. In turn, these reorganisations have important implications for the quality of manufacturing investments in, and trade performance of, particular regions and nations.[3] Yet relatively little is known about the basis on which companies make decisions regarding restructuring for the Single European Market and the actual and possible impact of regional, national and EU policy to enhance industry embeddedness and competitiveness in particular regional settings. It is with these questions that this book concerns itself.

Background

Regional economic integration is perhaps the most salient feature of the contemporary international economy. It is most accurately conceived as an ongoing economic and political process but is also conveniently interpreted as a state of affairs such that the process can be divided into a number of stages. The differences between the two ways of conceiving of regional economic integration can be illustrated in a couple of ways with reference to Europe. First, what is today referred

---

3   Throughout this book the separate and distinct manufacturing establishments of
    multinationals in Wales are referred to variously as investments, operations, factories and
    plants (see also Chapter 5).

to as the European Union (EU) was once referred to as the European Community (EC) and before that as the European Economic Community (EEC). This re-titling seems to bear little relation to the state of affairs reached at various times in the EU. The title European Union as applied today is certainly inaccurate. It is instead a signal of future intentions regarding economic union. Second, the Single European Market did not come into existence on the 1st of January 1993. Indeed, with a small number of the original 279 measures (plus a small number of subsequent measures) remaining to be adopted by the Council of Ministers and with a larger number of directives yet to be transposed into national legislation (Barnes and Barnes, 1995: 77) let alone enforced at the start of 1995, it remains to be fully established. In other words, regional economic integration as a process need not be unidirectional.

To a large degree, the contemporary regionalism has been forged from a political will both, in a positive sense, within trade blocs (towards removing barriers to trade) and, in a negative sense, between trade blocs (in terms of a strategic reaction). Naturally, then, there is some concern that the current regionalism is associated with a protectionist turn in international trading relations. However, the carving up of the international economy into such trade blocs and the prospect of increased protectionism is, as Hirst and Thompson (1992, 1994) note, far from inevitable. There are a number of good reasons why the implications and trajectory of regional economic integration are unclear. First, investment has begun to replace trade as the main force behind regional economic integration. Compared to trade, investment is surrounded by less protectionist sentiment and is more susceptible to multilateral regulation. Second, bloc-wide regulatory institutions are in their formative years and their character, scope and powers remain unclear. Third, nation states remain important in the regulation of trade and investment in the emergent trade blocs. As such, whether the current trade bloc centred economic integration is associated with the protectionism alluded to above depends on the form of integration within each of the trade blocs.

However, it is also true to say that a large element in such regionalism is 'natural' – deriving from the working out of corporate strategies and structure in relation to appropriate markets. This distinction between politically constructed (strategic) integration and natural integration emphasises the uncertain pace, form and implications of future regionalisation in the world economy. The tri-polar world economy emerging around the three main trade blocs need not herald the end to multilateralism if such integration is in large part natural rather than strategic in origin (Sapir, 1993). Multinationals are especially important within such natural integration – since it is they who are unique in their ability to integrate national territories as centres of consumption and production. Furthermore, it is they who often have the greatest influence on the development of competition and industrial policy of supranational regulatory bodies such as the Commission.

If multinationals are the most important contributors to processes of regional economic integration, then their contribution is growing both quantitatively and qualitatively. Whilst quantitatively the contribution of the stock of world foreign direct investment (FDI) to world output is small and stagnant, the contribution of foreign affiliates to world exports is large and growing (UNCTAD, 1994: 130). In this way multinationals are a very important element in the shallow economic integration embodied in trade flows. The contribution of multinationals to the UK economy may be particularly significant, with 80% of UK exports in 1988 accounted for by multinationals, a third of whom were foreign companies (Ietto-Gillies, 1993). Arguably, just as important, is the contribution of multinationals to regional integration in a qualitative sense. Here there appears to have been some evolution in the organisation of multinational companies away from overseas investment strategies based on stand-alone affiliates towards strategies involving simple and complex integration (UNCTAD, 1994).[4]

This book concerns itself with the role of multinationals in shaping patterns of trade, investment and regional development as part and parcel of processes of regional economic integration. An understanding of these issues involves a number of often quite distinct literatures. Certainly, there is little literature dealing specifically with the contribution of multinationals to regional economic integration (see Dunning and Robson, 1988). Furthermore, if regional economic integration is manifest in patterns of trade and investment then there has been little consideration of the complex relation between the two. Until comparatively recently, trade and investment have been treated as substitutes for one another and as a result there is relatively little literature which analyses the more complex and often complementary relationship between trade and investment, especially as orchestrated by multinationals. There is literature on the local and regional development impacts of multinationals (for a recent review see Young, Hood and Peters, 1994), but this tends to be rather unconnected with issues of trade and regional economic integration. The task of producing some theoretical synthesis of these relevant literatures is well beyond the scope of this book. Nevertheless, through the combination of a focused review of the existing relevant theoretical and empirical literature and the original empirical material on multinationals in Wales, the intention of this book is to offer some insights into the contribution of multinationals to European integration.

In this respect, one initial observation can be made. The two ways of conceiving of regional economic integration noted at the start of this chapter raises immedi-

---

4   The UNCTAD (1994) report speaks of multinational strategies involving: *stand alone affiliates*, where there is a clear division of tasks between the parent company and foreign affiliates and where the latter replicate, with important exceptions, much of the entire value chain of the parent company; *simple integration*, 'where affiliates undertake...a limited range of activities in order to supply their parent firms with specific inputs...' (UNCTAD, 1994: 138) and; *complex integration*, where multinationals are 'turning their geographically dispersed affiliates and fragmented production systems into regionally or globally integrated production and distribution networks.' (UNCTAD, 1994: 138).

ately two differing tendencies in the interpretation of the spatial implications of European integration. Changes in the geography of investment and industrial activity accompanying European integration cannot be detached from their long-term historical context and appear evolutionary when conceiving of regional economic integration as a process (e.g. see Gertler and Schoenberger, 1992); they might appear radical if regional economic integration is conceived in terms of distinct stages (as is most obvious in the Commission's own analyses of the SEM). This book tends toward the former interpretation of geographical changes in industrial activity when stressing the inertia inherent in multinational restructuring and economic development in Wales.

Structure of the Book

Chapter 2 provides a general framework for interpreting the metarial presented in the book. It sets European integration in the broader context of the regionalisation of trade and investment in the world economy and the regulation of the activities of multinationals. The chapter suggests that the ownership and vintage characteristics of multinationals are likely to offer some of the more important insights into the main dimensions of the restructuring of trade and investment by multinationals in the EU. It also discusses the influence of various regulatory bodies on multinational embeddedness and competitiveness.

Some of the basic theories and evidence regarding the connection between multinationals, trade, investment and regional economic integration are discussed at the beginning of Chapter 3. Thus, Chapter 3 looks first at customs union theory and issues of trade creation and diversion as a precursor to discussion of the central contribution of multinationals to such patterns of trade and investment in the EU. Finally, the regional development implications of multinational orchestrated trade and investment in the EU are examined. The focus in the chapter is upon European integration up until the 1980s and the attempt to complete the internal market of the EU.

Chapter 4 looks in more detail at the presumed effects of the creation of the Single European Market. The chapter first discusses the Commission's own analysis of the spatial and aspatial impact of its single market programme. The bulk of the chapter is, however, concerned with elaborating three lines of criticism of the Commission's analyses which, in turn, form the basis to the research presented in subsequent chapters. The chapter argues that because of the complex relationship between processes of competition and the exploitation of economies of scale, the continued fragmentation of the SEM into numerous distinct markets, and because of the attachment of multinationals to established centres of production, the process of industrial restructuring accompanying market integration will be protracted. These three influences on processes of industrial restructuring in the EU will work themselves out differently according to the ownership and vintage characteristics of multinational investments in the EU.

This book presents original research on the role of multinational manufacturing operations in Wales on patterns of trade and investment in the EU and on regional development. Chapter 5, therefore, provides some initial background to this original research. The chapter provides a review of existing published material on multinational involvement in Welsh manufacturing industry, with a view to detailing some of the historical and persistent, as well as some possibly recent and novel, characteristics of multinational investment over the years.

Chapter 6 briefly introduces the design of the original research into the impact of European integration on multinationals in Wales. Details of a postal survey of the larger multinational manufacturing investments in Wales are provided. Similarly, the basis to a number of case studies of corporate restructuring with a 'European dimension' involving Welsh operations is also discussed.

Original empirical material is presented in Chapters 7, 8 and 9. Each of these chapters relates to one of the lines of criticism raised earlier. In Chapter 7 the market orientation of multinationals in Wales is examined empirically. The trading patterns of multinational affiliates give an idea of the character, corporate role and competitive position of those affiliates. The chapter also considers whether the removal of remaining barriers to trade has had any significant impact on the competitive position of multinational manufacturing operations located in Wales.

Since multinational firms are the main orchestrators of trade and investment in the EU, the fortunes of manufacturing operations in different regions of the EU are interrelated. The prospects of Welsh manufacturing operations are therefore, to an extent, related directly or indirectly to the performance and capabilities of other parent company operations in the EU. Chapter 8, therefore, attempts to put the competitiveness of multinational manufacturing operations in Wales in some wider intra-corporate context.

Chapter 9 looks at the question of whether the local embeddedness of multinationals has any bearing on the competitiveness and security of multinational operations. There are contradictory schools of thought on this subject with, on the one hand, a long-standing tradition of empirical research with an underlying suspicion of multinationals as 'snatchers' rather than 'stickers' and, on the other hand, recent conceptual work which has tended to re-emphasise the local bases to multinational competitiveness. The chapter looks at the linkage patterns of multinational manufacturing operations in Wales as well as the policy infrastructure in support of multinationals in Wales compared to other EU regions.

Finally, Chapter 10 attempts to draw together the earlier conceptual discussions and the research findings contained in the book. The chapter first summarises the prospects for multinational manufacturing investment in Wales. It then reconsiders the extent to which 'ownership' and 'vintage' are of use in understanding the differential contribution of multinationals to European integration and peripheral region development. This leads on to a more speculative discussion of how processes of market integration and multinational restructuring may currently be working themselves out in the EU. At this point, the chapter argues that processes of European integration, multinational restructuring and their trade and investment implications cannot be separated from an understanding of regionalisation elsewhere in the world economy. It is important, therefore, for future academic research to focus on the precise implications of regionalisation on corporate strategies in terms of the extent and main dimensions of any connections, or trade-off, between integration of activities both within and between trade blocs. The chapter closes with a discussion of the possibilities for institutional infrastructure to enhance the competitiveness and embeddedness of multinational investments in Wales and other peripheral 'regions' in the EU.

CHAPTER 2

The Political Economy
of European Integration

Regionalism

At once the EU stands as the most potent symbol of, and the major force behind, the contemporary regionalisation of trade. The EU's sphere of influence in world trade has steadily grown to effectively undermine the purpose of the General Agreement on Tariffs and Trade (GATT) and multilateralism. Through both a widening (from the original 6 to the current 15) and deepening, the EU has become the major trade bloc in the world economy; one which has become powerful enough to frustrate the GATT under the leadership of the US. Furthermore, the EU's influence on world trade does not end there, it extends through its trade relations with much of the rest of the world.

Regional economic integration can be considered both as a state of affairs and as a process (Balassa, 1962, cited in Chisholm, 1995). Integration as a state of affairs can be conceived in terms of several stages of integration. There are four main stages of economic integration which are usually identified – the free trade area, the customs union, the common market and the economic union – though to this list we can add an initial and more general category of the regional trade bloc. The term trade bloc is general enough to encapsulate any of the four formalised states of economic integration but also allows one to consider groupings of countries which are not integrated by way of formalised arrangements but rather by *de facto* trade and investment patterns. Four general conditions make for a coherent trade bloc; similar levels of per capita GNP, geographic proximity, similar or compatible trading regimes, and political commitment to regional organisation (Schott, 1991: 2). As a first stage of regional economic integration we may have a collection of countries for which there are no common formal arrangements as in a free trade area but which satisfy the conditions above. At this point it is worth noting that the success of formalised regional trading arrangements (including the EU) derives in no small measure from such 'natural' tendencies towards economic integration in the world economy (Sapir, 1993). Thus, as Thomsen (1995) has argued, 'the growing regional integration that we observe, orchestrated in large part by multinational enterprises..., is a natural result of geographical and cultural proximity, not the outcome of political negotiations. Governments have played a role in the process, not by dictating where firms should sell their goods but by allowing firms to conduct business with their own natural partners.' (Thomsen, 1995: 109–110)

The Pacific rim trade bloc, which is commonly considered to be centred on the economic hegemony of Japan might be one example of an emerging trade bloc. Japan and a number of its Pacific rim partners are clearly integrated to a degree in terms of existing trade and investment patterns. However, here 'Japan's growing influence in Asia is based not upon explicit treaties of the type that westerners strive for...but on "murkier undertakings, like trust and personal favours"' (Hodder, 1994: 232). Clearly the next state of economic integration rests upon formal arrangements which allow nation states to set their own external tariffs and ensure the free movement of goods between markets – the free trade area. The UK opted not to join the EEC with its fuller commitment to regional economic integration in the form of a customs union by itself being instrumental in the formation of the European Free Trade Area (EFTA). A customs union extends the commonality of trading arrangements inherent in a free trade area to the realm of external tariffs of the member states by establishing them at a common level. The original six of the EEC created their customs union in very rapid time – establishing the common external tariff by 1968 in just ten years. It is generally held that this was possible for a number of reasons. First, rapid economic growth during the 1960s offset any negative impacts of integration on individual member states. Second, major industrial restructuring was not apparent given that the increased specialisation brought about by European integration was intra-industry rather than inter-industry in nature. Third, the existing levels of tariff protection operated by member states before the creation of the EU (6) were low and in any case there was continued protection in the form of a proliferation of non-tariff barriers (Hine, 1985: 62).

Since that time and culminating in the creation of the Single European Market (SEM) in 1993, the EU has been attempting to attain the next state of affairs, as far as economic integration is concerned, when creating a common market for goods and services and factors of production. The Community is now termed the EU in recognition of its aspirations to pursue the likes of monetary integration. In actual fact, as through the years from 1968 to 1992 when the EU (6) considered itself a common market, the EU is short of being a truly common market let alone an economic union.

Such formalised progress towards economic integration naturally has considerable effects on the patterns and determinants of trade and investment not only within trade blocs themselves but also in the wider international economy. It is, therefore, worth situating EU integration in the wider context of the growing regionalism in trade and investment in the world economy.

In a very general sense, economic integration has been occurring independent of any regionalisation in the world economy. As pre-capitalist and capitalist societies alike have created more and more complex divisions of labour so interdependencies between individuals, regions and nations have grown in the form of trade and investment. Economic integration on an international scale has a long history since capital in commodity form has long been internationalised through trade (Palloix, 1975, cited in Dicken, 1992). More complex forms of international economic integration are now evolving with the much more recent internationalisation of capital in the form of finance and direct investment. However, it would be wrong, as Hirst and Thompson (1992) point out, to assume that we live in a globally integrated economy since this requires truly global regulating institutions, truly transnational corporations operating on a globally-localised basis and a diminution of the influence of organised labour – none of which exist to any great extent in today's world economy. Instead they characterise the world economy as 'one in which the principal entities are nation states and [which] involves the process of growing interconnection between national economies' (Hirst and Thompson, 1992: 358–359). Though even here such interdependencies are less than one might think (Krugman, 1996: 9). So that 'The worldwide economy is one in which processes that are determined at the level of national economies still dominate and international phenomena are outcomes that emerge from the distinct and differential performance of the national economies' (Hirst and Thompson, 1992: 310). Rather than truly global economic integration they recognise a growing economic integration on a regional scale – although even such regionalisation has rather shaky foundations.

In some senses regionalisation of trade has a history equal in length to that of world integration but is probably best considered as a relatively recent phenomenon. For example, 16 customs unions were formed between 1818 and 1924 (Robson, 1987: 5). Today's regionalisation of trade (and investment) is probably best considered as being of a different order. First, the scale of integration – the size of the regional trade blocs being formed is much greater in geographical scope than in the past. Second, the blocs are qualitatively different in terms of the complexity of integration based not simply on trade but a greater or lesser articulation of trade, finance and productive investments. Third, whereas until recently some of the major regional trade blocs have been centrally planned, today's regionalism is founded more nearly on a purely capitalistic mode of production.

This in turn raises the important issue of the connection between the new regionalism and the capitalist mode of production. Classical economic discussion of regional economic integration concentrates on the trade diverting effects of customs unions – the trade creating effects being left unrecognised. Perhaps because of this there is certainly a strand of economic thought which views customs unions, and presumably other forms of economic integration, as essentially protectionist. This is certainly one way to view the current regionalism in the world economy – as a result of periodic crises within the capitalist mode of production. Today's regionalism, it is argued, has its parallels in the protectionism which became rife during the recessionary years of the 1930s. At this time the UK was unable, as a failing world economic power, to champion the cause of free trade whilst the US, the leading world economic power, was unwilling to do so. Today, as the US looks towards economic integration with Canada and Mexico under the North America Free Trade Agreement it is unable to champion the GATT cause of multilateral trade liberalisation whilst Japan, currently the leading world economic power, is unwilling to do so (Gibb, 1994). However, as we will see shortly, the theory of customs unions also tells us that formalised regional economic integration can be trade creating. As such, regional trade blocks occupy an ambiguous position in relation to multilateral trade liberalisation. This in turn means that their relationship to the capitalist mode of production may be rather more complex than simply a set of strategic responses to the changing terms of trade. In particular, there is a suggestion, as yet underdeveloped, that regional economic integration is intimately linked to the rise of a new mode of capitalist production and the establishment of a new regime or long wave of capitalist economic expansion. So for Gibb and Michalak 'when the relationship between regionalism and multilateralism is examined in relation to different systems of production, organisation and consumption, it is possible to identify a fundamental change in the nature and organisation of the capitalist economy' (Gibb and Michalak, 1994: 252).

The remaining sections of this chapter explore the natural and political (or regulatory) basis to the current regionalisation in trade and investment. The next section considers two important perspectives from which to view contemporary multinational-led industrial restructuring in the EU. It suggests that, on the face of things, vintage and ownership provide two important insights into multinational-led restructuring in Europe.

Multinationals and Industrial Restructuring

We need to understand how patterns of trade and investment accompanying European integration are orchestrated by multinationals. In this respect there are perhaps two key dimensions to analysing the process of European integration. First, we need to consider how patterns of trade and investment have changed over time as multinational strategies and structures have changed over time. This is a question of understanding how the different vintages of multinational investment have a bearing on trade and the characteristics of production in EU regions. We also need to consider how different multinationals contribute differently to the process of integration. There are important differences in individual investments according to industry sector but multinational firms often-times operate in more than one sector. Arguably, the main differences between multinational firms are in terms of their ownership and the differences in productive systems, innovation, work practices and culture which compose the country of origin of those firms. There is, then, a question of the ownership of multinationals and how this impacts on trade and investment and market integration in the EU. This is not just a question of how different vintages and nationalities of investment are affected differently by the process of European integration but also how they themselves have a bearing on processes of market integration.

There are perhaps two aspects to the 'vintage effect' in terms of the evolving characteristics of multinational manufacturing investments. The first meaning relates to the age of a particular investment in relation to some fixed process of evolution of multinational investments. In other words, new plants tend to have different characteristics to older plants. As plants age they change their characteristics through a process of *in situ* reorganisation. The assumption here is that the overall investment strategy of multinationals remains essentially fixed over time. That is the overall strategy for serving markets and organising production remains fixed but that the characteristics of individual plants evolves over time. Once one relaxes this assumption about the overall strategy of multinationals a second meaning of 'vintage effects' becomes apparent. If overall strategies change over time then the characteristics of new investments will also vary over time. Here 'vintage effects' take the form of 'real' differences between old and new multinational investments.

Because there are these two meanings to 'vintage effects' – there being evolution at the level of individual investments and at the level of corporate strategy including investment decisions – it is difficult to disentangle the precise effect of vintage on the changing nature of multinational investment activity. The two meanings or aspects to 'vintage effects' tend to cancel each other out so that *in situ* reorganisation of a particular operation can rarely be separated from the context of changing corporate strategy whilst 'real' differences between old and new investments may be eradicated by *in situ* change.

Our main understanding of *in situ* reorganisation of individual investments over time comes from product cycle theory (Vernon, 1966). Here new multinational investments begin by producing standardised or mature products and, with age, progress to producing newer products and gain certain functions such as research and development. However, by the end of the 1970s it had become apparent that such subsidiary life cycles were not fixed, as overall multinational strategy had changed somewhat from the initial post-war period to which the product cycle theory pertained (Vernon, 1979). Decentralisation of new products and functions such as research and development had accelerated, so changing the characteristics of new investments in more recent decades.

Our main understanding of changing corporate strategies and the characteristics of new investments derives from recent debates relating to changing norms of competition in capitalism and the regulation of the capitalist world economy. In this debate there is undoubtedly a tendency toward overgeneralisation and loss of detail regarding the variety of corporate strategies over time. Nevertheless, few would doubt that there has been somewhat of a dissolution of a quite pervasive production paradigm (Fordism) based upon vertically integrated mass production and marketing. Rather, debate centres on what may be to a greater or lesser extent replacing Fordism. Here a variety of possible successors to the Fordist mode of production have been proposed. At the risk of oversimplifying this debate, the new norms of production and competition centre on flexibility. Smaller scale vertically and horizontally disintegrated production is seen to offer the flexibility needed to service increasingly fragmented demand in advanced economies. Changes in the nature of markets and the development of technologies have created pressures for multinationals to change their strategy and structure with implications for the characteristics of their individual manufacturing sites. The potential characteristics such new or, as Amin *et al.* (1994) term them, 'quality' investments of multinationals are discussed in a little more detail in Chapter 4. For the moment it suffices to note that it has been suggested that multilocational and multinational firms have adopted more decentralised corporate structures and have increasingly localised and reintegrated elements of their production and non-production activities. Vintage may therefore be an important consideration in understanding the markets served by, the scale, productivity and functional capabilities and also the embeddedness of, multinational investments.

Multinationals potentially break the link between the competitiveness of companies and countries. This is not to say that multinationals transcend national economies completely but rather that their strategically relevant territories coincide only imperfectly with those of national and supranational governments, labour organisations and consumers (Ietto-Gillies, 1993). The contribution of multinationals to European integration is more than that of simply a mixed response to initiatives taken by the Commission but also what they bring to their host economies in terms of productive systems, work practices etc. from their domestic sphere. From the growing literature on comparative business systems it is clear that

> 'The nation state is the dominant collectivity for organising so many of the social institutions which impinge directly on economic activities, such as legal, educational and financial systems, as well as itself constituting one of the major influences on firm structure and behaviour...' (Whitley, 1992a: 37)

In other words 'Most firms are embedded in a distinct national culture of business that provides them with intangible but very real advantages.' (Hirst and Thompson, 1995: 430). Whitley (1992a) argues that the nature of firms (for example their legal basis and form), their authoritative coordination and control systems and the organisation of markets each vary between national business systems. In this way, as Dunning's (1979) eclectic framework of international trade and investment makes apparent, nation specific institutional arrangements, work practices and labour organisation etc. can have an important bearing on the 'ownership advantages' upon which firms internationalise.

In this way, different types of multinationals, as defined by ownership, can contribute different things to the process of market integration in Europe. US firms, for example, by virtue of their ownership advantages in terms of economies of scale (derived from their large domestic market) and their long experience as multinationals have been at the forefront of integrating markets and production within the EU. They have probably exerted a subtle effect on the mind-sets or even the preferences of consumers, and the organisation and conduct of labour organ-isations and even national governments across the EU. In contrast EU firms have, until recently, remained entrenched within their respective home markets and have had perhaps the obverse effect to US multinationals in reinforcing national differences in consumer tastes and systems of government and labour organisation. The recent arrival of Japanese manufacturing firms in the EU represents a new set of influences upon processes of integration which are, as yet, unclear. Debate is centred on what the contribution of Japanese multinational 'transplant' investment might be and whether it represents a radically different set if influences from US or EU multinational investment. There is a suggestion that the perceived differences between Japanese and US and EU investment may be rather more apparent than real; a reflection of the difference in the vintage of investments. Evidence from the US does suggest that Japanese foreign direct manufacturing investment is indeed rather different from other foreign direct investments. The evidence from the EU is a little less clear, being shrouded as it is in the complications of competition policy (local content and anti-dumping measures). Encarnation and Mason, how-ever, are clear that there are significant differences between Japanese multinationals on the one hand and US and EU multinationals on the other and that

> 'such persistent differences cannot be discounted as mere "vintage effects", vestigial remnants reflecting an earlier stage in a multinationals evolution, but instead may actually grow larger with the proliferation and maturation of Japanese investment abroad'. (Encarnation and Mason, 1994: 441)

Consideration of 'ownership' is therefore important to an understanding of multinational restructuring. Commenting on the orchestration of European inte-gration, Middlemas (1995) reminds us that 'it is probably still true to see the great majority of firms...as retaining their national identity, however much their patterns of behaviour and affinity have become international and European.' (Middlemas, 1995: 496).

There is one final implication of this line of analysis. The interaction of multinationals with host economy business systems, in turn, makes it quite possible for elements of the host economy to be transferred to the domestic economy of multinationals. Thus, 'In a sense, the structure and organising principles of oligopolistic worldwide industries are the outcomes of competition between different ways of organising economic activities in different business systems.' (Whitley, 1992a: 38). Thus, the question of whether the creation of the SEM has altered multinational strategies must be placed in a broader world context – altered European strategies being part and parcel of a renewed attempt by US and

European firms in particular to become globally competitive (Middlemas, 1995: 673). In terms of the empirical focus of this book, ownership continues to offer some important insights into the markets served by, the scale, productivity and functional capabilities as well as the embeddedness of multinational manufacturing investments – albeit that the organisation of different multinationals in the EU needs to be seen in a wider context.

The contemporary regionalisation in the world economy is also, in part, politically constructed. As the following section describes, the competitiveness and embeddedness of multinationals are influenced by the supranational, national and local regulatory environments in which they operate.

Regionalism, Regulation and the Multinationals

By now, progress towards multilateral trade liberalisation and its coupling with paradigmatic forms of mass production and consumption and international regulation of trade have been widely documented (e.g. Glyn *et al.* 1990; Peck and Tickell, 1994). It is also clear to see that, to a degree, the contemporary regionalisation is associated with a step back from integrated world production under the short-lived 'global Fordism' of the late 1960s and 1970s (Lipietz, 1987) and the rise of strategies of global-localisation or 'glocalisation' centred on new forms of production (Swyngedouw, 1992; Ruigrok and Van Tulder, 1996). However, the connection, if any, between a possible new mode or long wave of post-Fordist accumulation and regional economic integration has yet to be specified in much detail.

Initial accounts of what is perceived to be a newly emerging global-local order have envisaged a diminished role for the nation-state as a regulatory body (e.g. Jessop, 1994; Ohmae, 1993). The new 'institutional fix' for post-Fordist capitalism is one in which there has been a 'hollowing out' of the nation state and the transfer of many of its functions to regional or local institutions on the one hand and to supranational regulatory bodies such as the Commission on the other (Jessop, 1994). In similar vein Smith (1995) suggests that regionalisation raises policy issues regarding industry development at the macro (i.e. national or supranational level and at the micro or meso (local/regional) level. The examples Smith gives here are strategic trade policy at the macro level and the fostering of localised external economies in industrial clusters at the micro or meso level.

However, the bases of the current regionalisation of investment and trade and their regulation are highly fragile (Hirst and Thompson, 1992) so that it is best to characterise the current situation as one of global-local disorder (Peck and Tickell, 1994). Whilst there are a number of ways in which multinationals can become embedded within particular regulatory environments, the ability of institutions at the local or regional level to effect such embeddedness is likely to be highly circumscribed. Rather, different institutions operating at different geographical scales will be able to effect embeddedness in different ways. Conversely, one implication of this is that firms, and multinationals in particular, may be able to exert considerable influence over the actions of regulatory bodies. In other words, there is the potential for *institutional or regulatory capture* by multinationals. The discussion which follows looks at three levels at which institutions may have some bearing on multinational competitiveness and embeddedness of multinationals – the supranational, national and local or regional levels. Arguably, institutional capture is a feature of the relationship between multinationals and governments at each of these levels.

At the broadest geographical scale there are supranational policies which may impinge on issues of multinational embeddedness and competitiveness. It is argued that there has been a functional expansion of often long-established supranational bodies which have gained a renewed interest in 'structural competitiveness in the economic spaces they manage' (Jessop, 1994: 270). Here considerable weight is placed upon the contemporary regionalisation in the world economy and upon the EU as an exemplar of the evolution of supranational regulation. In particular, the EU's recent attempts to encourage the formation of globally-competitive EU multinationals through a combination of the SEM initiative and competition and industrial policies have been cited as instances of an emerging supranational level of regulation (Jessop, 1994).

Strategic trade policy is another area in which supranational bodies such as the Commission may increasingly have a role to play. Trade policy has come to the fore at the level of nation states and trade blocs because of academic arguments which stress its value in shaping national competitiveness through first-mover and lock-in advantages in imperfectly competitive industries. Certainly, trade and investment related policies have been used, arguably quite successfully, to promote the competitiveness of, or protect, industry at a national level. In the late 1970s and early 1980s Cambridge economists were arguing for such strategic trade policies to protect UK industry in relation both to EU and world competitors. Arguably, Britain bore the brunt of industry restructuring and capacity reduction in the EU at that time because of its non-interventionist stance on trade compared to other member states. Whether desired or not, the possibilities for such unilateral trade and investment measures in the UK are now much more circumscribed. Instead, the logic of, and possibilities for, such strategic trade policy appear to have shifted from the sphere of nation states to the sphere of the major trade blocs.

This interest in strategic trade policy raises the very real prospect of an increasingly antagonistic and protectionist edge to regional economic integration. However, Hirst and Thompson (1994) argue that such strategic regional integration is less likely given that investment has now displaced trade as the main force behind world and regional economic integration. Given this and given the apparent limitations of dealing with investment related matters under the GATT, interest in strategic trade policy may be overtaken by the more pressing need for such supranational (inter-trade bloc) regulation of investment.

There are similar pressures for the regulation of investment at an intra-trade bloc scale. Within the EU a common approach to the treatment and regulation of multinationals may be needed to establish the framework for policy at lower levels, since economic integration means that national or regional policies have spillover effects (Cooper, 1986 cited in Streeten, 1992). There are a number of ways in which national or regional policies may be distorted or have unintended consequences and these militate in favour of the setting of some sort of common framework for trade, regional and industrial policy at the EU level. Perhaps the most obvious and relevant example here would be the need to establish some EU-wide framework within which regional policy can operated. Thus, Amin *et al.* (1994) recommend that the EU has a role to play in setting ceilings on levels of financial assistance to mobile investment and in setting the basic criteria upon which investment would qualify for such assistance. This might go some way to eliminating the bidding-up of financial assistance to mobile investment which has accompanied the increasingly intense inter-regional competition for such investment within the EU.

However, there are also limits to which there is a coherence apparent within such supranational regulation of economic activity. As Whitley reminds us, 'the institutionalisation of relatively free movement of goods and services through the European Community will not, in itself, lead to a pan-European business system…' (Whitley, 1992b: 278). If any such pan-European business system exists it is on an informal level, with different histories and styles of participation in the Commission's policy-making apparent among firms of different national origin. Nevertheless in this way, multinationals operating in the EU 'have changed the EUs political market place probably irreversibly, because all serious players…have engaged themselves permanently on a large scale and with substantial resources, to the evolution of means of influence over their common regulatory environments.' (Middlemas, 1995: 675). The coupling of such informal orchestration to more formalised elements of EU policy has created conflicting policy aims as seen for example between EU regional policy and competition and industrial policy (Amin, Charles and Howells, 1992).

In the face of those instances of supranational regulation of multinationals which do exist, others have argued that 'the balance of power has shifted from the MNE towards the nation state' (Rugman *et al.* 1986, quoted in Ruigrok and van Tulder, 1996). This reflects, among other things, the fact that internal corporate strategies can only be imperfectly executed in the face of government regulation and the constraints on strategy created by differing national and supranational bodies. Recently, then, there has been some re-affirmation of the importance of the nation-state as a body involved with the regulation of multinationals (Hirst and Thompson, 1995). Thus,

> 'in a world in which the nation-state is more circumscribed in its policy choices, the role of policy is, if anything, more rather than less important; locational advantage relies more on physical and social infrastructure, which

governments have a role in creating, rather than on natural resources or other inherent advantages.' (Campbell, 1994: 202)

On the one hand, and as described above, this role derives from the potential role for national governments in creating, in Dunning's terms, the ownership advantages upon which firms internationalise. However,

> 'TNCs are "produced" through a complex historical process of embedding in which cognitive, cultural, social, political and economic characteristics of the national home base play a part. TNCs...are bearers of such characteristics, which then interact with the place-specific characteristics of the countries in which they operate to produce a particular outcome.' (Dicken, 1994: 118)

On the other hand, then, national governments have a role to play in creating the locational advantages with which multinationals engage with in their host economies. The extent to which this is the case depends on the openness of national business systems and local business cultures to the elements of alien business systems transplanted by multinationals.

> 'The more open and pluralistic an economy is, the more likely it is to accept – or at least acquiesce in – the transplanting of new firm-market relationships. Conversely, where institutions are cohesive, integrated and have generated a distinctive business system, it is more likely that MNCs will have to adapt their mode of operation to the prevailing pattern.' (Whitley, 1992b: 277)

In this respect, there have been some persistent differences in the attitude of national governments specifically as regards multinationals (Bailey, Harte and Sugden, 1994). Furthermore, if nation states have a continuing policy role in relation to multinationals due to their administration of territory and population, then, as Hirst and Thompson (1995) note,

> 'The key to the success of TNC FDI is not whether it simply seeks a low-cost location to generate maximum profit advantage but how it adapts its strategy to fit into the particular institutionalized national environments of business and innovation into which it settles.' (Hirst and Thompson, 1995: 289)

The UK's long-standing non-interventionist attitude to both outward direct investment by UK firms and inward foreign direct investment (FDI) means that the UK economy, as a melting pot of multinational business practices, provides one of the best opportunities to consider the impact of different multinationals on processes of European integration. It also highlights the fragile and rather limited basis to the UK economy as a location for multinational investment.

Perhaps the most salient area in which there is a continuing and vital contribution to industry embeddedness and competitiveness at a national level is in terms of education and vocational training as a key input to production. Here it becomes apparent that UK government policy over a long period has contributed to the poor vocational skills available to modern manufacturing industry in the UK (Rubery, 1994). There might also be a role for national policy in terms of the monitoring of the activities of multinationals and their contribution to economic performance. This is something which Amin *et al.* (1994) suggest has been lacking and might usefully form part of EU policies towards mobile investments. Here again there have been important differences between EU-member states in terms of their monitoring of, and intervention in, the activities of multinationals within their territories (Bailey, Harte and Sugden, 1994). In the UK, the generally liberal attitude toward both outward and inward direct investment has a long history and is deeply entrenched. Calls for improved monitoring of multinational investments may therefore face important cultural/ideological obstacles. Furthermore, and as described later, some of the undisputed benefits of recent foreign investment in the UK are intangible in nature and therefore rather difficult to monitor either by national or regional bodies. Thus, whilst improved monitoring especially in member states with generally liberal attitudes towards multinationals may help engender a slightly more discerning attitude to investments made by such companies

'It is unlikely...that tighter implementation of incentives and institutional proactivism are sufficient to attract high quality investment or maximise its contribution to a host region. The type of project a region can expect depends on the quality of supply-side resources it can offer.' (Amin *et al.* 1994: 51)

In the UK, then, it appears that there is actually very little for multinationals in many industries to adapt to, or engage with, in terms of a distinctive business system. This becomes apparent when considering some of the most pertinent areas of national economic policy and underlines the fact that the UK may indeed be little more than a low cost location within Europe.

Finally, considerable weight has been placed on the increasing involvement of local and regional institutions in attempts to restore the competitiveness of their locally-based firms within the context of the continued internationalisation of industry (e.g. Albrechts and Swyngedouw, 1989; Jessop, 1994). 'This involves more than a simple "technical fix" and requires local states to engage in other fields of public policy, ranging from basic infrastructure provision to cultural policy' (Jessop, 1994: 272). Here, Jessop cites the increasing involvement of local and regional institutions in the likes of labour market policies, education and training, technology transfer, local venture capital etc. The role of such local and regional initiatives in regional economic development and industrial competitiveness has been widely presumed and celebrated. It is precisely these sorts of initiatives which form the basis of a new policy orthodoxy and renewed optimism surrounding the regenerative capacity of peripheral 'regions' such as Wales in the UK (e.g. Cooke, Price and Morgan, 1995; Morgan and Rees, 1995; Rees and Morgan, 1991). Central to this new orthodoxy appear to be a concern with the creation and coordination of local institutional infrastructure with which to promote successful clusters of industry.

Jessop's (1994) key account of the post-Fordist state tends, as Peck and Tickell (1994) note, to imply some symmetry in the emerging regulation of contemporary capitalism. However, Peck and Tickell argue that 'The global-local nexus is...a lopsided concept, comprised on the one hand of powerful processes of global disorder and on the other hand of largely reactive, and typically shallow, local responses' (Peck and Tickell, 1994: 298). They characterise the situation as one in which there have been 'a handful of genuinely innovative local experiments and a raft of pale imitations' (Peck and Tickell, 1994: 298). Their discussion highlights the likely transitory nature and essentially limited capacity of local and regional initiatives in fields such as technology transfer, education and training, supplier and indigenous firm development to engender regional economic development. In particular the resources available to such local and regional institutions are dwarfed by the economics of production on an international scale.

Conclusion

This chapter has suggested that European integration needs to be situated in the much wider context of an increasingly integrated world economy, one important, though relatively opaque, aspect of which is the contemporary regionalisation of trade and investment and their regulation. Regionalisation of trade and investment is, in part, a natural process to which multinational investments of different ownership and vintage are likely to have contributed in different ways. However, it is also true to say that the activities of multinationals are regulated to a greater or lesser degree by local, national and supranational bodies. In this way the competitiveness and embeddedness of multinational investments has been, and can be, shaped, to an extent, by a variety of regulatory institutions. Seemingly, the relative powers and influence of regulatory institutions at each of these various geographical scales may have changed. This study concentrates on examining the contribution of local and regional institutions to multinational embeddedness.

In the chapters which follow some greater empirical detail is provided on the role of multinationals in engendering European integration through trade and investment. In particular, the following chapter examines some of the empirical detail relating to the trade and investment effects of European integration and their impact on regional development within the EU.

From the Customs Union
to the Single Market

Introduction

Greater regional integration in Europe began to replace the national integration and protectionism which had characterised the immediate pre-World War II period with the formation of a number of pan-national organisations prefiguring the EU as it stands today. Formal arrangements for regional integration, such as free trade areas and customs unions, hold an ambiguous position with respect to the liberalisation of world trade. The precursor organisations to the EU, and the European Coal and Steel Community (ECSC) in particular, violated the principles of the General Agreement on Tariffs and Trade (GATT) but the political advantages of Western European peace appear to have overridden concerns over the economically discriminatory impact of such organisations. Thus, whilst customs unions can be recognised within the GATT framework, the EU, when formed in 1958, was never formally recognised by GATT (Barnes and Barnes, 1995).

With the formation of the EU (6) customs union, the initial impetus to liberalise trade among the original six member states focused on eliminating tariff barriers. In this respect the original members and those joining in 1973 were highly successful. However, this success in removing internal tariff barriers to trade needs to be set against the simultaneous proliferation of non-tariff barriers to trade. In 1966 the proportion of imports to the EU affected by non-tariff barriers was (at 20.8%) lower than for the US and Japan and the world as a whole, but by 1986 (at 54.1%) it was higher than the US, Japan and the world as a whole (Barnes and Barnes, 1995: 362). In some senses the regional integration that occurred up until the 1980s was of a rather weak form and certainly did not circumscribe the ability of nation states to shape intra-community trade by way of these non-tariff barriers.

The impact of the EU in terms of trade and investment – especially in the formative years of the EU (6) – also needs to be seen in a broader international context. The initial growth in intra-EU trade and regional convergence within the EU coincident with the formation of the customs union of the original six, for instance, took place against the backdrop of generally healthy rates of economic growth among advanced economies under what has commonly come to be regarded as the Fordist mode of accumulation (Glyn *et al.* 1990). Similarly, the stagnation of intra-EU trade and regional divergence of the 1970s and 1980s has to be seen in the context of a crisis in this hegemonic mode of accumulation and intensified international competition from Far Eastern economies.

Trade Creation and Diversion

A significant element of our understanding of the economic, and more particularly, the trade implications of regional economic integration comes from the theory of customs unions. Before considering customs union theory and the concepts of trade creation and trade diversion it is worth briefly considering the relationship of customs unions to world trade liberalisation under the aegis of the GATT. The General Agreement on Tariffs and Trade is concerned with multilateral trade liberalisation based on the principles of non-discrimination and reciprocity. The rationale for such trade liberalisation lies in orthodox economic theory which suggests that there are gains in trade if free trade is allowed to engender specialisation in production according to the principles of absolute or comparative advantage. Orthodox theory rests on numerous assumptions, some more implausible than others, and is usually demonstrated using simple two-country examples – nevertheless it captures the essence of why free world trade is held to be so desirable.

Customs unions occupy an ambiguous position with regard to such multilateral trade liberalisation and the potential gains to trade. Internally, between member states, a customs union is trade liberating. Outwardly, between member states and the rest of the world, a customs union is protectionist. To the extent that customs unions encourage trade liberalisation there may be gains to trade or what is referred to as trade creation. However, to the extent that customs unions discriminate against non-member states and so distort patterns of specialisation based on absolute or comparative advantage, there may be no such gains to trade but rather trade diversion.

Orthodox theory and the idea of gains from trade rest on some large assumptions. Consumption patterns, for instance, are assumed to be constant and not to differ between trading partners. So orthodox theory is primarily concerned with the production of goods and more particularly geographical or national variations in production costs. Variations in product costs arise from differing factor endowments and technical know-how among trading partners. Countries specialise in the production and trade of goods for which they are well endowed in terms of land, labour, capital or technological expertise. There may be understandable differences in these factor endowments and technological capacities between advanced economies and lesser developed economies but the differences will be much less pronounced between individual advanced economies. Yet a large proportion of world trade takes place between advanced economies, of which a large proportion is made up of manufactured items which require similar factor requirements and technological know-how. The reason for this is that a large proportion of world trade is intra-industry trade as opposed to the inter-industry trade supposed in orthodox theory. That is, much of world trade consists of different varieties of the same generic products. To understand such intra-industry trade we need to consider differences in consumption patterns across trading partners and not just production issues.

A customs union can consist of two or more countries which agree to abolish all tariffs and quantitative restrictions on trade between themselves and establish a common external tariff on imports from non-member states. Until recently the weight of opinion, including classical economic thought, presumed that customs unions, because they were concerned with removing barriers to trade internally, were predominantly trade creating. Not until Viner's (1950, cited in Hine, 1985) work was it firmly established that the trade effects of customs union formation included elements of both trade creation and trade diversion. The establishment of a customs union can lead to an increase in trade between member states but not all of this is properly considered to represent trade creation or gains to trade in the orthodox sense. Trade creation would occur where, for instance, consumers in one member state with higher production costs for a particular item switch consumption to items produced from lower cost sources in other member states. However, it may be equally that increased trade between member states results from the substitution of low cost imports from non-member states by high cost imports from a member state as a result of the common external tariff. The increase in trade between member states does not represent gains to trade but rather is a diversion of trade. For Viner the appraisal of the trade effects of a customs union rests on a quantitative assessment of the balance of these trade creation and trade diversion effects. If, on balance, a customs union is trade creating then it has a beneficial effect on world trade.

Viner's analysis has since been extended to include consideration of the 'dynamic' effects of customs union formation and economic integration more generally on production cost issues. Viner's analysis concentrated on demonstrating the possibility of trade creation and diversion given a once and for all re-allocation of resources. However, these 'static' once and for all effects are only part of the picture regarding the potential gains to trade from regional integration. It is quite possible that the so-called 'dynamic' effects of changes in consumption, economic growth and economies of scale are more significant, if somewhat long-term in nature. First, a reallocation of resources towards more efficient member state production can engender further economies of scale. Second, immediate price reductions from the 'static' reallocation of resources and ongoing price reductions from increased economies of scale can produce an increase in consumption, trade and economic growth. One implication of this is that what we have until now termed trade diversion may, under certain circumstances, actually include an element of trade creation! In analysing trade diversion Viner was concerned solely with production costs. However, even if there is a shift from low cost imports from a non-member state to a high cost member state in production cost terms, the consumption effect can produce some gains to trade. If the consumption effect of lower prices outweighs the loss of trade due to higher production costs, trade diversion may actually be beneficial in terms of trade expansion and economic growth.

The contribution of customs unions to world trade depends on the quantitative balance between trade creation and diversions effects. As a guide there are a number of general conditions under which customs unions will, on balance, be trade creating. First, if the member states are producing a similar range of products but at different costs there is scope for competition as well as a degree of complementarity – stimulating both inter- and intra-industry trade. Second, if the customs union is large in relation to the outside world – here there is less scope for trade diversion. Third, if the internal tariffs on products traded between the member states are high but the initial tariffs on products traded mainly with the rest of the world are low there is likely to be less trade diversion (Hine, 1985: 21–22).

On the face of it, the EU (6) as formed in 1958 satisfied the second and third of the above conditions and has, through subsequent enlargements, satisfied the first condition. As such it seems likely that the original customs union of the EEC and its subsequent enlargements have been, on balance, trade creating. Certainly the pattern in Figure 3.1 seems to support this. Figure 3.1 illustrates how trade among EU member states has grown in relation to their trade with the rest of the world. This growth in intra-EU trade is often taken as an indication of the growth in trade accompanying European integration. Thus, Figure 3.1 also shows that the growth in intra-EU trade was most dramatic in the formative years of the EU(6), slowed somewhat during the recessionary years of the mid-1970s until the early 1980s when it then picked up a little. However, as we have discussed, only part of this growth in trade may be the result of trade creation. For an appreciation of the balance of trade creation and diversion embodied in the general pattern evident in Figure 3.1 we need to consider the large number of quantitative studies which have attempted to estimate the balance of trade creation diversion effects of the EU.

Naturally, estimating the balance of such trade creation and diversion effects is fraught with difficulties. The different types of analysis used (*ex ante* or *ex post*) and the different methodologies and data used yield many differing estimates. The difficulties have not dissuaded economists from trying to quantify the trade effects of European integration though very little can be said as a result of the numerous studies produced.

Two of the earliest studies of the trade effects of the formation of the EU(6) set the pattern for the large number of subsequent studies. Scitovsky (1958, cited in Chisholm, 1995) was highly sceptical of the potential trade creation effects of the customs union of the original six. Balassa (1962, cited in Chisholm, 1995), however, believed the gains from formation to be much greater than estimated by Scitovsky though in actual fact, compared to the range of estimates produced by

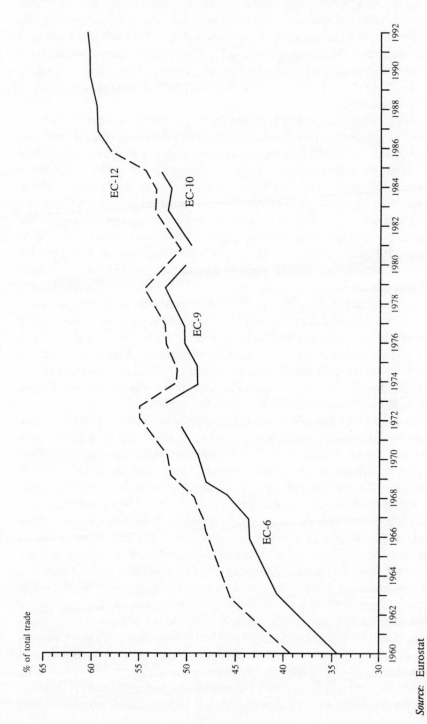

Source: Eurostat

Figure 3.1. Intra-EC trade in goods, 1960–1992

subsequent studies, their estimates varied little. Instead, as Mayes (1978) has graphically demonstrated, the range of estimates of the balance of trade creation and diversion effects has increased over time and with the increasing number of studies published. All that might reasonably be concluded from these studies is that the impact of the EU(6) has been positive – that is, on balance, trade creating (Robson, 1987: 245). Little or nothing can firmly be said about the magnitude of such trade creation.

Evidence concerning the trade creating and trade diverting effects of the EU(6) can also be gleaned from studies of the UK's accession – though the evidence here is sparse. Entry into the EU appears to have altered the UK's trade patterns significantly or at least returned them to a previous state of affairs. As Chisholm notes, 'the reorientation of Britain's trade with Europe up until about 1970 was no more than a return to the position which had obtained prior to the first World War' (Chisholm, 1995: 29). There certainly has been a dramatic growth in the UK's trade with the original six from roughly 10% of total UK trade in 1950 to 40% in 1990. Imports from the EU have increased more rapidly than the UK's exports to the EU. Furthermore, there appears to have been little in the way of trade diversion as a result of the UK's accession since, although UK exports to the rest of the world have declined, imports from the rest of the world have remained at their previous levels. The result of these trends has been a growing trade deficit in manufactured goods so that it is difficult to detect the effect of the customs union and integration during this period from the effects of growing worldwide integration and the UK's loss of competitive position within world manufacturing. It is likely then that the impact of the UK's accession has been small but positive in terms of trade creation (Chisholm, 1995: 67).

The various estimates of trade creation and diversion with the formation of the EU customs union and ensuing processes of integration need to be situated in a broader economic context. European integration needs to be conceptualised alongside worldwide integration (Dicken and Oberg, 1996). As we saw earlier, in a very general sense much of industry worldwide has become more integrated. This is particularly the case regarding trade and investment between the advanced economies. It is difficult to disentangle the specifics of European integration from the generalities of world integration. Thus Jacquemin and Sapir (1988) pose the question of the trade impact of European integration in this wider context of world integration. They ask whether European integration has been at the expense of world integration or whether the EU has become more integrated into the world economy. Their analysis looks at shares of domestic production, Community imports and extra-Community imports for four major EU nations (Germany, France, Italy, UK) over the period 1973 to 1984. They find that 'expenditures in all the four largest European countries are devoted less and less to goods produced domestically and more and more to products coming from both community partners and the rest of the world' (Jacquemin and Sapir, 1988: 129). In other words there is double trade creation taking place. In particular they note the falling share of domestic producers in each of the four main nations and qualify the extent to which this may be a product of European integration.

'This conquest of the domestic manufacturing market by foreign producers may not be entirely attributable to European integration – or lack thereof. Besides a change in competitiveness within the manufacturing sector, between domestic and foreign suppliers, there could have been changes in the allocation of resources within a member country, between manufacturing and non-manufacturing activities.' (Jacquemin and Sapir, 1988: 130)

There are two main trends they pick out. First, that the share of domestic suppliers has been continually falling with European integration since 1958. Second, after an initial phase where there was rapid growth in intra-community trade, there has been a second phase where rises in intra-community trade have faltered and stagnated whilst extra-community trade has risen more rapidly. This is the much lamented product of what is sometimes referred to as 'Eurosclerosis' and the stimulus to the desire to complete the internal market. However, such a stagnation in the growth of intra-EU trade may, as we have seen above, have more to do with the EU's increasing integration into the world economy and the competitive position of its industries *vis-à-vis* its main competitors – the US and Japan (see also Dicken and Oberg, 1996: 111–112). Jacquemin and Sapir reinforce the idea by providing an analysis disaggregated by industry. This confirms that there are some sectors where there continues to be some form of trade diversion (including aerospace and agricultural produce over which there has been much trade friction with the US). However, in others (chiefly electronics goods) intra-Community trade has been falling behind extra-Community imports (notably from places like Japan). EU producers in these sectors have been highly protected by way of anti-dumping duties, voluntary export restraints (VERs), etc. and yet Japanese producers have been able to penetrate the European market. This underlines the strength of Japanese compared to European industry in these sectors.

Trade and Investment

In the previous section we considered some of the aggregate studies of the effect of customs union formation and subsequent integration upon trade. These quantitative studies of trade are paralleled by an equally large and yet virtually unconnected set of quantitative studies of the effect of European integration on patterns of foreign direct investment. These sets of studies have remained virtually separate, in part, because of much economic theory treating trade and investment as substitutes for one another. Yet there is a growing recognition, in both theoretical and empirical terms, that the relationship between trade and investment is more complicated in as much as they can be complementary. Understanding the relationship between trade and investment requires an understanding of multinational companies since these are the main orchestrators of both trade and investment in the world economy and in the EU. Thus, the analysis of trade and investment takes one into the realms of the corporate organisation of production – something which is not readily analysed with recourse to aggregate statistics. Instead primary survey or corporate case study material is needed to adequately explore the connection between trade and investment.

Before going on to consider the connection between trade and investment as orchestrated by multinationals we need first to establish some general conclusions regarding the quantitative impact of European integration on patterns of FDI. This leads naturally to a discussion of more qualitative issues – that is, of the character of FDI. Finally, a number of taxonomies of multinational investment are considered and their connection to the evaluation of patterns of European trade and investment discussed.

Yannopoulos (1990) has reviewed the evidence regarding the formation of the EU(6) and its impact on foreign direct investment. There have been a large number of studies attempting to discern a distinct European integration effect on levels and geographical patterns of foreign direct investment. The earliest of these have focused on US FDI into Europe since Japanese FDI at the time of formation of the EU(6) customs union was negligible, and given that immense data problems surround the study of intra-European FDI. There has been a quite extended debate over the impact of the customs union on levels and patterns of US FDI in Western Europe. The conclusion of this debate appears to be that the locational pattern of US FDI changed significantly after the formation of the EU(6) and that the EU(6) attracted significantly more of the growth in total US FDI than did European Free Trade Agreement (EFTA) countries (Yannopoulos, 1990: 240). Here, D'Arge (1969 cited in Yannopoulos, 1990) has suggested that EFTA countries benefited from a once and for all increase in US FDI but that the formation of the EU(6) had resulted in both a once and for all increase as well as an ongoing increase in US FDI. Certainly in the early years of the EU(6) there appears to have been some diversion of US FDI from other European countries to EU(6) countries. In some respects this is not altogether surprising since the UK, as a major non-EU(6) nation at the time was and still is the major destination for US investment in the World and in Europe and we would expect some gradual diversion of investment away from the UK as other markets became important in their own right. The precise aspects of the customs union which may have prompted this shift in US FDI have also been explored by way of quantitative studies. Scaperlanda and Mauer (1967, cited in Yannopoulos, 1990) found no evidence that tariff discrimination had had any effect in prompting tariff-jumping US FDI. This leaves market size and market growth as possible determinants of the increase in US FDI – factors which are likely to have become progressively more important considerations in FDI with the deepening and widening of the EU.

A more limited number of studies have dealt with changing patterns of intra-EU FDI – that is foreign direct investment by EU companies in other EU countries. The limited number of studies is due in part to the problems of collecting reliable comparable data for each of the member states (e.g. see Thomsen and Woolcock,

1993). Dunning and Robson (1988) suggest that the formation of the EU(6) will have had two opposing effects on intra-EU investment. On the one hand, the lower costs of exporting with the removal of tariff barriers may have encouraged some retrenchment of investment within home economies. On the other hand, reduced transfer costs offer the prospect of better co-ordination between EU plants giving rise to more extended divisions of labour based on product or process specialisation and encouraging some new intra-EU FDI. The earliest evidence of changing patterns of intra-EU FDI comes from Franko's (1976) study of European multinationals. His study suggested that there had been a rapid growth in the number of overseas manufacturing subsidiaries of EU multinationals after the formation of the EU(6). The data regarding the UK's accession to the EU provide some further, though extremely limited confirmation that European integration has stimulated intra-EU FDI. Yannopoulos (1990) for instance suggests that there was a sizeable increase in UK FDI in the EU but no similar surge in EU FDI in the UK in anticipation of accession.

More recently there does seem to have been renewed activity in terms of intra-EU FDI which, in part, has been related to the growing spate of mergers and acquisitions between EU enterprises. Here, the available evidence suggests that because intra-EU patterns of trade and FDI are very similar – focused on flows between the major economies and in particular between economies which are physically or culturally close – trade and investment are in fact complementary (e.g. Molle and Morsink, 1991). Molle and Morsink (1991) go on to suggest that the relationship between trade and investment is not proportional but rather trade relations need to reach a minimum level before investment takes place and beyond this, further integration does not necessarily give rise to larger flows of intra-EU FDI.

Molle and Morsink (1991) also go on to identify different groupings of EU nations according to their net balance of inward and outward intra-EU FDI. Greece, Portugal, Spain and Ireland are essentially recipient countries for intra-EU FDI, whilst the Netherlands and Germany are on balance investor countries from which much intra-EU FDI originates. The UK, Italy, France and Belgium are 'crossroads' countries which have a balance of inward and outward intra-EU FDI. They also note that the situation has been changing since the early 1970s into the 1980s with the Netherlands and the UK moving more towards key investor countries.

Japanese manufacturing FDI has risen quite dramatically over the past two to three decades, seemingly accelerating continuously over this period. Japan's manufacturing FDI has risen particularly rapidly within the EU during the 1980s and this leads one to associate this rise with processes of European integration in general and the creation of the SEM in particular. However, Japan's manufacturing FDI needs to be put in a global context (Dicken, 1988) since flows of Japanese manufacturing FDI into the EU are lower than those with the US or East Asia.

Ozawa (1991) and Dicken (1988) identify three phases of Japanese manufacturing FDI. The first began in the 1960s and continued into the early 1970s and consisted of the transfer of labour intensive, low technology activities to East Asia. The second phase lasted from the early 1970s to the early 1980s and consisted of a surge in resource-based and capital intensive activities such as steel, chemicals and petroleum. The most recent stage, during the 1980s and 1990s, has involved large scale FDI in consumer product activities in advanced economies including the EU. It is this most recent stage of Japanese FDI which is coincidental with renewed efforts at European integration. However, there are few empirical studies of the sort carried out to detect any connection between the levels and motives of US FDI and the formation of the EU(6).

There are two main ways in which processes of European integration can affect the, to use Dunning's (1979) terminology, locational advantages of the EU as a destination for manufacturing FDI. First, there is the need to manufacture inside the EU due to any barriers to exporting into the EU – the trade diversion effect may stimulate inward FDI. Second, the very size and growth rate of the EU market may stimulate inward FDI. The available evidence gives rise to some debate regarding the connection between European integration and the quantity of Japanese FDI in the EU. Thomsen and Nicolaides (1991, cited in Balusabramanyam and Greenaway, 1992) argue that European integration has had no effect on the quantity of Japanese manufacturing FDI in Europe and only an effect on its timing. They associate growing levels of Japanese manufacturing FDI in the EU with a more general tendency towards the internationalisation of production on the part of Japanese firms. In this sense, Japanese FDI in Europe may be market oriented but not in relation to the growth rates within the EU but with the dictates of internationalisation according to the product cycle (Thomsen, 1993). Others have detected some connection between the levels of Japanese manufacturing FDI in the EU and the existence of external trade barriers. This is not simply a question of tariff jumping but rather the proliferation of non-tariff barriers to Japanese imports into the EU such as voluntary export restraints (VERs) and anti-dumping actions (Heitger and Stehn 1990; Kume and Totsuma 1990 cited in Balasubramanyan and Greenaway, 1992: 186) – though this may simply be a reflection of the industry composition of recent Japanese manufacturing FDI in the EU. According to this view, Japanese manufacturing FDI in the EU is largely a defensive measure. This protectionist face of the EU coupled with domestic pressures to internationalisation is behind Dicken's (1988) thinking when he suggests that 'all the evidence suggests that most Japanese firms would have preferred to serve markets in industrialised countries by exports from, Japan or the Far East on a continuing basis' (Dicken, 1988: 648).

At present there are just the merest signs that Japanese manufacturing investment in the EU is becoming more offensive in nature. At least this is the assumption according to product cycle theory – whereby firms will start to decentralise newer product technology and research and development functions more rapidly as they gain experience (Thomsen, 1993; Vernon 1979). Whether any locational change in the intra-EU destination of Japanese manufacturing FDI will accompany such a qualitative change in investment strategies is harder to determine.

The assumption thus far is that trade and direct investment are separate from, or substitutes for, each other. However, the relationship between trade and investment is more complex given that they can sometimes be complementary to one another. This can be seen in the fact that although foreign direct investment can be justified in order to protect markets won through exports (thereby replacing trade) it can also be important in creating or extending overseas markets and hence supporting continued exports from domestic operations. One further implication of this is that foreign direct investment and investment in domestic operations have important impacts on each other.

Yannopoulos (1990) has attempted to link forms of multinational investment to trade effects. He identifies four types of investment:

1. defensive import substituting;

2. offensive import substituting;

3. reorganisation investment;

4. rationalised investment.

The first form of investment is a response to the trade diversion effects of customs unions and itself results in one set of trade relationships being replaced by another once the investment has taken place. This form of investment may have been of importance in the past history of European integration, but Yannopoulos sees it becoming progressively less important. The second form of investment is related to the growth of markets and income which may be a secondary product of market integration. This form of investment need not reduce trade but may restrict trade expansion. Yannapoulos suggests that this type of investment is characteristic of the current state of affairs in the EU. The third and fourth forms of investment may both be complementary to trade. If the first two types of investment have dominated in the formative years of the EU, the latter two types of investment are precisely those types seen to lead to a significant restructuring of EU industry post-1992. Reorganisation investment is a response to pressures to re-group production into fewer sites following trade creation and competition within the EU. Rationalised investment results from the dynamic effects of regional integration – increased price competition from trade necessitates a search for lower cost centres of production.

More straightforwardly an understanding of the changing characteristics of new investment by multinationals can be gained from the literature on changing multinational strategies. Regarding subsidiary roles Hood and Young (1988) and Young, Hood and Dunlop (1988) have taken this line of research the furthest in relation to multinational investment in the UK and the EU. Their work suggests that the roles given to subsidiaries have changed over time to reflect both changing corporate strategies and market circumstances. For instance, Hood and Young

(1988) suggest that multinational investment in the UK has evolved through several stages from: the 'marketing satellites' of pre-1950 which were geared solely towards the UK market; through the 'miniature replicas' of the 1950s and 1960s geared towards the UK and some European markets; to the 'rationalised investments' of the 1970s and 1980s where there is a growing specialisation and division of labour by product or function. Naturally each of those subsidiary roles have different characteristics in terms of the nature of production and functional capabilities, the markets served and the degree and potential degree of local embeddedness. Drawing upon such literature and that on recent developments in multinational organisation more generally, Amin *et al.* (1994) also suggest that the shift away from market-oriented investments to product-specialist investments has given rise to what they term 'quality' mobile investment. Such quality investments have increased in number from the 1970s onwards and are most prevalent in, for instance, the electronics, automotive and pharmaceuticals sectors.

There are a couple of points to note regarding the changing characteristics of multinational investments and their possible trade impacts. First, there appears to be some conflict between the theory and the evidence regarding the changing nature of multinational investments. For whilst some elements of corporate strategy appear to have changed many of the most notable investments in various 'regions' of the EU are far from the 'quality' investments anticipated in the literature (Amin *et al.* 1994). Second, there are some minor differences of opinion over the timing of the emergence of new forms of multinational investment. Thus Hood and Young (1988) and Amin *et al.*'s (1994) work tends to suggest that the rationalised forms of investment which Yannopoulos (1990) sees dominating future multinational investment in the EU have already been prevalent for some time.

Owens (1980) has analysed the relationship between overseas and domestic investment decisions by multinationals (see also Buckley and Artisien, 1988). In detail, foreign direct investment decisions can impact on the domestic operations of multinationals in a number of ways. Quite apart from any direct diversion of investment from domestic operations, foreign direct investment can result in subsequent changes in the level of output and exports of domestic operations, changes in the spatial allocation of product ranges and changes in input sources for company plants. Owens identifies a number of factors which influence both whether there is investment diversion and subsequent knock-on effects on domestic operations. Chief among these are differing international conditions for investment (including regional comparative advantage) and the relationship between overseas and domestic operations – their comparative size, age, location etc. Owens's (1980) study of foreign direct investment by UK firms in Ireland found that a large proportion of investment decisions involved some direct diversion of investment from domestic locations. Furthermore, for these and the remainder of overseas investments which did not involve such immediate diversion of investment, there were nevertheless important knock-on effects on domestic operations. Most important of these effects were transfers of resources (i.e. key personnel, equipment), reorganisation of markets, product rationalisation and, to a lesser extent, changes in output, sourcing and functional status of domestic operations.

Owens's study illustrates that the overseas and domestic operations of multi-nationals are intimately linked. In economies dominated by multinationals, few investment, closure or rationalisation decisions or changes in the competitive position of individual plants will be isolated from developments elsewhere in the corporate sphere. Such interdependency ensures that most domestic and foreign operations of multinationals, most of the time, are in greater or lesser competition with each other for investment and product, market and functional responsibilities. Whilst regions are often by-passed in such inter-plant competition, as Owens suggests, there nevertheless appears to be some scope for policy to influence multinational investment and rationalisation decisions given that regional com-parative advantage plays a part in the competitive position of operations.

Trade, Investment and Regional Development

Thus far we have considered processes of regional economic integration in the EU and their impact on patterns of trade and investment in the EU. It is also valuable to consider whether the trade and investment effects of integration have a regional dimension for the EU as a whole. Integration has offered, and can continue to offer, benefits but the gains to trade and expansion in employment may be unequally distributed at a national or regional level.

On this question of the geographical or regional impact of regional integration, the available theory, though not the weight of evidence, is neatly divided. This in itself perhaps says something about the simplicity of theory – a simplicity which may be out of all proportion to the complexity of processes of industrial restructuring and locational change which accompany regional integration. Thus, on the one hand, there is orthodox neo-classical theory which suggests that regional economic integration will produce convergence of national and regional employment and income around some equilibrium. Whilst there is some limited empirical support for this theory few would take it seriously, preferring instead to point to the uneven nature of capitalist economic growth. Thus, on the other hand, we have a variety of theories and theses which argue that regional integration has led, or will lead, to increased polarisation of economic activity into 'core' and 'peripheral' regions.

Convergence Among EU Regions

Orthodox neo-classical theory suggests that there is an eventual but nonetheless automatic adjustment of markets with economic growth. The evidence does suggest that there has been some convergence of regional income during the formative years of the EU. Thus Keeble et al.'s (1982, 1988) studies suggest that there was some convergence of regional GDP per head in the period 1973 to

1977 but renewed divergence from 1977 to 1983. However, it is difficult to disentangle any effect European integration may have had from the more general economic stability and high growth rates which characterised the world economy at this time. Thus, Dunford (1994) suggests that European integration combined with the final years of the Fordist mode of accumulation to create high growth and regional convergence in the EU (6) during the 1960s and early 1970s. Since the 1970s, however, there has been much slower growth and a less consistent pattern in the growth of regional income. An initial period of divergence at the end of the 1970s and into the 1980s (due in part to a restructuring of Fordist industry recently established in peripheral regions) appears to have been succeeded by some further convergence. In sum, all that might reasonably be suggested here is that there have been elements of both convergence and cumulative causation at work among the regions of the EU as with advanced economies in general (Chisholm, 1990 cited in Chisholm, 1995).

Cumulative Causation and Uneven Regional Development in the EU

This group of theoretical and empirical literature can itself be divided into two groups. First, there are those studies which posit the existence and reinforcement of an obvious core-periphery type arrangement. Second, there are those studies which are perhaps more complex in stressing the importance of agglomeration based upon localised external economies and export specialisation which can lead to clusters of successful industries in even physically remote regions of the EU.

CORE-PERIPHERY

A number of different studies have examined regional variations in accessibility and income and unemployment in Europe. These studies have been suggestive of some sort of polarisation of economic activity on the basis of physical distance. Clark et al. (1969) identified an emerging economic core of Europe. This study of accessibility was updated by Keeble et al. (1982, 1988) who detected signs of further concentration of economic activity in the core 'golden triangle' as well as some changes in the potential of peripheral regions – including the increasing peripherality of Scotland.

Others have suggested that regionalisation in the world economy is accompanied by the formation of macroeconomic corridors (Andersson, 1990, cited in Rimmer, 1994). One such corridor stretching through much of EU territory from London to cities in northern Italy and subsequently celebrated as the 'blue banana' has been identified (Brunet and Salloix, 1989, cited in Lever, 1995). More recently, and as if to play-down the potentially highly uneven nature of the benefits from European integration, the Commission has identified a second banana stretching along the Mediterranean coast from Valencia in Spain to middle Italy (CEC, 1991). In this way metaphors appear to have been used graphically to broaden the benefits from European integration (Williams, 1993). Other metaphors – such as the 'bunch of grapes' – have also recently been used to describe contemporary patterns of regional development in the EU. These again tend to diffuse criticism of the processes of European integration leading to regional uneven development in the EU.

Chisholm (1995), examines trade figures for Europe in some detail and attempts to analyse the geographical impact of trade creation and diversion. When considering the process of regional integration and associated trade creation and diversion Chisholm notes how 'Geographically, the main benefits to be derived from these trade effects will be along the internal frontiers and especially in any area where a large amount of frontiers is located' (Chisholm, 1995: 10). However, as we have seen there is little hard evidence to suggest that the magnitude of trade creation associated with European integration is at all significant. It is therefore hard to imagine that integration would have much of an effect on patterns of regional development. Here Chisholm's conclusions are worth quoting at length.

> 'The theory of economic integration leads one to expect that there will be clear and measurable benefits for the participating countries, and also that these benefits will be geographically concentrated in the "central" areas within the union where there are many political frontiers. In practice, the expected benefits are hard to quantify and appear to be smaller than many would wish us to believe…it follows that peripheral regions – or countries – have little to fear from economic integration solely on account of their relative location.' (Chisholm, 1995: 5)

Chisholm's conclusions on the basis of an examination of the trade impacts of European integration are further confirmed when he later considers regional variations in transport and production costs and economic performance.

Cutler *et al.* (1989) have also examined patterns of European trade but argue strongly that processes of European integration have had geographically uneven effects and in particular have favoured the concentration of economic activity and growth in Germany. They argue that the gains from freer trade within the EU have been captured largely by Germany. Their argument rests not on conventional analyses of trade and regional economic growth but on their own interpretation of how shifting patterns of trade are connected to transfers of output within Europe.

Cutler *et al.* note that Germany has taken an increasing share of extra-EU exports (an increase of 10% as compared to an 18% decline for the UK) and has a large and stable share of intra-EU exports.

> 'Through success in world export markets, the Germans tap a powerful stimulus which has multiplier effects on their rate of domestic output growth and that allows them to achieve what they regard as adequate growth rates without recourse to expansionary domestic fiscal or monetary policies.' (Cutler *et al.* 1989: 15–16)

As a result virtually all EU-member states have run up large trade deficits with Germany. These trade deficits, they argue, represent a net transfer of output to

Germany through trade. This transfer of output has occurred because, despite their economic strength, German firms have not engaged in significantly increased intra-EU FDI – that is until very recently when domestic wage costs have become too high. Instead, gross fixed capital formation has been much higher domestically than abroad. This again is a situation which contrasts with the UK whose firms have increasingly internationalised during the 1980s, and who, as a result, have contributed to a situation whereby gross fixed capital formation overseas was frequently higher than domestic fixed capital formation during the 1980s (Dunning, 1988). Thus, Cutler *et al.* argue that intra-EU trade has resulted in net transfers of output from most member states to Germany (See also Ziebura, 1982). The spatial polarisation which Cutler *et al.* see is therefore quite stark. 'Within Europe, the disparity in manufacturing performance between Britain and West Germany is such that the intra-European transfer of output is increasingly concentrated along the one axis between these two countries' (Cutler *et al.* 1989: 20).

AGGLOMERATION, EXTERNAL ECONOMIES AND CLUSTERS OF INDUSTRY

However, processes of cumulative causation may work in a more subtle way – one which is unrelated to physical centrality or peripherality measured in terms of distance. As Keeble suggests,

> 'The complexity and variety of economic forces currently at work in Europe's regions are too great to be encompassed by any single all-embracing theory of economic change…the result is a regional mosaic of different development trajectories within Europe, in the evolution of which both macro-economic forces and local socio-economic characteristics are important.'
> (Keeble, 1991, quoted in Bachtler *et al.* 1993: 82)

The interpretations of cumulative causation and regional development outlined above take little account of the detailed way in which industry organises itself in space and the role that multinationals play in processes of cumulative causation. Cumulative causation is based on external economies which tend to be highly localised and engender regional clusters of industry specialisation. Spatial polarisation in Europe may therefore be more evident at the level of urban and regional industrial structures irrespective of physical centrality or peripherality. Few would argue that tracts of Belgium are anything other than peripheral or problem regions despite their being physically central to the economic core of the EU. Similarly, some successful regional clusters of industry are physically quite remote from the economic core of the EU. This in turn suggests that the 'bunch of grapes' metaphor may be quite appropriate to explaining the polarisation of economic activity in the EU – including multinational manufacturing investment. Thus, 'even as capital becomes more mobile TNCs and their affiliates will continue to derive their competitive advantage, in part, from interacting with the local economy.' (Kozul-Wright, 1995: 161). An important question, therefore, is how multinationals contribute to, or detract from, the formation and development of such regional clusters.

Porter (1990) and Krugman (cited in Martin and Sunley, 1995) and Storper (1992; 1995) have each stressed the contribution of industry clusters or regional export specialisation to patterns of trade and national economic performance. In Porter's analysis, the competitive advantage of nations is synonymous with the performance of indigenous industry – multinationals being an exogenous influence on national economic performance (Young, Hood and Peters, 1994). Krugman's analysis doesn't really distinguish between indigenous and multinational firms and their contribution to regional export specialisation based on external economies. However, his analysis may be more appropriate than Porter's given that it is explicitly framed to take account of imperfect forms of competition and economies of scale – rather than assuming perfect competition. According to Krugman intra-industry trade, which we have seen is the defining feature of trade between advanced economies, represents specialisation to take advantage of increasing returns to scale. If firms in a region begin to be successful in export markets there can be cumulative gains to trade which are captured by those firms – rather as Cutler *et al.* suggest has happened at the national scale within the EU. Exports are crucial, given economies of scale, to processes of cumulative causation.

Krugman has produced two variants to his theories of cumulative causation and spatial polarisation. The first simply suggests that trade coupled with conditions of imperfect competition, scale economies and variations in transport costs can lead to core-periphery type development. Krugman suggests that the forces generating this core-periphery pattern in Europe have probably reached their limit and that cumulative causation is now producing a pattern of regional export specialisation – the outcome of which is more unpredictable. The second variant of this model suggests that trade coupled with internal and external economies produces specialised 'core' regions which may then be quite susceptible to 'shocks'. His analyses have suggested that internal and external economies of scale can complement each other in the formation of regional specialisms. As Martin and Sunley (1995) have argued, the sort of regional instability alluded to above is likely to depend on the type or mix of external economies upon which such regional specialisation is based. The prospect of shocks undermining successful regions in itself highlights the fact that processes of cumulative causation are themselves prone to disruption.

Others have looked more explicitly at the contribution of multinationals to uneven urban and regional development. Here interpretations focus on the division of labour within multilocational and multinational companies. The division of labour within large companies finds spatial expression in the hierarchy of national (e.g. Massey, 1979, 1984; Pred, 1976) and international (e.g. Hymer, 1979) urban-systems. At the apex of such hierarchies are nationally or internationally important cities which act as command and control centres of large companies. Concentrated in the same or nearby cities might be important non-manufacturing functions such as research and development and sales. Routine production activities would tend to be concentrated at the bottom of urban hierarchies in smaller urban areas in peripheral regions. In this way

> 'Through the internationalisation of business hierarchies and networks the European regions are becoming more and more integrated with each other on a functional basis within transnational corporate divisions of labour. As a result, uneven spatial development is less a matter of inter-regional competition than a question concerning the impact on local economies of the uneven distribution of tasks within a Europe-wide integrated corporate production system.' (Amin and Malmberg, 1992: 411)

Amin and Malmberg (1992) eschew any all-embracing theory of spatial development in Europe based on an analysis of the division of labour within multinationals and go some way toward considering recent developments in multinational organisational forms – including the partial and uneven replacement of hierarchies by networks. Nevertheless, in aggregate, the hierarchical arrangement of economic activity alluded to above is apparent in one recent study of the location of multinational firms in the European urban system (Rozenblat and Pumain, 1993). Their survey, covering 94 of the largest 300 firms in Europe, suggested that in the region of one-half of all headquarters of these firms were located in London and Paris alone. They also found that three-quarters of multinational affiliates were located in urban agglomerations with over 200,000 inhabitants. One implication of this is that the factors contributing to the agglomeration of economic activity in Europe may be quite widespread and not especially unique. In general, the pattern which emerges suggests that internationalisation is closely, though not inevitably, associated with metropolitanisation. If this is the current pattern, then some consider that urban regions are the spatial units at which processes of European integration work themselves out (Cheshire, 1995) and that further European integration is likely to increase polarisation within the European urban system. Arguably, then, 'Europe is in the middle of a transition from a hitherto prevalent system of inter-regional hierarchies of power and opportunity to a trans-regional hierarchy of unevenly distributed possibilities' (Amin and Thrift, 1995: 45).

Cantwell's (1988) model of cumulative causation based on multinationals is a more formal but more limited (in terms of conceptualising the division of labour within multinationals) rendering of the same approach. Cantwell's model is a rather simple one based upon a distinction between two types of activity; research and development (R&D) and production. The peculiar contribution of multinationals is that the link between R&D and production associated with indigenous industry in national economies can be broken due to the division of labour in multinationals and the mobility of their investments. Put simply, Cantwell's model suggests that vicious and virtuous circles of economic development are associated with locations with weaknesses or strengths in R&D activities respectively. Processes of cumulative causation are centred on R&D activities and in this respect multinational investment decisions can act to complement or counteract indigenous strengths or weaknesses in R&D. He identifies two main implications of the division of labour within multinationals as it impinges on national or regional economic performance. First, and irrespective of processes of regional integration, multinationals will tend to locate their R&D activities in existing centres of R&D activity. In this way, indigenous R&D and that of multinationals are complementary and reinforce one another. Second, European integration presents incentives for multinationals to create a greater division of labour and hence may exacerbate tendencies for multinational investment patterns to reinforce processes of cumulative causation. Naturally, in this simplistic form Cantwell's model comes close to the neo-marxist literature on multinationals and dependent development (Young, Hood and Peters, 1994). Whilst multinationals historically have derived much of their technological expertise and competitive advantage from their domestic economy, Cantwell (1995) suggests that they are increasingly establishing globalised networks of research and development activity.

> 'In the past, foreign technological activity exploited domestic strengths abroad... At that time the capacity to develop internationally dispersed innovations derived from a position of technological strength in the firm's home base, and led to similar lines of technological development being established abroad. By contrast, today, foreign technological activity now increasingly aims to tap into local fields of expertise...' (Cantwell, 1995: 172)

Thus, in globalising their research and development activities, multinationals complement similar activity existing in host economies and contribute to a 'virtuous circle' of development centred on technological external economies.

Such interpretations of the role of multinationals in urban and regional development in the EU have their limitations. Not least of these is the inherent tendency to assume that processes of cumulative causation perpetuate an existing urban and regional hierarchy of activity (e.g. see Walker, 1989). As Cantwell himself concedes his model would need to take account of the many other activities inherent in the division of labour within multinationals. It may be that some of the more profound forms of corporate reorganisation are centred on activities – for example, distribution – often overlooked. Finally, to gain insights into the more subtle way in which multinationals effect a division of labour we need to consider theories or taxonomies of these different types of activity as they are represented in different forms of multinational investment. Of particular importance here is the extent to which the various elements of corporate divisions of labour have been, and currently are, more or less uncoupled within individual investment decisions. Fuller consideration is given to these issues in Chapter 4.

Conclusion

European integration and its impact on trade and investment patterns needs to be placed in a wider global context. More particularly, patterns of trade and investment can only be understood with reference to the changing competitive position of domestic and multinational European manufacturing firms *vis-à-vis* imports and competition from US and Japanese firms.

The relationship between trade and investment in Europe has changed over time and is complicated by the growing importance of multinationals within the EU. For US multinationals direct investment initially appears to have been largely a substitute for trade though the relationship between the two may have become complementary in more recent years. This pattern appears to have been repeated for Japanese firms though there is already an important element of complementarity between investment and trade due to the competitiveness of Japanese manufacturing firms. Furthermore, the widespread persistence of multiplant operations within Europe will ensure a complex complementarity between multinational orchestrated trade and investment. The connection between trade and investment promises to become more complicated with the growth of intra-EU FDI which until recently has been relatively unimportant. An understanding of the impact of FDI upon domestic investment therefore appears particularly important to understanding the likely impact of intra-EU FDI.

There is little theory which deals explicitly with the role of multinationals in regional economic integration and still less which also addresses itself to the spatial distribution of economic activities within multinationals. Theories which point to the self-reinforcing tendencies towards spatial polarisation tend to be inadequate to capture actual patterns of regional development in the EU. From a review of the literature, the evolving investment patterns of multinationals in relation to European integration appears to be contributing to the formation of specialised local/regional industrial clusters based upon localised external economies. It is how multinationals contribute to the formation, growth or indeed decline of such regional clusters which is of importance.

Chapter 4 discusses in more detail some major dimensions of corporate restructuring by multinationals in relation to the latest stage of European integration – the completion of the internal market. The chapter takes issue with the Commission's analysis of the likely extent and timing of restructuring. In particular it suggests that restructuring will be a product of the complex relationship between economies of scale and firm competitiveness, the persistence of several markets rather than a truly single market, and the attachment of firms to particular production locations.

CHAPTER 4

The Single European Market and Multinational Restructuring

Introduction

We have already seen how the creation and enlargement of the EU customs union produced some gains to trade for member states. The magnitude of these gains is debatable but is typically associated with movements in intra-EU trade, the growth of which began to diminish from the mid 1970s and into the early 1980s. During this time intra-EU trade went hand in hand with the falling competitiveness of EU industry in relation to US and more particularly Japanese and other Far East industry. Coincident with this economic stagnation in the EU was a 'sclerosis' in the EU decision-making apparatus which had held up progress toward, among other things, harmonising standards for trade in goods and services. The attempt to create truly EU-wide technical standards for goods and services traded within the EU was extremely slow and cumbersome. Eventually (with the Cassis de Dijon case) case law provided a more rapid and politically acceptable means of harmonising standards by establishing the principle that any product currently produced in a member state should be free to circulate within the EU. One obvious interpretation of this state of affairs was that poor economic performance was, at least in part, a function of the Commission's lack of progress in creating a truly common market. In any event this was the interpretation to emerge from a consensus of public and private sectors within the EU – albeit a consensus fashioned largely by the Commission itself (Tsoukalis, 1993).

Key to remedying the economic ills of the EU was therefore the completion of the common market. The EU had long since titled itself as a common market but much needed to be done to remove the many remaining non-tariff barriers to trade, and facilitate the free movement of factors. In this respect the Commission's interpretation and presentation of the problem facing the EU resonated with most national macroeconomic policies of the time since it was supply-side orientated. It also resonated with a general reluctance on the part of the established members to increase the EU budget dramatically by presenting the task ahead in terms of 'rules and not money'. In 1985 the Commission presented its White Paper on Completing the Internal Market which contained 279 separate measures to be adopted by 31 December 1992. These were subsequently supplemented by a small number of further measures. The measures related to the removal of four sets of remaining barriers to trade in goods and services. First, there were remaining variations in technical regulations between member states. Second, there were delays and burdens at frontiers due to customs checks and different administrative procedures. Third, there were important restrictions on competition for public purchases. Fourth, there were restrictions on the freedom to engage in some service transactions. The White Paper proposals were accepted by the 12 member states under the Single European Act in February 1986 which itself came into force in July 1987. By the beginning of 1993, 95% of the original 279 measures in the White Paper had been adopted by the Council of Ministers (CEC, 1994b).

The Commission's Analysis of the Single European Market

Since the Single European Act was passed and prior to the actual 1992 deadline, the Commission has been engaged in an attempt to quantify the effects of further European integration with the completion of the Single European Market. The initial analysis which was published in summary form in 1988 (CEC, 1988) was based on just seven members and not the twelve which signed up to the Single European Act. This analysis consisted of micro and macroeconomic assessments involving surveys of industrialists and econometric modelling to quantify the overall benefits from a more integrated EU market. Omitted at this stage was any consideration of the distribution of these benefits. Thus, more recently the Commission has focused its analytical work on assessing the sectoral and national distribution of the benefits of the SEM.

The Commission's initial analyses of the possible benefits from creating the SEM identify three sets of savings or sources of economic growth in the lead up to, and in the aftermath of, 1992. The various estimates of these benefits are shown in Table 4.1. First, there are the static microeconomic effects of the elimination of remaining barriers to trade. Here the Commission has made estimates of the cost savings open to industry with the elimination of these barriers. So, for instance, removal of physical barriers to trade – essentially custom checks and import/export paperwork – would, they suggest, lead to a saving in the order of 1.8% of the total value of goods and services traded. Overall, the removal of all barriers, including technical and physical barriers, to trade, is estimated by industrialists to result in a saving on total industry costs representing between 2.2% and 2.7% of EU GDP. The several industry studies which were also conducted as part of the empirical analyses confirm these overall cost savings with removal of existing barriers producing savings between 1 and 2% of total production and distribution costs for firms in the food and beverages, pharmaceutical, textiles and clothing and construction materials industries and up to 5% for the car industry.

Table 4.1 Estimated benefits from the completion
of the Single European Market

	bn ECU	% GDP
Stage 1: static microeconomic effects	74–91	2.2–2.7
Stage 2: dynamic microeconomic effects	127–187	2.1–3.7
Stage 3: macroeconomic consequences		4.5–7.0

NB Figures are for EU (12)
Source: CEC (1988)

These direct static effects from the elimination of remaining barriers are only part, and probably a minor part, of the possible gains from further market integration. Potentially much greater, though also much harder to estimate, are the secondary or dynamic effects of industry reorganisation once barriers are eliminated. The idea is that the removal of barriers to trade would permit and encourage some reorganisation of business, the exploitation of economies of scale and the elimination of x-inefficiency. Here the Commission's analysis provides for a number of different scenarios. The most pessimistic of these estimates entertains a saving of 2.5% of GDP, the most optimistic a saving of up to 6.5% of GDP.

Finally, the third part of the Commission's analysis uses macroeconomic simulation to arrive at estimates of the benefits of further European integration. They present two main scenarios. First, there is the scenario of passive macroeconomic policy which yields similar benefits to those estimated in the overall microeconomic analysis. Second, there is the scenario of active macroeconomic policy whereby a more expansionary stance in national economic policies is permitted by the positive effects of integration and which produces benefits of up to 7% of GDP.

Two initial points of criticism can be made which relate directly to the Commission's own figures and assumptions. First, there is the assumption that resources made redundant by the secondary dynamic effects are redeployed. If they were not, then the costs – essentially costs of unemployment – would detract from the estimated savings. Yet there is no reason to expect that those made unemployed would all find work, especially in the current highly competitive world economy. Second, the Commission's own analysis admits to a wide margin of error (plus or minus 30%) which means that, viewed pessimistically, the benefits to further European integration may be as little as 3.15% of GDP (i.e. 30% less than the passive macroeconomic scenario).

Nevertheless, the Commission argues that 'the largest benefits suggested...are unlikely to be overestimates of the potential benefit of fully integrating the Community's market' (CEC, 1988: 20). This is, they argue, because their analysis of the secondary or dynamic impact of integration excludes some important considerations, namely: 1. the effect of technological change on competition and economies of scale; 2. the sorts of learning economies evident in high technology industries and; 3. the reorganisation of business strategy and structures within Europe; all of which they suggested will have a further positive effect. In sum, they believe that

> 'In the present condition of the European economy the segmentation and weak competitiveness of many markets mean that there is large potential for the rationalisation of production and distribution structures leading to improvements in productivity, and reductions in many costs and prices.'
> (CEC, 1988:21)

Subsequent to this initial analysis of the trade and economic effects of the creation of the SEM detailed above, the Commission turned its attention to analysing the distribution of potential benefits across industry sectors and member states. The benefits estimated in the initial analysis are crucially dependent upon competition accompanying both the direct and secondary microeconomic effects. However, the Commission also concedes that 'the optimum market structure from the stand point of integration ought…to promote *strategic rivalry* between a *limited number* of firms' (CEC, 1988: 89, emphasis added). Such oligopolistic market structures may, however, be quite anti-competitive. Here is a quandary in which the Commission finds itself. In many respects European integration is geared toward rationalisation of industry structures and the emergence of fewer larger firms – something which the Commission accepts as being potentially favourable to processes of innovation but which is likely to have distinctly unfavourable effects on peripheral regions (e.g. Amin, Charles and Howells, 1992) and nations.

The Commission identifies 40 industry sectors which, on the basis of their facing significant non-tariff barriers or for which such barriers that exist prevent exploitation of economies of scale or permit price dispersion, are most sensitive to the measures included in the White Paper. These so-called most sensitive sectors fall into three main groups: 1. 'high technology public procurement markets'; 2. 'traditional public procurement and regulated markets' and; 3. 'sectors with moderate non-tariff barriers.'

These 40 sectors represent sensitive industries at the EU-wide scale and their importance within each member state varies. The importance of the sensitive sectors varies in importance from a high of 55% of industrial employment in Germany, to 50% in the UK, to a low of 39% in Spain. Northern member states appear to be potentially prone to reorganisation of public procurement sectors (CEC, 1990: 29). Deletions and additions to their list of 40 sectors are made to take account of the peculiarities of each member state. Once the list of sectors has been adjusted in this way to produce lists of sectors which are sensitive at a national level the position of Portugal and Greece in particular changes since the importance of sensitive sectors in these two countries increases.

Taking this adjusted list of 40 sectors the Commission's analysis proceeds by three stages. First, they look at the current structure of trade and production specialisation of each member state. Here the UK appears to be very poorly or very well placed in only a few industries. The UK possesses little in the way of a distinct competitive advantage in selected industries and overall is perhaps at a slight competitive disadvantage in most of the sensitive sectors. It is poorly placed with respect to textiles and clothing and footwear but well placed in chemicals, pharmaceuticals and telecommunications (CEC, 1990: 34). The balance of strong and weak sectors is illustrated graphically in Figure 4.1. This confirms the slightly weak position of the UK and the particularly weak position of Portugal and Greece.

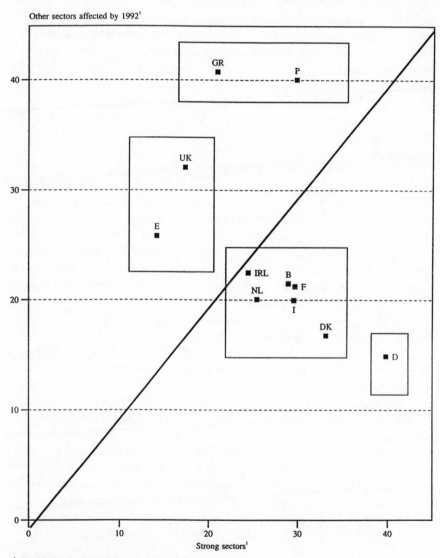

Other sectors affected by 1992[1]

Strong sectors[1]

[1] Identified on the basis of the composite static indicator score

Source: CEC (1990)

Figure 4.1. Postion of countries in the run-up to 1992 - Share in industrial employment

The second of the Commission's three stages of analysis is an examination of the determinants of historical trends in export performance of member states in the sensitive sectors. From their principal components analysis the UK's position appears to be good in relation to high technology and labour intensive sectors but poor in terms of those involving high capital intensity and neutral in terms those for which economies of scale are important (CEC, 1990: 48). The Commission notes that for the majority of member states' trade in the sensitive sectors is intra-industry in nature but that for Portugal and Greece it is mainly inter-industry in nature. This leads them to believe that there may be some relocation of activity in certain sectors to these southern member states due to lower labour costs there. Their findings here are supported by those of Neven who argues that 'the main beneficiaries of the 1992 programme are...likely to be the southern European countries, both in terms of exploiting comparative advantage and in terms of exhausting scale economies.' (Neven, 1990 quoted in Chisholm, 1995: 74). Against this it can be argued that the poor transportation and communications infrastructure in these countries may counteract labour cost savings.

The third element of the Commission's analysis of the distribution of the benefits from the 1992 programme represents an attempt to assess the dynamic effects. Here they adopt a more qualitative approach examining merger and acquisitions and FDI statistics and the results of surveys of industrialists. The data in Figure 4.2 indicate that national merger and acquisition activity in the EU was most important in the early to mid-1980s. In the latter half of the 1980s mergers and acquisitions of EU-wide and international scope have grown in importance. It is this trend which the Commission sees as evidence of important restructuring accompanying the creation of the SEM.

The Commission also cites the changing motives for merger and acquisition activity in the EU (see Figure 4.3). A desire to rationalise operations was the most important motive for merger and acquisition activity in the mid to late 1980s. This has given way to strengthening of market position and expansion as the major motives for merger and acquisition activity in the 1990s.

The Commission has tended to interpret these data in terms of a distinct phase of mergers and acquisition activity *leading up to* the deadline for completion of the SEM. In some ways this is a curious line of interpretation since it tends to argue against there being significant potential for restructuring accompanying market integration. Given the marginal impact on levels of industry concentration ratios (recorded in CEC, 1994a: 31) that this merger and acquisition activity will have contributed to, it would appear that the restructuring accompanying the creation of the SEM has been relatively small scale and short-lived. The Commission's interpretation can be contrasted with the findings in one recent survey of leading manufacturing companies in Europe in which 55% of firms had overcapacity, of which 15% had severe overcapacity; this despite more plant closures than openings in the last decade (Collins and Schmenner, 1995). This would tend to suggest that

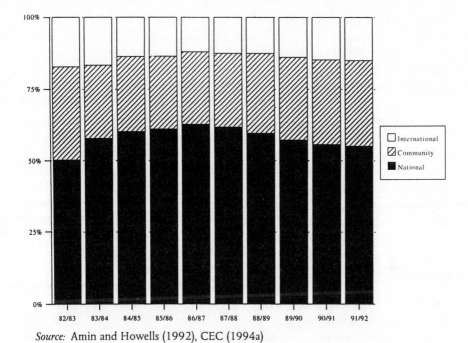

Source: Amin and Howells (1992), CEC (1994a)

Figure 4.2 National, community and international mergers and acquisitions involving EU companies

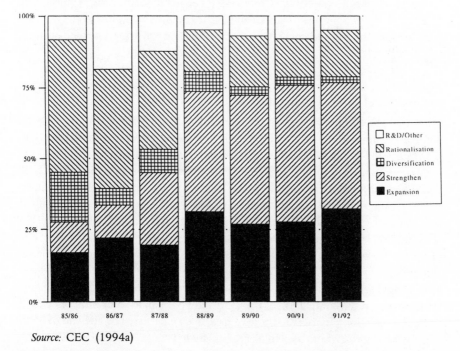

Source: CEC (1994a)

Figure 4.3 Reasons for merger and acquisition activity involving EU companies

there is still considerable scope for rationalisation it is just that such rationalisation is slow to take place.

According to the Commission's own surveys of leading industrialists in the EU, the impact of the SEM initiative appears to be greatest in relation to decisions regarding products and the restructuring of production plants with 63% and 61% of industrialists surveyed suggesting that the SEM would have some effect on these aspects of business respectively. However, over half the surveyed industrialists also thought that distribution and research and development would be likewise affected in some way by the SEM. As Collins and Schmenner (1995) argue it is relatively easy to centralise aspects of sales and marketing (and distribution?) but very difficult to base a business on the manufacture of pan-European products. There are some variations in the opinions of industrialists in different member states which may shed some light on the different proclivities of firms for restructuring according to ownership. 82% of German industrialists suggested that the SEM would have a bearing on production plants. For the UK this figure was only 43% (CEC, 1990: 55). Furthermore, there may be differences between for example US firms and Japanese firms compared to those from member states in terms of which functions will be most affected by the creation of the SEM. One study of US firms suggests that the creation of the SEM will have its major impact upon pricing and distribution and not upon production since many of these firms have already standardised production on a worldwide let alone an EU-wide basis (Krum, 1991).

Some initial criticisms of the Commission's economic justification for its efforts to create a single European market have been noted. However, this chapter now turns to some more fundamental criticisms of the Commission's prognosis of the impact of '1992'.

Economies of Scale, Competition and Restructuring

From the preceding discussion it is apparent that the main ways in which the completion of the single market is presumed to have an effect on industrial activity is through the static reallocation of resources/rationalisation accompanying the SEM programme and through on-going or dynamic gains from economies of scale and future rationalisation. Clearly, in the Commission's analysis, the main impact of the creation of the SEM and further economic integration is upon the supply side – that is production activities. Leaving aside the Commission's neglect of consumption – side issues which we can examine in a lot more detail below, there are problems with the interpretation of the impact of the SEM on production activities.

To begin with we can take the Commission's own estimates of the cost savings associated with the completion of the SEM and put them in some kind of context. Since the remaining barriers to trade to have been eliminated by the end of 1992 add up to only 2.7% to the total cost of traded items only the most minute opportunities for reaping economies of scale should have been left unexploited

(Pelkman and Winters, 1988 cited in Holmes, 1989). Furthermore, these cost savings are potentially overshadowed by other factors. The Commission's estimates suggest that the harmonisation of border controls will result in savings of roughly 1.8% on the cost of traded items. At the time, these savings were, for example, well within the permitted deviations within the EMS. In other words, currency fluctuations may be more significant in altering the competitiveness of traded items than the physical barriers to trade which have persisted until recently (Kay, 1989).

The Commission's own figures on minimum efficient technical plant sizes (METS) across EU industries, also give further grounds for doubting that significant restructuring centred on the exploitation of economies of scale will be apparent after 1992. The Commission's re-examination of minimum efficient technical plant sizes in EU industries makes it apparent that economies of scale are only important in a small minority of industries. There are very few industries indeed for which the METS is at all large in relation to the entire EU market. For instance, there are no industries for which the METS is such that the EU market as a whole can only support one plant. Yet the logic of the economies of scale argument leads one in the direction of rationalisation of industry output into fewer larger plants with just a single EU-wide plant presumably being some sort of optimum. Such 'Euro-plants' have a troubled history and they are likely to appear only very slowly and not before time. The Commission's own figures make it apparent that national markets let alone the EU market as a whole can support numerous plants operating at their minimum efficient technical size.

Some of the industries in which there do appear to be unexploited economies of scale are in the public sector or those affected by issues of public procurement. Here the process of rationalisation and restructuring is critically dependent upon the political commitment to the removal of such barriers of trade. However, progress in opening up various public sectors in the member states has been painfully slow. Thus, some time before the actual 1992 deadline, Kay was arguing that '"completion of the internal market" is a description of a legal and administrative process, rather than an economic outcome' (Kay, 1989: 4). Certainly, for these public sector oriented industries, completion of the internal market requires considerable commitment *in practice* from local, and national governments.

Furthermore, when examining the figures of the METS for plants in various industries, we can note that the METS has generally increased but for some industries, notably cars, it has actually fallen. In other words there seems some limited tendency toward smaller plants in some industries. This evidence can be put in a broader context. It is argued quite widely now that new production methods are being very widely instituted by Western manufacturing companies. These new production methods rely less on the exploitation of economies of scale, and more on responsiveness to changing consumer demand and flexibility in production. In general, adoption of such methods of production leads toward smaller plant sizes and in some instances to the exploitation of economies of scope. These forms of production organisation are exemplified in different ways by

Japanese manufacturing firms and the contemporary industrial districts of Italy and elsewhere (Scott, 1988). To an extent, the success of these producers undermines the idea that significant cost savings can be made through the rationalisation of production into fewer larger plants and the exploitation of economies of scale (see the debate between Gertler, 1988, 1989, 1992 and Schoenberger, 1988).

In fact, as Cutler *et al.* (1989) note the available evidence on the connection between plant size and productivity is not straightforward. There is a technical sense in which economies of scale are a function of the physical capacity of plant and equipment (e.g. see Gold, 1981). However, for many industries the better part of what economists term economies of scale centre on 'learning curve' effects and operational efficiency including plant utilisation. Instead of stressing the technical basis to the concept of economies of scale, Cutler *et al.* (1989) stress the operational basis to economies of scale and factory productivity. They argue that estimates of METS abstract from the problem of operational efficiency and the widespread feature of capacity underutilisation. As Collins and Schmenner note, 'In moving to pan-European operations, the generous buffer capacities typically present in the independent, country-based plants are squeezed out of the reduced number of plants that the company decides to keep in operation.' (Collins and Schmenner, 1995: 259). In other words, the exploitation of economies of scale within any rationalised pan-European organisational structures which may be emerging are based upon fuller utilisation of production capacity and not necessarily upon plant size. In questioning the view that economies of scale are significant Cutler *et al.* do 'not wish to invert the myth of scale and to endorse the newly fashionable notion of "flexible specialisation..."' (Cutler *et al.* 1989: 65). Rather, they wish to draw attention to the various sources of productivity of which scale, in a technical sense, may be one. Equally important, then, may be the capital and labour skills employed or more likely the capital-labour combination and place specific forms of learning.

There is also ambiguity over the impact of processes of integration on firm as opposed to plant sizes. There seems little doubt that European integration has prompted an increase in firm sizes – at least the rising number of mergers and acquisitions of a European-wide scope is strongly suggestive of this. Arguably, most European firms are quite large even if plant sizes are small. Further rationalisation at the firm level – through merger and acquisition activity – may have little connection with the exploitation of economies of scale at the plant level. Indeed merger and acquisition activity may have a dampening effect on competition – reinforcing oligopolistic market structures and hence negating any tendency towards rationalisation of the number of plants and an increase in their size.

This brings us to the assumption that exploitation of economies of scale will be driven by heightened European competition. It is unclear whether and in what way market integration is accompanied by the maintenance or enhancement of competition or in what way the exploitation of scale economies and competition may be related. Rationalisation of production by companies into fewer larger factories, may be unprofitable if there is oligopolistic reaction by competitors (Holmes, 1989). Arguably such oligopolistic or anti-competitive practices are quite widespread within the EU. Scherer *et al*.'s (1975) analysis of multiplant operations makes it quite clear that multiplant firms rarely operate on strictly efficiency grounds. They found that multiplant firms in Europe in particular tended to operate more plants than necessary as a result of market failure or anti-competitive practices rather than as an attempt to offer greater product variety. Instead, 'National boundaries constitute a kind of focal point around which tacit or explicit bargaining over spheres of influence can coalesce (Scherer *et al*. 1975: 388, quoted in Holmes, 1989). Such oligopolistic market structures may therefore mean that 'the profits from continuing price discrimination may be greater than the cost savings from standardisation and rationalisation' (Holmes, 1989: 530). Thus, the emergence of rationalised and integrated production in the EU is largely limited to those industries in which there are economies of scale and low barriers to entry (Millington and Bayliss, 1996).

The assumption in the Commission's analysis of the impact of the SEM is that competition is essentially market-based and responsive to the price mechanism. However, in the large, often multinational, firms which are the main orchestrators of European integration, competition may at least partly, if not primarily in some cases, be intra-corporate in focus. This means that a number of factors additional to scale and unit cost enter the equation regarding which plants to operate and which to close. Whilst 'plant specific economics' may be the most important of considerations in plant closures (Schmenner, 1982, cited in Watts and Stafford, 1986), there is also an apparent tension between the economies of scope available to a multinational operating a group of plants and the economies of scale available at individual plants (e.g. see Charles, Monk and Sciberras, 1989).

So far we have examined the issue of the exploitation of economies of scale and pressures of competition within a single market from the supply-side perspective. We can now also consider the connection of economies of scale with the nature of demand or consumption within the SEM.

A Single European Market?

We have already noted that the Commission's prognoses of restructuring accompanying and following the creation of the SEM are based almost exclusively on production or supply-side considerations. Even when examining the supply-side effects of the SEM there appear to be good reasons to believe that the cost savings and presumably the extent of restructuring accompanying further economic integration will not be great. Considering the demand-side effects of the creation of the SEM throws yet further doubt on the impact of further European integration. The potentially rather limited impact of further European integration and industry restructuring in general and multinational activity in particular resolves itself into the question of whether there is any such thing as the Single European Market?

First, whilst there are some examples of companies managing to create 'Euro-brands', not all products are or will become standardised, and hence subject to mass consumption with intense price competition predicated on economies of scale and minimisation of costs of production. Indeed, if anything, the reverse may be the case. Japanese manufacturers, for example, are widely held to have de-matured certain products – notably consumer electronics and cars (Taylor, 1986). Furthermore, and in general terms, there is the consumption-side corollary to the flexible forms of production which some see as emergent in the world economy. It is argued that the flexible forms of production alluded to above have their origins in the fragmentation of mass markets and differentiation of consumption patterns (Piore and Sabel, 1984; Scott, 1988). This thesis has been subject to fierce criticism and has undoubtedly been overstated by its proponents. Yet few would doubt that a halt to mass consumption has probably occurred even if this doesn't necessarily mean increasingly customised consumption. If we can accept this basic change in consumption patterns then the cost savings achieved by the removal of remaining barriers to trade and through the exploitation of economies of scale may be irrelevant to current norms of competition based more on product quality rather than price.

The main effects of 1992 are therefore in terms of uniting a diverse set of consumer tastes in one large market (Geroski, 1989). The market is undoubtedly large but not necessarily a single market in the sense of there being a ready demand for a very limited number of highly standardised or homogeneous goods. Arguably, trade liberalisation through the removal of remaining barriers will expose producers more fully to a diversity of consumption patterns. The barriers themselves are not the reason for such a diversity of consumer tastes. Instead, long-standing differences in habits, language, culture, climate and income have existed and will continue to exist after the removal of barriers in 1992. The impact of the SEM could be in terms of competition but not solely in terms of price.

Because consumption patterns vary according to such factors as language, climate, culture and income, there is also a geographical aspect to this question of whether there is a single European market. Such differences coupled to the need to add value locally by way of, for example, after-sales service, force multinationals to have a 'presence' in local markets (Buckley and Artisien, 1988). Thus, whilst there has been some evolution of subsidiary roles within Europe away from stand-alone plants operating in individual countries (Hood and Young, 1988), there is still a need for multinationals to have a presence in local markets – albeit that these local markets may now cover several national markets. Here, we can conceive of a number of sub-European markets or market clusters formed of EU member states and non-member states. We noted earlier that the geographical patterns of trade and investment within the EU are very similar which in turn suggested that the two were complementary (Molle and Morsink, 1991). Thus 'A good deal of the patterns of investment in Europe can be explained by the size of the host country market, together with some measure of proximity such as distance or a common language or border' (Thomsen and Woolcock, 1993: 47). When the patterns are examined further it is possible to be a little more precise about a number of possible sub-European market clusters (e.g. see Guido, 1991; Petri, 1994; Thomsen and Woolcock, 1993; Wijkman, 1990). This observation in itself undermines the misleading notion of the EU as a single market or indeed the relevant market for which corporate strategy is composed. These European sub-markets have in the past cut across the boundaries of the major trade groupings of EFTA and the EU and today include both member and non-member states of the EU. It may be these market clusters which are more meaningful to treat as coherent markets both in terms of consumption patterns and the organisation of production.

The debate here' is really over the precise groupings of countries into the relevant clusters. On the basis of trade patterns alone Wijkman (1990) speaks of the 'Northern periphery' (the UK and Nordic Countries), 'core Europe' (the original six plus Switzerland) and the 'Southern Periphery' (composed of Portugal, Spain. Greece, the former Yugoslavia and Turkey), with the latter grouping being the only one of the five based on one-sided flows of trade and investment with the rest of Europe. Thomsen and Woolcock (1993) on the other hand identify four market clusters centred on the UK, France, Germany and the Netherlands.

Perhaps more important and more interesting than debate over the precise number and form of these market clusters is consideration of their implications for conceptualising industrial restructuring (the rationalisation and investment decisions of multinationals) accompanying processes of European integration. The existence of these market clusters suggests that 'there appear to be limits to the degree to which firms will treat Europe as one market, and for larger countries this limit may already have been reached' (Thomsen and Woolcock, 1993: 61). Just as significantly, the notion of market clusters 'alters the notion of the periphery in Europe' (Thomsen and Woolcock, 1993: 67). In particular, not all countries or regions which are physically peripheral, or even currently peripheral in terms of lacking clusters of competitive industries, need remain peripheral. Peripheral countries such as Ireland and Portugal are well-placed to serve their respective market clusters and may benefit precisely from this role. This certainly questions the notion of cumulative causation based on a physical peripherality and instead opens up the possibility of new economic development based on regional export specialisation away from existing centres of industry.

If patterns of investment are tied to locations as centres of consumption so too may investment be tied to locations as centres of production. The next section examines the way in which multinational investments may become tied to particular centres of production even within peripheral regions.

Multinational Embeddedness

Implicit, to a large degree, within orthodox analyses of the impact of the SEM – including those of the Commission – is that factors of production, and capital in particular, are perfectly mobile. Resource allocation occurs instantly or at least rapidly in the case of the indirect second stage effects where the exploitation of economies of scale is expected to lead to further rationalisation. This also accords with assumptions contained in neo-Marxist analyses of industrial location which predominated in the 1970s and early 1980s (e.g. Perrons, 1981; Frobel *et al.* 1980). In the more extreme of these analyses of regimes of accumulation and the new international division of labour there was an implicit sense of the extreme or hyper-mobility of capital – which was free to uproot itself and seek out more propitious locations.

However, in many senses the term 'mobile investment' is a misnomer. Productive capital in the form of inward investment is really only perfectly mobile in this sense when on paper. In reality there are many reasons why, once an investment is made, it becomes rooted or embedded to a greater or lesser degree in a particular location. Depending on one's object of analysis, location can be viewed as a factor contributing to plant rationalisation and closure or survival and continued investment (though as Watts and Stafford suggest, the latter may well be far less prevalent (Watts and Stafford, 1986). Thus Hirst and Thompson note, 'the real question to ask of MNCs is not why they are always threatening to up and leave a country if things seem to go bad for them there, but why the vast majority of them fail to leave and continue to stay put in their home base and major centres of investment' (Hirst and Thompson, 1992: 368).

More recently, then, the academic and business literatures have come to stress the prevalence of corporate strategies of global-localisation (e.g. Cooke and Wells, 1992; Mair, 1993). The renewed emphasis on local forms of accumulation has been widely interpreted alongside flexible forms of production as representing something of a departure from the singular emphasis upon the globalisation of the 1960s and 1970s and which now seems a misplaced reaction to the falling profitability of many western companies. Of interest here is not debate about the macroeconomic regulation of national and world economies but the question of how local embeddedness mediates processes of rationalisation accompanying European integration.

The issue of embeddedness resolves itself into the question of why, when an industry or a firm has selected a location, does it stay there a long time? This is the very question which Alfred Marshall set himself at the turn of the century when trying to understand the dynamism of Britain's successful industrial districts. Marshall's inductive approach – a descriptive account of the benefits of locating in established centres of production – established the concept of 'external economies'. Thus, our understanding of embeddedness must begin with a discussion of the orthodox analysis of external economies or 'agglomeration factors' as these were termed by Weber (1929). However, more recent literature on the social, institutional and political origins of industry embeddedness as well as on sunk costs and locational inertia and the spatial division of labour and the branch plant syndrome can also shed light on the issue of embeddedness.

The Technological, Social and Institutional Bases to External Economies

Alfred Marshall identified three main types of external economies in his descriptions of Britain's successful 19th century industrial districts; those relating to local labour markets, those relating to inter-firm and inter-industry linkages and technical externalities. This conception of external economies has barely been extended since this time. Recently it has once again been revived as a means of analysing the persistent tendency for industry to agglomerate (Scott, 1983, 1986, 1988). Scott has restated the importance of external economics to an understanding of agglomerated forms of production including some celebrated contemporary industrial districts. Scott's analysis provides a more formal transaction cost based microeconomic interpretation of externalisation and linkage formation coupled to a macroeconomic analysis of contemporary industrial restructuring and the rise of new industrial spaces (Phelps, 1992a). Scott's analysis pertains to situations in which small firms dominate and in which there are competitive market structures. The relevance of this macroeconomic analysis to the large tracts of rationalised forms of production in peripheral regions is less clear. In part this is due to the limiting distinction between market and hierarchy implicit in the transaction cost based analysis of externalisation and linkage formation within Scott's analysis – one which does not admit of situations intermediate between market and hierarchy. Since Scott's initial analysis of contemporary instances of agglomeration it is probably fair to say that subsequent literature has diverged into two slightly different strands.

On the one hand, a number of commentators have taken up the idea that there are network forms of industrial organisation which are intermediate between the markets and hierarchies of Scott's transaction cost based analysis. This strand of work has often addressed itself explicitly to the emergence of more embedded forms of production in peripheral regions. A number of commentators (e.g. Sabel, 1989; Storper and Harrison, 1991; Cooke and Morgan, 1993) have stressed the prevalence of network forms of industrial organisation intermediate between the markets and hierarchies of transaction cost economics. These authors indicate that such network forms of industry can, and to some extent are, taking shape in some peripheral regions. Perhaps the characteristic form such network forms of production take within the peripheral region setting is that of the subcontracting complex (e.g. Sabel, 1989). Such 'branch industrial complexes' are highly centralised – being focused on one or a limited number of large, often externally controlled branch plants. Whilst there is growing evidence to attest to some forms of externalisation and linkage formation in peripheral regions (Phelps, 1993a, b; Turok, 1993; Clarke and Beaney, 1993) there is also a very real concern that such branch industrial complexes are simply an extension of the branch plant syndrome to the wider economy (Amin and Robins, 1990).

On the other hand, others have developed an earlier strand of thinking regarding the origins of certain of the contemporary industrial districts in particular (Brusco 1982), and ideas of industry embeddedness in general (Granovetter, 1985). This body of work has tended to focus exclusively on highly successful agglomerated forms of production, but nevertheless offers some insights into the possible embeddedness of industry in a peripheral region setting albeit those elements which are likely to be missing in the peripheral region context. The emphasis in the influential California School's transaction cost analysis of external economies and agglomeration was on the dense inter-firm and inter-industry linkages noted by Alfred Marshall in his description of external economies. However, contemporary to the California School's accounts of agglomeration was a less influential set of accounts focusing on the technological and labour market externalities described by Marshall and hence upon the less quantifiable, less tangible features of agglomeration. This body of literature has concentrated on, for instance, localised transfers of knowledge and technology, the social and cultural basis to embeddedness and the role of institutions in the competitiveness of certain contemporary industrial districts. The transaction cost analysis of the California School has given way to, and incorporated elements of, these diverse literatures (see Storper, 1995).

One strand of thinking here is that which focuses on patterns and processes of localised learning and technological development as the key determinant of industry embeddedness. The literature here ranges from the largely European work on innovative milieux which, Storper (1995) notes, is rather better at identifying locational *patterns* of learning and technology transfer as defining features of successful contemporary agglomerations than at identifying the *processes* by which innovation and growth take place. Here it seems likely that institutions again can play a central role though not all processes of localised learning are formally orchestrated as Saxenien has shown in the case of Silicon Valley (Saxenien, 1992). Storper (1992; 1995) has perhaps gone furthest in stressing the central role of technological external economies to industry embeddedness and regional economic growth. Here, Storper's emphasis upon specialisation in international trade as this amplifies productivity, innovation and returns to scale echoes Krugman's 'new trade theory'. In this way globalisation of economic activity is linked to regionalisation by way of localised technological learning (Storper, 1992; 1995). It is these technological externalities which Storper sees as being longer-lived in contemporary instances of agglomeration than, for example, inter-firm and inter-industry linkages. The geographical constraints on untraded interdependencies are more enduring than the geographical constraints on input-output linkages (Storper, 1995).

Somewhat in contrast, Scott, for example, has chosen to concentrate on the extent to which contemporary agglomerations are crucially held together not by market forces but by relationships of trust. Here Scott builds upon the work by Dore (1986) which stresses the social rather than the economic bases to transactions which underpin much of Japanese industry. The high trust environment in Japanese industry and in some contemporary agglomerations is probably a specific example of the social and cultural practices in which industry becomes embedded (Granovetter, 1985). These distinctive social and cultural practices in which industry becomes embedded may naturally be quite place specific. Most commentators have identified the extent to which the social and cultural bases to embeddedness and competitiveness differ at a national level (e.g. Whitley, 1992a) but there may also be differences at the local and regional levels.

Finally, others have chosen to concentrate on the institutional basis to industry embeddedness. Here the defining features of agglomeration are seen to be the product of effective institutional capacity or 'thickness' (Amin and Thrift, 1994). The success of some contemporary industrial districts stems from the manner in which production is orchestrated by various locally-based institutions (e.g. Brusco, 1982; Scott and Paul, 1990). These institutions can play a vital role in ensuring the effective functioning of local factor and intermediate input markets. Institutional capacity or thickness is not related simply to the profusion of relevant institutions but their effectiveness and the degree of coordination among them (Teague, 1994). This analysis of the institutional basis of agglomeration has much in common with a body of literature on, for want of a better expression, the politics of local economic development. This literature suggests that the relationships between institutions and industry embeddedness are not one way. Rather the 'local dependence' of many firms and industries means that they often have a vested interest in making local institutions work to their own ends (Cox and Mair, 1988; 1991). Private sector industry if it is at all locally dependent will have some interest in determining the functioning of local factor and intermediate input markets. To effect this, private industry will often therefore become involved in local politics and economic strategy making. In this way private and public sectors can come together in partnerships, 'networks' (Wood, 1993) or 'growth coalitions' (Molotch, 1976). Here, then, private industry shares with other local public and private institutions an interest in promoting local economic development since 'Capturing agglomeration economies requires a high level of political and social consensus' (Teague, 1994: 290). The evidence from the US suggests that it is primarily industry with considerable land or property based interests which have become involved in such growth coalitions. That is not to say that large and small manufacturing firms will have no interest in such coalition building since many such firms have significant ties to local land and property markets (Adams, Russell and Taylor-Russell, 1994). However, the evidence from the UK suggests that, as yet, there is very little in the way of such coalition building (Harding, 1991) whilst some of the greatest institutional capacity in the UK exists in the peripheral 'regions' such as Scotland and Wales (Morgan, 1993).

Potentially of greater relevance to understanding the likely extent of and possibilities for multinational embeddedness in peripheral regions of the EU are literature which concentrate economies internal to the factory or firm and their connection with location. We will look inside the firm rather than at its many relationships with other firms and organisations. Here there are two main bodies of literature which can assist in an understanding of industry embeddedness. The first is a large body of empirical and conceptual literature on the 'branch plant syndrome'. The second is the emergent literature on 'sunk costs' and locational dynamics.

The Embedded Branch Plant?

From the literature on the branch plant syndrome evident in many older industrial or peripheral regions of advanced economies, there is the basis of an understanding of how the organisation of production internal to large firms leads to development *in* rather than the development *of* local and regional economies (Sayer, 1985). For large multisite often multinational companies, the internal corporate economy supersedes the external local or regional economy as a source of many key inputs including, for example, finance, intermediate material and service inputs and even labour. Individual plants will be more or less embedded to the extent that the internal corporate economy supersedes the local or regional economy.

This potential lack of embeddedness of the production outposts of large firms manifests itself in a number of characteristic deficiencies of branch plant type investments. From the large literature on this topic, five closely related deficiencies of branch plants can be identified. First, branch plants are considered to be 'truncated' compared to indigenous firms (Britton and Gilmour, 1978; Hayter, 1982). That is to say, they lack certain manufacturing and non-manufacturing functions – most notably sales, marketing, research and development (e.g. Hood and Young, 1976). Second, and closely related to this 'truncation', there is a suggestion that branch plans are less innovative or technologically sophisticated than indigenous firms (e.g. Thwaites, 1978). Third, a large literature has been devoted to examining whether branch plants are less integrated into their host economies by way of localised backward linkages (e.g. Marshall, 1979; O'Farrell and O'Loughlin, 1981; Stewart, 1976; Britton, 1976). Fourth, there are long-standing concerns over the quality of employment provided by branch plans compared to indigenous firms. The suggestion here is that the employment created by branch plant investments is essentially low-skill, low-pay, low value-added assembly work. Finally, and as an outcome of some of the above deficiencies and the lack of embeddedness, branch plants are considered to be a relatively unstable source of employment in their host economies. The mobility of branch plant investments means that they are 'snatchers' rather than 'stickers' (McAleese and McDonald, 1978).

These various deficiencies have been subject to considerable empirical scrutiny from which it can be concluded that the contribution of branch plants to local or regional development has generally been underrated. For example, foreign 'branch plants' in the Scottish electronics industry were found to have greater local backward linkages than indigenous UK branch plants (McDermott, 1976) whilst the innovativeness of branch plans in the regions of England compared favourably to indigenous single-site firms (Oakey *et al.* 1982). The equivocal nature of the large body of empirical material on the branch plant syndrome must surely be a product of a number of conceptual difficulties and prejudices underlying much of this work. First, then, branch plants are compared unfairly with often idealised notions of indigenous firms. It is quite clear for instance that many small firms are 'truncated' in the sense that they lack certain functions due to an inadequately developed internal corporate division of labour. Second, an estimation of the contribution of branch plans to local or regional economic development is thwarted by the difficulties of ascertaining the counterfactual situation of 'what would have been' in the absence of such investment.

The various deficiencies of branch plants have come to be regarded as a product of a spatial-functional division of labour within large companies (Massey, 1979; 1984). Crudely put, this division of labour finds spatial expression in as much as rationalised forms of branch plant production predominate in peripheral regions whilst less rationalised forms of production and more particularly key functions such as sales, marketing and research and development are found in core regions. Naturally, the precise way in which companies organise their internal divisions of labour can produce qualitatively different types of investment in different regions. Here the large literature on corporate structure and strategy and on subsidiary roles provides ample detail on the different types of investment undertaken by large firms. More recently, this accepted framework for interpreting the centrality of large corporations to issues of local and regional economic development has been questioned (e.g. Storper and Walker, 1989; Walker, 1989). Two direct criticisms have been made. First, the spatial divisions of labour approach focuses on divisions of labour internal to companies to the exclusion of external of inter-firm and inter-organisational divisions of labour. Second, the approach has often been deployed in a way which assumes a unidirectional tendency towards an increasing division of labour, fragmentation of tasks and presumably the spatial separation of activities.

Indirect criticisms of this approach are also evident in as much as recent theoretical and empirical literature has begun to speak of the prospects of development at the periphery of many advanced economies including the upgrading and increased embeddedness of branch plant investments. So for example some commentators have pointed to changing corporate structures and strategies which involve a flattening of internal hierarchies and a resynthesis of corporate divisions of labour popularised in the term 'global localisation' (e.g. Morris, 1992). Such changes in corporate structures and strategies are likely to manifest themselves at the level of individual company sites in terms of, for instance, increased decision-making autonomy, functional upgrading perhaps in terms of research and development and/or sales and marketing – though as yet the evidence is rather limited (e.g. Clarke and Beaney, 1993; Phelps, 1992b). In this way rationalised branch plants may be transformed into 'technical branch plants' (Glasmeier, 1988) with greater technological capacity, though it has long been recognised that such upgrading is related to the age of investments. Indeed, such a resynthesis of corporate divisions of labour and increased plant-level autonomy may go hand in hand with reciprocal flows of information, expertise and strategic decision-making from individual plants to corporate headquarters as is the case with global subsidiary mandates (Roth and Morrison, 1992).

Similarly, and at a less abstract level of analysis, others have detailed the way in which the organisation of production at branch plants has become more flexible (Milne, 1990; Peck and Stone, 1993; Potter, 1995). The point here is that many of the new manufacturing innovations and practices said to epitomise new norms of flexible accumulation are also evident at branch plants with important implications for industry embeddedness in peripheral regions. Here at least there is some debate since Williams *et al.* (1991) argue that the Japanese transplant investments in the UK and US – which are said to exemplify such best practice – resemble warehouses rather than factories. Here again there seems to be an issue about the connection between ownership and vintage and the character of branch plant investments and their embeddedness. Williams *et al.* appear to be suggesting that there are differences between Japanese and other branch plant investments. However, many of the Japanese transplants in Europe and North America are relatively recent and so their 'warehouse' status may be a product of their vintage.

Finally, a number of researchers have looked at one direct, if limited, manifestation of the changing corporate organisation of production in general and embeddedness in particular. Industrial linkages, especially backward linkages, are an important indicator of embeddedness. They may be important in both employment and expenditure terms but also in less tangible ways such as the transfer of knowledge and best practice. Little evidence is available on the contribution of branch plants to localised transfers of technology and best practice. The evidence which does exist on the changing linkage patterns of branch plants suggests that there has been little in the way of any improvement in levels of local sourcing in peripheral regions (e.g. Phelps, 1993a, b; Turok, 1993). Seemingly, embeddedness in terms of local sourcing is not related to the vintage of investments since, by virtue of *in situ* linkage change, longer established branch plants appear to source as much locally as those more recently established.

Sunk Costs and Locational Inertia

Since, as Sayer notes (1982), 'there is an internal [i.e. necessary] relation between investment and location…', we need to consider what type of investment ties firms and industries to particular places. Here the emergent literature on sunk costs (Clark, 1994; Clark and Wrigley, 1995) appears most pertinent. This strand of work represents an expansion of earlier work within the radical tradition, pointing to the connection between investment (primarily in terms of natural resources, land and property) and the spatial fixity of capital (Harvey, 1982; 1985). This earlier work tended to stress the *absolute* immobility of capital but there are many ways in which capital is *relatively* immobile due to investment decisions (for example, in relation to training of local labour, intangible learning effects in production, etc.). Here Clark and Wrigley argue that the concept of sunk costs is an important one in bridging firm-specific case studies with more abstract notions of spatial fixity and plasticity. Sunk costs by definition tend to have limited transferability and recoverability and tend to be long-lived and impose recurrent financial need. Clark and Wrigley (1995) identify three types of such costs, each of which can effectively engender a greater or lesser degree of locational inertia.

First, there are set-up sunk costs. One example here would be the training costs of inward investors. These might be considerable where there are significant skills to be acquired, but presumably for the majority of inward investments centred on low-skill jobs such sunk costs are not particularly great. More significant in terms of set-up sunk costs may be the costs of acquiring or leasing local land and property. Significantly, a considerable portion of such set-up sunk costs may be borne by local and central government, through regional development grants and the assembly and provision of sites and premises (Peck, 1996).

Second, Clark and Wrigley identify accumulated sunk costs. Included under this heading would be the untraded interdependencies – the localised sources of innovation and information exchange – which Storper suggests are the basis of Marshallian technological spillovers within the contemporary industrial districts. Also included under this heading is the larger element of what economists generally term economies of scale. There is a technical sense in which economies of scale relate to the physical capacity of plant and equipment (e.g. see Gold, 1981). Such technical economies of scale are probably best considered as set-up sunk costs but can nonetheless be significant in tying particular firms and industries to particular places. the best example here would be the petrochemicals and chemicals industries. However, for many industries the better part of what economists term economies of scale centre on learning curve effects and operational efficiency including plant utilisation. Such learning economies are a product of the social relations of production constituted between firms, workers and institutions in particular places. In contrast to set-up sunk costs, which may be relatively minor for inward investments, these accumulated sunk costs may become important even to some of the more rationalised forms of inward investment. The unique combination of capital and labour and productivity achieved in one location may be difficult to achieve in another location even if equipment can be transferred.

Finally, Clark and Wrigley identify 'exit' sunk costs which become apparent when a factory shuts or a firm withdraws from a market or industry. The best examples here are the costs embodied in severance pay and pension provisions. Again, even for branch plants such sunk costs are usually not insignificant. The annual reports of major companies are, from year to year, replete with provisions made for 'restructuring'.

There are, then, a number of ways in which companies invest considerable amounts of time and money in particular places – that is, when those investments are composed of a significant element of sunk costs. These sunk costs may be significant even for the most rationalised forms of production in peripheral regions. This in turn suggests that such branch plant investments involve more than minimal risk to their parent companies and indeed imply a certain commitment to a production location.

Conclusion

The Commission has presented a rather simplistic scenario of industry restructuring accompanying market integration in Europe; one which points to quite rapid and radical restructuring through trade and investment with consequent benefits to producers and consumers alike.

In this chapter it has been argued that, for a number of reasons, processes of industrial restructuring are more complex than assumed by the Commission and will be more drawn out. First, the relationship between competition and the exploitation of economies of scale at firm and plant level in the EU is more complex than assumed by the Commission. A variety of sizes of firm and plant with a variety of functions, production technologies, worker skills and practices and combinations thereof, will persist into the long-term future in the EU. In part this is underpinned by the fact that for many manufactured items there is not, and never will be, a single European market. Thus, second, the fragmented nature of markets within the EU will persist to support a diversity of corporate organisational forms and strategies. Third, firms, multinationals included, may be constrained both in the short-term and the long-term in their abilities to restructure due to their embeddedness in regional economies. Such embeddedness can represent a constraint not merely in negative terms, as regards the costs involved in withdrawing from particular locations, but also in positive terms, regarding the dependence of multinational companies on particular locations for their competitive advantage.

Earlier in Chapter 2 we saw that ownership and vintage of multinational investments are two important considerations when attempting to understand the role of multinationals on trade, investment and European integration. More specifically, then, consideration of the ownership and vintage of multinationals is likely to shed light on the main ways in which restructuring takes place in relation to markets, scale and competition effects, and locational inertia. Furthermore, the activities of multinationals are influenced to an extent by the different regulatory environments in which they operate. One influential, though debateable, development in the regulatory environment faced by multinationals is the enhanced role of local or regional institutions in industry competitiveness and embeddedness. This, then, forms the focus of the original empirical material contained in the following chapters.

As a prelude to this original material Chapter 5 provides some essential background to the Welsh economy. It provides a discussion of the existing published literature on the role of multinationals in Welsh manufacturing industry. The chapter identifies a number of persistent traits of, and concerns regarding, the involvement of multinationals in Welsh manufacturing industry.

Multinationals in Wales

Introduction

The aim of this chapter is to provide a background to some of the issues raised and discussed in the original research presented in later chapters. This chapter examines the changing nature of multinational manufacturing investment in Wales as this has been reported in the existing published literature. Here, the information concerning foreign manufacturing firms is clearly more detailed than the available information on the arrival, employment and other impacts of UK multinationals. Of necessity then, the chapter draws upon indirect indications of the likely contribution of UK multinationals to the Welsh economy. Information on the contribution of foreign-owned manufacturing investments in Wales is more detailed though, here, the bulk of literature has been published since 1980. The chapter considers the changing nature of multinational involvement in the Welsh economy in terms of the main phases of such involvement.

Wales's integration into an international division of labour has been comparatively recent. Unlike the other UK regions, Wales had no major indigenous but rapidly internationalising companies. Equally, foreign direct manufacturing investment in Wales took place rather later than in the other UK regions. So, for example, Monsanto's chemical plant in Ruabon which was established in 1895 post-dates the investments by Colt manufacturing at London (1853) and Singer at Clydebank (1867) (Bostock and Jones, 1994). Since this time and up until the 1980s Wales could be considered to be a laggard region in terms of the attraction of overseas manufacturing investments. Figure 5.1 shows that the number of foreign-owned manufacturing establishments in Wales grew only very slowly in the pre-World War 2 (WW2) period. Indeed, during the pre-WW2 years only East Anglia and the North and South West regions of England had fewer foreign-owned manufacturing plants (Bostock and Jones, 1994: 114).

By 1992 the total employment in foreign-owned manufacturing operations in Wales had grown to 68,000. At the time, this figure represented 29.5% of total manufacturing employment in Wales and serves to underline the important contribution of foreign companies to the manufacturing sector.

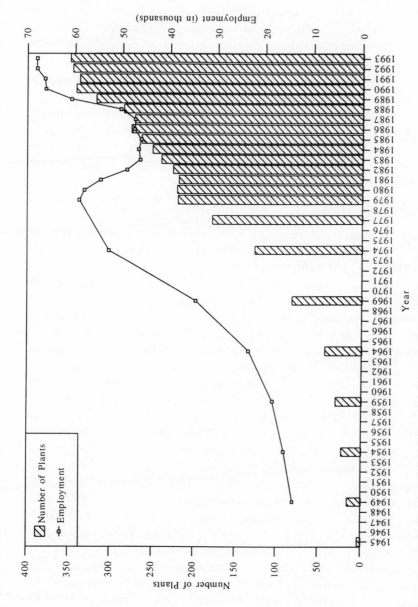

Source: Davies and Thomas (1976), Adams (1983), Welsh Office (unpublished tables)

Figure 5.1 Numbers of foreign-owned manufacturing operations and associated employment

As early as the late 1930s it was anticipated that the main way in which the Welsh economy could be diversified would be through the establishment of branch factories primarily of Welsh firms and those headquartered elsewhere in the UK (National Industrial Development Council of Wales and Monmouthshire, 1937). This of course has very much been the history of industrial diversification in Wales as in other peripheral UK regions. It was a strategy which soon generated concerns over the long-term implications for regional economic development. Yet, by the late 1960s the Welsh Office was arguing that

> 'Much of the increased manufacturing activity has been undertaken by companies which had previously operated outside Wales. Experience has shown that there is no ground for the fears once held…that enterprises so established might be specially liable to feel the cold wind of temporarily unfavourable economic conditions. On the contrary the majority have put down roots and conferred considerable benefits on the Welsh economy.'
> (Welsh Office, 1967: 48)

This appraisal of the situation might hold for the new industries and multinational investment attracted to Wales in general. Arguably, however, the overall health of this emerging branch plant economy in Wales owes more to the stability and quality of manufacturing investment from overseas companies than to that from UK multilocational and multinational firms.

It is difficult to ascertain the importance specifically of UK multinationals to the Welsh economy. There simply is no comparable data to that on overseas manufacturing operations. Data on inter-regional movement of manufacturing activities can provide a very rough indication of the involvement UK multiplant companies. However, not all of these movements will be by UK multinational companies and some will even be transfers by overseas multinationals already operating in the UK. Such inter-regional movements made a regular contribution to total employment growth in Wales through much of the post World War 2 period to date. Indeed such moves were far more important to Wales as a source of jobs than they were to any other UK region (Pounce, 1981: 33). All that can be suggested is that UK multinationals, as a sub group of such inter-regional moves, are likely to have been a highly important source of employment. However, in other respects the contribution of UK multiplant firms, including UK multinationals, to the Welsh economy may not have been all that could be desired. For example, it has recently been argued that the branch plant syndrome applies most closely to the operations of UK multiplant firm in Wales and not necessarily to the plants of overseas firms (Welsh Affairs Committee, 1988).

In comparison to the foreign-owned sector in other UK regions and in comparison to the performance of UK multiplant and indigenous firms, the overseas sector in Wales has provided a quite stable source of employment. Wales has a poor record of firm formation and, as with most UK regions, has suffered from the poor internationally competitive position of many UK firms. In contrast there have been few periods when there has been significant employment contractions in the Welsh foreign-owned manufacturing sector. In this respect Wales may be slightly unique among peripheral UK economic planning regions given that the employment contribution of the foreign owned sectors in Scotland and the northern region of England, for example, has been more volatile. However, it should also be remembered that, put in a broader context, each phase of overseas manufacturing investment in Wales has been far from that needed to balance job loss in traditional industries and even job loss in preceding rounds of inward investment (Morris, 1987).

Whilst the employment contribution of foreign-owned firms in Wales has been quite stable, the other indirect benefits may be less impressive. The foreign-owned sector provides the major source of inward investment to Wales and Wales has become the most successful UK region in attracting overseas investment, however, it has been noted that the capital intensity of recent investments is rather lower than is the case in other UK regions.

In reviewing the growth and development of multinational involvement in Welsh manufacturing industry, this chapter is concerned with examining the changing nature of such investments. Specifically, this chapter is concerned with evaluating recent claims regarding the nature of inward investment to peripheral regions such as Wales. Several commentators argue that general organisational trends toward the localisation of global corporate structures are offering up possibilities for less branch like investments in peripheral regions including Wales (e.g. Morris, 1992; Mair, 1993). So, for example, it is suggested that branch plant type investments may be less truncated than has previously been the case or that existing investments are being upgraded in one way or another. In this way branch plants in peripheral regions may be more locally embedded in terms of the presence of key functions, backward material linkages etc. than has been the case with previous rounds of investment. The material in this and subsequent chapters allows some evaluation of these claims in relation to Wales where, as Lovering notes, there has been quite a marked shift in the way in which the economy has been depicted both by academics and in the media in recent years (Lovering, 1996).

UK and US Investment and the Branch Plant Syndrome in Wales

In reality the post war period up to the 1970s might contain several distinct stages of growth in multinational involvement in the Welsh economy. For example, Davies and Thomas (1976) identify five phases of growth in overseas industry in Wales up until the 1970s. Their five phases are delimited on the basis of the quantity of foreign direct investment within Wales and not the quality of such investment. In the large literature on the subject, quality of investment has usually been judged in terms of employment stability and quality, innovativeness, linkage formation and degree of functional truncation. The changing quality of investment is in any case difficult to discern and, as such, is open to differing interpretations. Furthermore, because of the lack of data, it is difficult to ascertain changes in the quantity or quality of investments by UK multinationals and the extent to which these have countered or complemented foreign involvement.

Given the lack of data and published material on the subject, all that can reasonably be said about the involvement of UK multinationals on the Welsh economy is that investments by such companies reached their high water mark by the 1960s and 1970s (see Table 5.1). Over half of the Welsh manufacturing operations of UK multinationals responding to the author's survey began manufacture during the 1960s and 1970s (see chapter 6 for further details). It is also during this period that investments by UK multinationals were at their most important in relation to the total investment by multinationals in Wales. So, for instance, fully 54% of establishments responding to the survey and beginning manufacture during the 1960s were UK-owned.

Table 5.1 Date of establishment of UK-owned mutlinationals

	Number	Percent of UK-owned multinationals	Percent of all multinationals
1990s	2	4.8	15.4
1980–89	7	16.7	20.6
1970–79	10	23.8	31.3
1960–69	13	30.9	54.2
1950–59	4	9.5	28.6
Pre-1950	6	14.3	35.3
Total	42	100.0	31.1

Source: Author's survey

In the immediate post-war period, Wales, as with other peripheral UK regions attracted investments from US companies (Dunning, 1958). In this respect, Wales 'played the role of a minor Scotland in the post-war years' (Bostock and Jones, 1994: 115). However, it is also fair to say that, due to the minimal amount of FDI attracted in the pre-war period, Wales could be described as a laggard region in terms of attracting overseas investment. In the immediate post-war period Wales possessed a location quotient for US investment well below unity (Dunning, 1958: 85). Unlike some other peripheral regions, the 1950s were a relatively dormant period for the Welsh economy in terms of gaining overseas investment. During the 1960s and 1970s Wales experienced a surge in overseas manufacturing investment as these flows of investment began to decentralise from core to peripheral regions of the UK (Dicken and Lloyd, 1980: 1411).

During the post war period and up until the 1970s multinational involvement and especially overseas investment was concentrated in sectors such as mechanical engineering and metal manufacture. Chemicals industries and the electrical and electronic and vehicle and component manufacturing industries also received important shares of overseas investment and have subsequently become the most important sectors for overseas manufacturing investment in Wales. These sectors, along with the emergent electronics industry, have remained the most important in multinational investment in Wales. US companies dominated in the move of overseas investment into Wales up until the 1970s and continue to dominate during the 1980s and 1990s though to a much lesser extent.

Commenting on the impending accession of the UK to the EU, the Welsh Council was anticipating that Wales would benefit from industrial growth due to market expansion and increased flows of inward investment (Welsh Council, 1971). An increasing number of investments from European firms began to be made during the late 1960s and 1970s but prior to 1980 Wales still had a share of foreign direct investment from EU companies which was well below the UK average. In 1973, for instance, EU-owned manufacturing establishments accounted for 13.0% of the total of foreign-owned manufacturing employment in the UK but only 3.1% in Wales (Watts, 1980: 5). Naturally, German companies were among the main EU investors in Wales during this period. Five German firms set up in Wales the 1960s and 14 in the 1970s creating a total of 21 by 1978. The motives for West German manufacturing investment in Wales did not differ from those of foreign or UK firms in general (Davies, 1978). Perhaps more surprisingly, and against the backcloth of impending world recession, the first Japanese manufacturing plants were established in Wales in the early to mid 1970s.

It is more difficult to establish the quality of overseas investment up to the mid 1970s. Some clues as to the character of overseas investment in Wales can nevertheless be pieced together from the available published material. In the main, overseas investment in Wales has a number of positive characteristics and compares favourably with that in other peripheral UK regions. The earliest indications suggested that research and development activity was unevenly distributed across sectors and firms in Wales (Welsh Office, 1967: 58). Davies and Thomas's (1976) study suggested that 47% of surveyed overseas plants had some sort of research and development activity. A little later Hood and Young's evidence seemed to confirm that levels of research and development were comparatively healthy in Wales (Hood and Young, 1983: 201–202). However, Young has since been more critical of the quality of overseas manufacturing investments in Wales compared to those in Scotland.

Hood and Young (1983: 214) also found that overseas plants in Wales had relatively healthy export orientation compared to plants in other assisted regions. Other positive traits of overseas investment in Wales appear to be the smaller average size of overseas plants in Wales (which may suggest that Wales has had fewer of the classic large branch plants) and, significantly, the higher levels of reinvestment compared to other assisted regions. This last point is worth noting as it is one strength of the overseas sector in Wales which has persisted into the

1980s and 1990s and which offers opportunities for the upgrading of overseas industry in the future.

Nevertheless, there are a couple of less positive characteristics of overseas investment in Wales which might be detected from the literature. Overseas investment in Wales has been relatively truncated in terms of decision-making and sales functions and only weakly embedded in terms of backward material linkages. Here, Hood and Young's (1983) work on overseas investment in the UK suggested that Welsh plants were less likely to act as UK headquarters or sales offices than plants in other assisted regions. Similarly, one aspect on which policies to encourage industry upgrading in Wales would need to concentrate is the local sourcing of materials and components. Welsh overseas plants had some of the lowest levels of local backward linkage compared to other assisted regions in the Hood and Young study. Furthermore, there appear to be persistent problems in improving such levels of local sourcing.

Japanese and European Investment

Japanese manufacturing investments in Wales during the 1980s and 1990s continue to be fewer in number than those of North American companies and European companies. However, because of their perceived symbolic importance our main sources of information regarding inward investment into Wales during the 1980s and 1990s relate to Japanese manufacturing firms. Overseas investment now represents the vast bulk of inward investment into Wales and hence there continues to be a lack of information regarding the investment decisions of UK multinationals.

From Figure 5.1 (above) we can see that over the period 1979 to 1993 the number of foreign owned manufacturing establishments increased by 59% but that employment grew by only 15%. So whilst Wales has become a major UK location for inward investment, the average size of such investments is now less than in previous rounds of investment. The increasing capital intensity of overseas investment in Wales is, however, relative since it has also been claimed that inward investments into Wales have been less capital intensive than those in other regions (Welsh Affairs Committee, 198: x). The question arises, therefore, as to the nature of current inward investment and whether this is qualitatively different from that in previous rounds of investment.

The arguments here are contradictory. Qualitative changes to the stock of multinational investment in Wales can come from two sources. First, there may be *in situ* upgrading or reorganisation of existing multinational investments in Wales. Here there are a number of reasons to suspect that such *in situ* change will be quantitatively important. There is evidence from other peripheral UK regions that such *in situ* changes to work practices, management philosophies and linkage structures have been a quantitatively important element in industrial restructuring (e.g. Peck and Stone, 1993; Phelps, 1993a). Also the 'demonstration effect' of

Japanese investments in Wales seems beyond doubt. The case study evidence which does exist suggests that *in situ* restructuring of work practices, linkage structures and gains in autonomy and technological capacity have all been evident at the Welsh operations of multinational manufacturing companies (e.g. Price, Cooke and Morgan, 1994). Similarly recent evidence on occupational change in the automotive and electronics industries (those dominated by domestic and foreign multinationals) in Wales suggests some limited *in situ* upgrading of workforce skills (e.g. Morgan, 1991; Panditharatna and Phelps, 1995). Finally, evidence of recent productivity gains in Welsh manufacturing industry is also suggestive of *in situ* restructuring of industry including multinational investments.

Second, it has been suggested that recent investment may be qualitatively different – less branch like – from previous rounds of investment even in peripheral regions.

Again there is some evidence from other peripheral UK regions to suggest that this is indeed the case (Peck and Stone, 1993). In one study of training requirements of recent inward investors it is suggested that such investments are 'far removed from the "screw-driver" operations which were...associated with earlier phases of inward investment' (Rees and Thomas, 1994: 52).

However, it seems fairly clear that examples of this sort of qualitatively superior form of inward investment are restricted to some of the more notable high-profile investments in Wales such as Bosch and Sony. The branch factory syndrome is more evident in the UK-owned sector whilst in general Wales is not considered a candidate for European headquarters or research and development centres given the lack of skilled workers.

From Table 5.1 (above) it is apparent that there are continuing if rather modest (compared to overseas investments) numbers of plants being opened or acquired by UK-multinationals in the 1980s and 1990s – though these now account for only a minor share of total multinational investment in Wales. Evidence pertaining to UK-owned manufacturing establishments in one recent survey of industry in Wales (Simpson, 1987) provide the only indirect indication of the likely quality of investment by UK multinationals. That survey found that the Welsh manufacturing operations of UK headquartered firms sourced on average 26.4% of their inputs locally; the corresponding figure for foreign-owned manufacturing establishments in Wales was 15.9%. However, the export performance of UK-owned manufacturing establishments in Wales (13.1%) was poorer than their foreign-owned counterparts (23.4%) (Simpson, 1987: 54). The survey also indicated that the locational attraction of Wales to UK-owned establishments was primarily in terms of labour costs, more so than for overseas-owned establishments (Simpson, 1987: 105).

Despite the rapid growth of overseas manufacturing investment in Wales during the 1960s and 1970s it is only in the 1980s and 1990s that Wales has come to the fore as a location for overseas-owned manufacturing employment. The very high levels of foreign investment attracted to Wales during the 1980s and 1990s have pushed Wales from being a laggard region in terms of foreign manufacturing employment to the leading region in terms of the concentration of overseas-owned employment. The relative importance of foreign-owned manufacturing employment (as measured by the location quotient) in Wales has been in-line with, or greater than, that in other peripheral regions in the UK since the 1960s. However, during the 1970s, the relative importance of foreign-owned manufacturing employment barely changed. During the 1980s, there has been a quite rapid growth the location quotient for foreign-owned manufacturing employment in Wales (see Table 5.2). In the mid to late 1980s and into the 1990s, Wales has become the most popular destination for foreign direct investment in the UK. This is reflected in the fact that Wales now has the highest location quotient for foreign-owned manufacturing employment of all UK regions.

Table 5.2 Location quotient for foreign-owned manufacturing employment in Wales

1963	1973	1983	1993
1.30	1.27	1.34	1.87

Sources: Dicken and Lloyd (1976); Hill and Munday (1994); Stone and Peck (1996)

Table 5.3 Breakdown, by nationality, of the foreign-owned manufacturing sector in Wales

	1973	1977	1986	1993
US	85.9	71.7	⎤ 66.2	⎤ 52.5
Canada	(a)	9.4	⎦	⎦
EU	3.1	9.4	13.4	21.3
Japan	⎤ 11.0	⎤ 9.5	8.6	16.5
Other	⎦	⎦	11.7	9.7

NB figures may not sum to 100 due to rounding errors.
(a) included with 'other'
Sources: Hood and Young (1983); Watts (1980); Welsh Office unpublished tabulations

Historically, it is US firms which have provided the bulk of flows of foreign direct investment within the world economy. As such, and until very recently, a very high share of employment in the foreign-owned manufacturing sector in Wales has been provided by US companies (Table 5.3). However, following from the initial Japanese investments in Wales in the 1970s, the 1980s witnessed a large influx of further primary and secondary Japanese investment as well as German and French investments. As a consequence the ownership profile of the foreign-owned manufacturing industry in Wales has altered quite markedly during the 1980s. In

1977, the vast bulk of employment in foreign-owned manufacturing establishments was in North American and more particularly in US-owned operations.
By 1993 the North American-owned proportion of foreign-owned manufacturing
employment had dropped by nearly 30 percentage points.

Table 5.4 provides the components of change for the foreign-owned manufacturing sector in Wales (FOS) for the period 1979 to 1993. The superior employment performance of the FOS in Wales (and the northern region of England)
compared to other peripheral regions has been underpinned by new investments.
This is apparent given the surplus of new openings over closures in Wales shown
in Table 5.4. However, other components of change are perhaps more important
in understanding the dynamics of FOS employment in the peripheral regions of
the UK (Stone and Peck, 1996). Thus, Stone and Peck identify acquisition and *in
situ* change as important contributors to overall changes in FOS employment in
the peripheral regions of the UK.

During this period the EU-owned manufacturing sector in Wales accounted
for 98.9% of total employment gain in the FOS. The Japanese-owned manufacturing sector accounted for a similar proportion of the total gain (94.4%) whereas
the North American-owned sector lost a larger amount of employment than was
gained in the FOS as a whole.

The first main observation to be made from the data contained in Table 5.4 is
that acquisitions, although numerically less important than new plant openings,
have nevertheless been the main source of gains in FOS employment during the
1980s and early 1990s. Acquisitions provided 50% of the total gain (the sum of
employment from plant openings, acquisitions and expansions) in FOS employment during the period. This suggests at the outset that the contribution of new
plant openings to qualitative changes in the stock of multinational investment in
Wales may be quantitatively quite small, since new plant openings accounted for
only 32.5% of employment gains.

The second main observation that can be made is that expansions have gained
in importance during this time period. Over the period 1979 to 1993 employment
from expansions accounted for 12.5% of the total gain in FOS employment but
for the latter part of this (1985 to 1993) they accounted for 23.4% (Welsh Office,
unpublished tables). This reflects the growth in expansions or repeat investments
as a mode of foreign investment into the UK as a whole. Over the period 1984
to 1991 45.6% of foreign investments into the UK were in the form of expansions
(Pieda, 1993, cited in Morgan, 1996: 18). Over the period 1985 to 1993
expansions provided 37.1% of the number of foreign investments in Wales. This
last figure is lower than the national figure and may be a cause for concern
depending on how one interprets it. Thus, if expansions are associated with
qualitatively superior investments, then Wales would appear to be adversely placed
compared to the UK as a whole. This is particularly the case given that new plant
openings as a mode of entry appear to have been less important in Wales than in
the UK as a whole during the latter half of the 1980s and into the 1990s. Thus,

Table 5.4 Analysis of employment change at overseas owned manufacturing plants in Wales, 1979 to 1993

Employment in 1979	Employment change 1979–93							Emp in 1993
	New plant opening	Closures	Acquisitions	Divestments	Expansions	Contractions	Net change	
N. America 45,500	+5,600	-4,900	+10,600	-9,600	+2,100	-13,700	-9,800	35,700
Europe 9,300	+4,200	-1,500	+9,900	-2,000	+1,800	-2,000	+10,300	19,600
EEC [5,600]	[+2,600]	[-1,000]	[+7,900]	[-200]	[+1,000]	[-1,500]	[+8,900]	[14,500]
non-EEC [3,600]	[+1,500]	[-500]	[+2,000]	[-1,800]	[+800]	[-500]	[+1,500]	[5,100]
Japan 2,700	+6,900	0	*	*	*	*	+8,500	11,200
Other 1,500	+100	-300	*	*	*	*	0	1,500
Totals 59,000	+16,800	-6,700	+22,400	-12,400	+5,600	-16,800	+9,000	68,000
Percentage change over 1979	+28.5%	-11.4%	+40.0%	-21.0%	+9.5%	-28.5%	+15%	

Source: Welsh Register of Manufacturing Employment

Wales compares poorly to the UK as a whole in relation to expansions and the diversification of its stock of overseas firms through new plant openings.

There are, however, some revealing variations in mode of entry according to origin of foreign owned establishments in Wales. For instance, acquisitions are a more important mode of entry for EU-owned establishments than for North American or Japanese-owned establishments. Nearly 69% of employment gain in the EU-owned sector was provided by acquisitions (new plant openings accounted for 23%). Furthermore, this acquisition activity may be closely associated with processes of rationalisation since contractions and outright closures are a more important form of employment loss in the EU-owned sector than in the North American-owned sector.

Acquisitions are also the main mode of entry for North American firms but new openings are also important, providing 31% of employment gains in the North American-owned sector. Naturally, the dominant mode of entry in the Japanese-owned sector is new plant openings. Problems of disclosure mean that figures cannot be put on the contribution of various components of change, though it is important to recognise that an important share of employment gains in the Japanese-owned sector during this time will have been due to *in situ* expansions of existing operations.

Beyond the Branch Plant Economy? Japanese Investment in Wales

We have seen that new plant openings are spread quite evenly between the three main origins of investment; North America, the EU and Japan. As such, if qualitatively different forms of investment are associated with new openings then we would expect multinationals from each of these sectors to contribute to less branch plant like investment. It is also fair to say, however, that such new openings are particularly important in the Japanese-owned sector. The Japanese-owned sector provides an interesting bench-mark against which to speculate regarding the broader nature of inward investment in the 1990s. Since the dominant (almost exclusive) initial mode of entry of Japanese firms in Wales is that of new plant openings and since most of the detailed information we have regarding inward investment applies to the Japanese sector, it should be possible to make some judgement as regards the quality of inward investment to Wales in the 1980s and 1990s.

Wales has attracted the largest regional share of employment in Japanese manufacturing firms of all the UK regions and the second largest share of numbers of plants. To date, there have been over 30 Japanese manufacturing investments in Wales, mainly in the plastics, chemicals, automotive and electronic industries. At the outset it can be suggested that it is beyond doubt that these Japanese investments have been responsible for the introduction and diffusion, by way of example, of new work, management and procurement practices in Wales (Morgan and Sayer, 1985; Munday, 1995 *et al.*). However, beyond this the precise character of Japanese manufacturing investment and its contribution to the Welsh economy is less clear-cut.

According to Morris *et al.* Japanese manufacturing operations in Wales are 'developing away from the assembly-only stereotype and are employing, in some cases, large numbers of managers and engineers' (Morris *et al.* 1993: 24–25). They found that product ranges at Japanese plants in Wales have, through additional investment, been expanded (Morris *et al.* 1993: 19). They note that the performance of Japanese plants in Wales is a little lower than comparable parent company plants though there is no indication that the poorer performance has hindered the growth or development of Welsh operations (Morris *et al.* 1993: 55). The main examples of reinvestment and expansion are in the electronics industry in Wales where the likes of Panasonic, Aiwa, Brother have gradually expanded to produce a range of consumer electronics products. It is precisely these companies which Morris *et al.* see as key examples of the 'deepening' or 'maturing' of Japanese investment in Wales. Their data suggests that 10 out of 25 surveyed Japanese investments carry out some design work. However, there are relatively few research and development workers employed by just three Japanese firms. Here the 80 or so research and development workers employed by Sony dominate the figures (Sony is establishing its European R&D centre for consumer electronics in South Wales). The planned expansions of Japanese firms compared to North American firms in Wales have been much larger both in terms of employment and capital expenditure. Levels of reinvestment appear historically to have been important in Wales and Japanese investments appear to be continuing this tradition – which is an important one as far as policy is concerned since it represents a basis for industry upgrading. However, it is also true to say that the Welsh economy is apparently ill-equipped to continue to attract such repeat investments by Japanese and other firms. Thus, as the Welsh TUC has noted,

> 'We have seen some evidence in Wales of some companies that did start off with a relatively low-skilled, mundane screwdriver activity, who then brought into Wales some research and development activities. What we are finding is that the process of developing and improving upon the base inward investment has not been anywhere near the extent to which many of us had hoped... There is in Wales...now an identifiable skills shortage which is holding back the potential for securing some of the higher value-added, higher skill-demanding investment add-ons which we need in Wales if we are to start improving our overall employment mix.' (Jenkins in Welsh Affairs Committee, 1995: 85)

Thus, the Welsh TUC has voiced concern that a 'series of second phase investments by Japanese companies already well established in Wales, have been located increasingly on the European mainland' (Wales TUC in Welsh Affairs Committee, 1995: 83).

Furthermore, despite the upgrading which has occurred, Japanese firms continue to be truncated in some respects. For example, Morris *et al.* found that 'very few Japanese parent companies have gone far towards localising reporting structures' (Morris *et al.* 1993: 51). As such, Japanese plants in Wales enjoy lower levels of autonomy and decision-making authority (Morris *et al.* 1993: 54). As yet, then, there continues to be a difference in the Welsh experience of the academic and management rhetoric surrounding organisational decentralisation in large companies. Similarly, Japanese plants are not as locally embedded as they might be. Here Munday suggests that 'Whilst Japanese companies have attempted to buy as near to plants as possible, the local supply infrastructure has meant that this has been very difficult, and only a small proportion of components are bought in Wales' (Munday, 1990: 127–128).

Morris *et al.*'s figures suggest that Japanese plants source on average around 15% by value of their material inputs from Wales but that EU-wide levels of sourcing are more reasonable (Morris, *et al.* 1993: 46). These levels of local sourcing correspond to those of the foreign-owned sector generally in one recent survey of manufacturing industry in Wales (Simpson, 1987: 54). Of themselves, levels of local sourcing provide only a partial picture of the benefits of Japanese manufacturing investment in Wales. Within Wales a number of partial subcontracting complexes have grown up around major Japanese manufacturing operations. It may be as Munday *et al.* argue that 'Within these subcontracting complexes is the most substantive evidence of a significant "demonstration effect"' (Munday *et al.* 1995: 14). However, the significance of such complexes should not be overstated. The second wave of Japanese suppliers are a significant element in such subcontracting complexes and Munday's survey of such operations makes it clear that 'the nature of operations performed in Wales does not represent the best basis for an active subcontracting network using a wide base of skills.' (Munday 1995: 17).

The export performance of Japanese manufacturing operations also appears to be superior to that of the multinational-owned manufacturing sector in Wales taken as a whole. Export levels are particularly high among the Japanese consumer electronics operations in Wales. Compared to established US-owned operations there may be a vintage effect working upon export levels of Japanese consumer electronics plants, since they have been established from the outset to produce for export to the EU rather than the UK market.

The motivations for investing in Wales may provide some clues as to the nature of Japanese investment. Munday (1990), in his initial survey of Japanese firms in Wales, suggests that there are three main reasons why Japanese firms chose Wales: labour quality and cost, infrastructure and the so-called 'welcome mat' provided by Welsh institutions coupled with inward investment. More recently there is some disagreement over the likely locational attractions of Wales. Hill and Munday

(1991) confirm that it is government assistance and wage rates that have been the main attraction of Wales to Japanese manufacturing investments. However, Jim Taylor's (1993) study of the location of Japanese manufacturing investment in the UK tends to confirm only government assistance and not wage rates as a determining factor in location. Subsequent surveys (Morris *et al.* 1993) have suggested that proximity to customers has also become an attraction to locating in Wales, which in turn is likely to be a reflection of the arrival of component-producing plants.

The CBI identified four criteria which Japanese manufacturing investment should satisfy if, on balance, it was not to have a deleterious effect on established UK industry. They considered that inward investment should:

1. have high export potential

2. use a high proportion of local suppliers

3. create a net increase in jobs (once UK competitors have run-down operations)

4. not compete with UK firms (given the amounts of regional policy assistance received).

Overall, Munday (1990) suggests that Japanese firms in Wales have been successful in meeting these four criteria. However, this is not to suggest that there are not the same concerns regarding Japanese investment as there have been surrounding US investment in earlier decades. Thus, Morris *et al.* summarise the research on Japanese investments in Wales by suggesting that 'whilst there has been a substantial direct employment effect, question marks about the underlying quality of the Japanese investments still persist' (Morris *et al.* 1993: 51).

In sum, it seems premature to view Japanese manufacturing investments as anything other than quite rationalised forms of manufacturing investment. Furthermore, whilst there are obvious problems in taking this Japanese investment as indicative of recent manufacturing investment in general, nevertheless, apart from one or two notable exceptions, the branch plant syndrome persists as a feature of multinational manufacturing investment in Wales.

Conclusion

Multinational manufacturing investment is an important source of total manufacturing employment in the Welsh economy. Among some of the myths about the current state and prospects of the Welsh economy which appear to have blossomed recently, those relating to the regenerative capacity of foreign manufacturing investment have been some of the most notable (Lovering, 1996). As has been discussed, the wider benefits of such investment are debateable. Nevertheless, this review has suggested a number of features of multinational investment in Wales which offer some scope for industry upgrading.

The main locational advantages of Wales to mobile investment appear to be a combination of relatively cheap and available labour and financial incentives. These locational advantages appear to have been reinforced by productivity gains which have turned Wales from a relatively high unit labour cost location into a relatively low unit labour cost location. The small plant size of foreign owned manufacturing establishments in Wales (relative to that in other peripheral regions) need not therefore be a hindrance to competitiveness in an increasingly integrated EU market. Instead, the productivity gains experienced in Wales tend to highlight the contribution of new work-practices and management philosophies to competitiveness. However, it is still the case that Wales has been successful in attracting cost-minimising mobile manufacturing investment (Hill and Keegan, 1993, cited in Hill and Roberts, 1993). As others have suggested, there are severe limitations with the attraction of such cost-minimising investment. On the one hand, the competition for such cost-minimising investment is intensifying so that in an ever more integrated European space economy Wales as a location is drawn into competition with other low-cost locations (Thomas, 1996). Here, the recent reduction of Development Area status in Wales compared to other regions appears to have had and impact on Wales's share of inward investment (Morgan, 1996; Thomas, 1996) and presumably on the share of such investment in the form of new openings. Thus, even within a UK context, Wales may be losing out in the attraction of cost-minimising investments. On the other hand, such cost-minimising investment is very unlikely to bring long-term benefits to the Welsh economy. In the chapters which follow, the aim is to examine the competitive position of Welsh multinational manufacturing operations vis-à-vis company plants elsewhere in the EU.

It is also clear that multinational investment in Wales lacks decision-making autonomy, technical capabilities and sales capacity. Nevertheless, in other respects Welsh multinational manufacturing investment is less branch like. For example, foreign investment in Wales appears quite export oriented, possibly more so than in several other peripheral regions of the UK. This is a feature which may work to the advantage of Welsh industry, given the processes of economic integration in Europe. Again, issues taken up in the following chapters are those of the market orientation and corporate role of Welsh multinational outposts as well as the degree to which they are integrated with other parent company operations.

Finally, multinational companies are not deeply embedded in the Welsh economy. The most striking indication of this is the low levels of local sourcing materials by multinational manufacturing investments in Wales. Nevertheless, historically healthy levels of reinvestment by, together with the innovative management and procurement practices of, multinationals offer scope for the upgrading and embedding of industry. Here it appears that such organisational dynamics need to be matched by well developed institutional capabilities geared toward delivering a high level of aftercare (Morgan, 1993). In this respect Wales may compare favourably with other peripheral UK regions but may nevertheless lag behind innovative peripheral, let alone core, regions of the EU.

This book now turns to the presentation of original empirical material on multinationals, European integration and the Welsh economy. Chapter 6 briefly introduces the methodological background and detail to this empirical work.

CHAPTER 6

Background to the Study

Introduction

This study focuses on multinational enterprises as the main orchestrators of processes of regional economic integration in Europe. From the discussion in preceding chapters it is clear that the way in which multinationals organise production at and between sites has a considerable bearing upon aggregate patterns of trade and investment in Europe. Naturally, patterns of trade and investment vary according to industry sector as does multinational involvement, though, as far as multinationals are concerned, consideration of 'ownership' and 'vintage' also appeared to be important to an understanding the organisation of production.

One preferred strategy for empirical investigation of the contribution of multinationals to process of economic integration would be to examine particular companies with production operations in different EU member states. Such case studies would be sensitive both to issues of the organisation of production within multinationals as well as the complex way in which ownership and vintage have a bearing upon such organisations. A second option would have been to design a comparative regional study of multinational involvement in two or more regions of the EU. This is the approach taken in one recent study examining the nature of mobile investment in the EU (Amin *et al.*, 1994). That study examined the comparative quality of a limited number of high-profile inward investments in a number of EU regions. Various constraints dictated that the approach taken in this study is much more limited in scope.

The empirical strategy in this study was to examine the character of multinational manufacturing industry in just one region. In particular, the research is concerned with the implications of processes of European integration for peripheral region development. The prospects for peripheral regions are, as we have seen, rather unclear. In general it is probably fair to say that peripheral regions are the most vulnerable in relation to processes of integration. In detail, though, the position of peripheral regions is a little more ambiguous. At once, peripheral regions contain some of the most vulnerable, most rationalised and least embedded multinational investments and yet they may continue to attract such cost-minimising investment as a result of processes of integration. Furthermore, peripheral regions are rapidly acquiring the sorts of institutional capability deemed to underpin the economic vitality of certain core regions.

This ambiguity is quite apparent in relation to multinational involvement in UK manufacturing industry. One argument which has gained currency in academic and political circles is that the UK has increasingly assumed the role of a low cost, low technology, export platform for mainland European markets (De Smidt, 1992; Rubery, 1994; Williams *et al.* 1991) albeit one whose productivity levels have been rising during the 1980s and 1990s. As a whole, manufacturing industry in the UK therefore appears to be vulnerable to processes of rationalisation in European industry. However, the UK has continued to attract new investment from outside the EU – notably Japanese investment – and from within the EU.

The problems of occupying such a position within the European-wide division of labour become yet more apparent when considering the peripheral regions of the UK. This study focuses on one such UK peripheral region – Wales. There has been quite a long history of multinational involvement in Welsh manufacturing industry. Wales, as with other peripheral UK regions, has acquired large numbers of US-owned manufacturing operations as well as manufacturing operations of large multilocational and multinational UK firms. By now a vast literature has addressed issues of the quality of such US and UK investment in peripheral regions with the term 'branch plant economy' being applied to regions such as Wales. Implicit in such a label is the expectation that Welsh manufacturing industry is highly susceptible to rationalisation in general, and presumably, therefore to rationalisation associated with European integration in particular. However, Wales continues to benefit from inflows of new overseas investment – most notably from Japan, although also from Germany and France. Indeed, it has been the prime destination within Europe for Japanese manufacturing investment. At present such investment is probably little different from that of the US investments of earlier decades. However, debates rage about the character and contribution to regional development of Japanese manufacturing investment in particular and 'new' multi-national investment in general. Wales therefore provides an excellent opportunity to examine the impact of multinationals and processes of European integration upon peripheral region development. In particular, and because of the long history and mix of multinational involvement in Welsh manufacturing industry there is the opportunity to consider the ways in which ownership and vintage may have a bearing upon processes of integration and regional development. Finally, Wales has one of the most developed institutional capabilities of UK regions. The study therefore allows some consideration of the interaction of policy with corporate organisation.

The general approach taken in the research was to combine extensive and intensive forms of empirical investigation (Sayer and Morgan, 1986). Resource and financial constraints dictated that the rather blunt instrument of a postal survey would be used to build up a limited descriptive picture of the nature of multina-tional involvement in Welsh manufacturing industry and the impact of processes of integration on multinational manufacturing activity in Wales. This survey material provided the basis for a descriptive and exploratory account of the connections between the organisation of production in multinationals, processes of European integration and their possible impact on the Welsh economy. In particular, the survey material was useful in framing questions regarding the connection between ownership and vintage of manufacturing operations and processes of integration and regional development. For a more detailed and nuanced appreciation of the implications of European integration for manufacturing operations in Wales a limited number of company case studies were also undertaken. Here, the idea was to trace more accurately the decision-making processes regarding rationalisation and reorganisation of production on a European-wide basis in those instances in which there were implications for Welsh manufacturing operations. More particularly, the case studies were useful in exploring further some of the issues raised by the aggregate survey material especially issues related to the character of Welsh manufacturing operations. The rationalisation decisions made by multinationals are primarily intra-corporate rather than inter-corporate in focus with the fortunes of EU regions being interrelated through such internal corporate divisions of labour. Most studies which have explored the role of large firms and economies of scale in European integration have tended to adduce general trends regarding such internal corporate divisions of labour and their spatial ramifications. In the present study, however, the survey and case studies attempted to gain an insight into the extent and dimensions of inter-plant competition within multinational companies and inter-regional competition in terms of factor endowments and institutional infrastructure. In this respect the approach is somewhat unique.

Postal Survey Method

A list of all large (100 or more employees) Welsh manufacturing establishments which were part of multinational firms was compiled from lists supplied by the business services division of the Welsh Office and was supplemented and cross checked with information contained in local and national business directories. Multinationality and ultimate ownership of these establishments was determined using the sources mentioned above as well as *Who Owns Whom* (Dun and Bradstreet Ltd., 1994). However, 'ownership' defined in this way is not synonymous with 'control'. One concern of this study is to consider the relation between ownership and corporate organisation as this affects processes of integration and regional development. The implication here is that ownership somehow approximates to control. For example, an establishment whose ultimate headquarters is in the US but whose immediate headquarters (where virtually all the major decisions are taken) are in Europe might reasonably be considered a European firm. Discussing the effective locus of control within a large corporation and defining 'ownership' in these terms is a time consuming task which is not always possible without detailed knowledge of the corporation concerned. In defining ownership in terms of ultimate ownership the approach taken in this study is necessarily rather crude. Even with such a crude indication of ownership there were still problems in deciding upon whether establishments should be included in the survey sample frame. For instance, a number of establishments were part of holding or conglomerate companies; this being especially prevalent among UK-owned establishments. The questionnaire which addresses questions of comparative plant performance and corporate strategy was clearly far less relevant to the establishments which were part of such holding or conglomerate companies.

The final sample frame of multinational operations in Wales numbered 224 in total. In June/July 1994, questionnaires were mailed, in the main, to factory managers or managing directors at these establishments. The information requested on the questionnaire was kept to a minimum. The questionnaire itself was structured to gain information on the markets served by, and the comparative performance and embeddedness of, multinational investments. In trying to ascertain an idea of intra-corporate comparative plant performance, the questionnaire attempted to follow broadly the approach used by Hood and Young (1983). In this respect, Hood and Young's (1983) survey naturally has a major advantage over the present study in that it was conducted by way of face-to-face interviews – thus eliminating ambiguity about issues of comparability of plants. Two reminder letters were sent to remaining establishments which had not responded. A number of establishments had closed or were in the process of closing and a number had been wrongly identified as being part of multinationals and hence the original sample frame was reduced to 214. Eventually, useable completed questionnaires were received from 142 establishments giving an overall response rate of 67% (see Table 6.1).

Analysis of Responses to the Postal Survey

Tables 6.1, 6.2 and 6.3 give details of the sample frame and the responses broken down according to industry class, ownership and vintage. From Table 6.1 it is apparent that multinational involvement in Welsh manufacturing industry is concentrated into the chemicals industry (class 25), the electrical and electronic engineering industry (class 34) and the automotive components industry (class 35). Between them these three sectors accounted for 46.3% of the establishments in the sample frame and 45.8% of the total number of questionnaire returns. There are some sectoral variations in the response rate with the best response rates being recorded for class 26, the chemicals industries (class 25) and the furniture industries (class 46) and the worst response rates recorded for the computer industry (class 33) and the clothing and footwear industry (class 45). However, a chi-squared test suggests that these variations according to industry sector are not statistically significant.

Table 6.1 Survey responses by Industry Class

SIC (1980) Industry Class	Sent (a)	Received (b)	Response rate	Ratio (b/a)
22 Metal Manufacturing	6 (2.8)	3 (2.1)	50.0	0.75
24 Non-metallic mineral products	3 (1.4)	2 (1.4)	66.7	1.00
25 Chemicals	24 (11.2)	19 (13.4)	79.2	1.20
26 Man Made fibres	4 (1.9)	4 (2.8)	100.0	1.47
31 Metal Goods n.e.s	13 (6.0)	10 (7.0)	76.9	1.17
32 Mechanical engineering	8 (3.7)	5 (3.4)	62.5	0.95
33 Office machinery & data processing equipment	2 (0.9)	1 (0.7)	50.0	0.78
34 Electrical & electronic engineering	48 (22.4)	28 (19.7)	58.3	0.88
35 Motor vehicles & parts	27 (12.6)	18 (12.7)	66.7	1.01
37 Instrument engineering	6 (2.8)	4 (2.8)	66.7	1.00
41/42 Food, drink & tobacco	8 (3.7)	6 (4.2)	75.0	1.14
43 Textiles	3 (1.4)	2 (1.4)	66.7	1.00
45 Leather & leather goods	2 (0.9)	0 (0.0)	0.0	0.00
46 Timber & wooden furniture	9 (4.2)	8 (5.6)	88.9	1.33
47 Paper & paper products and printing	16 (7.5)	8 (5.6)	50.0	0.75
48 Rubber & plastics	19 (8.9)	14 (9.9)	73.7	1.11
49 Other manufacturing	16 (7.5)	10 (7.0)	62.5	0.93
Total	**214 (100.0)**	**142 (100.00)**	**66.4**	

Source: Author's survey

Table 6.2 Survey responses by date of establishment

	Received
Pre 1950	17 (12.0)
1950–1959	15 (10.6)
1960–1969	24 (16.9)
1970–1979	32 (22.5)
1980–1989	34 (23.9)
1990–	13 (9.2)
Not available	7 (4.9)
Total	**142 (100.0)**

Source: Author's survey

Table 6.3 Survey responses by nationality of ownership

	Sent (a)	*Received (b)*	*Response rate*	*Ratio (b/a)*
UK	63 (29.4)	37 (26.1)	58.7	0.89
US	49 (22.9)	37 (26.1)	75.5	1.14
EU	48 (22.4)	33 (23.2)	68.8	1.04
JAP	27 (12.6)	21 (14.8)	77.8	1.17
Other	27 (12.6)	14 (9.9)	51.9	0.79
Total	**214 (100.0)**	**142 (100.0)**	**66.4**	

Source: Author's survey

One concern of this research is to explore the possible connection between vintage of investments and the corporate role and character of such investment. Table 6.2 provides a breakdown of the sample frame and response rates according to the period of establishment of manufacturing operations. It proved difficult to compile accurate data on the period of establishment of multinational manufacturing operations in Wales. The problems were particularly acute for UK-owned establishments. Some data on date of establishment was provided by way of questionnaire returns whilst a variety of published and unpublished sources were used for the remainder of the sample-frame for which there were no responses. The data contained in Table 6.2 should therefore be regarded as indicative rather than a highly accurate portrayal of response rates according to vintage.

A second concern of the research was to examine whether 'ownership' matters in terms of the character of, and prospects for, multinational manufacturing investment in Wales. Table 6.3 provides a breakdown of the postal survey response rate by ownership category. The poorest response rates are recorded for UK-owned establishments and the diverse group of establishments which fall into the 'other' ownership category. With respect to UK-owned establishments a number of possible reasons for non-response can be offered. For instance, the fact that there tend to be multiple production sites in Wales owned by UK parent companies together with the possibly more rationalised nature of UK-owned establishments may be one explanation for the poor response rate for this ownership category. The best response rate was recorded for Japanese-owned establishments which may have an interest in maintaining good public relations in the region in particular and the UK in general. Again, however, a chi-squared test suggests that these variations in response rate according to ownership are not statistically significant.

Case Study Method

A number of company case studies were also conducted in order to add a little more detail to some of the issues raised by the postal survey material. During the course of the empirical research a small number of highly pertinent examples of corporate rationalisation and reorganisation involving Welsh manufacturing operations came to light. Hitachi's consumer electronic factory at Hirwaun for instance had gained responsibility for production transferred from its recently closed factory in Germany. In contrast, Ondawel, a Welsh-based manufacturing subsidiary of Wella in Germany could not take part in the postal survey since it was shutting its Welsh operation to serve the UK market from mainland Europe. The latter case suggested that a more systematic look at manufacturing plant closures might throw up examples of production reorganisation and transfers with a Wales – Europe angle. Building up a comprehensive list of the main closures would in itself have been a time consuming task. Instead the approach was to focus on some of the more notable recent closures as possible additional case studies. The former case suggested that a more systematic examination of some of the main multinational manufacturing organisations could produce further examples of where Welsh operations had benefited from transfers of production or functions on a European-wide basis. Again, this was potentially a time consuming business involving primarily a detailed examination of national and local press reports over a lengthy period of time. In the event, clues regarding certain companies were followed up and again this approach threw up a limited number of additional examples of corporate reorganisation involving a Wales–Europe dimension. Given the above, the limited number of case studies which are reported in this study are not intended to be in any sense 'representative'. Rather they represent some of the more notable of a limited number of examples of restructuring having some relation to processes of European integration.

Case study material was compiled from a number of sources. Initially background material was gathered from national and local press reports and from other published sources such as company annual reports and accounts and company histories. Here the London Business School's collection of company annual reports and accounts also proved a highly valuable source of information. Particular use was also made of the McCarthy newspaper clippings service which is held on microfiche (dating back to the 1970s) in the British Library Science Reference and Information Service at Holborn, London and on CD Rom data-base. This background information was supplemented, where possible, by interviews with staff at the relevant establishments and companies. In the case of establishments which had closed there were difficulties in obtaining an interview with an appropriate member of staff able to discuss the closure decision (e.g. see Fothergill and Guy, 1992). In certain instances, where few details of closures or transfers were reported in the press, these interviews were an important part of the case studies.

In general the case studies proved a very valuable addition to the aggregate survey material since as Schoenberger notes '[they]...can provide a qualitative context that amplifies and enriches the meanings derived from quantitative methods' (Schoenberger, 1991: 181). This was particularly the case as regards an understanding of the logic of decisions involving selective plant closures and transfers of production and the ways in which multinational manufacturing operations were embedded in the Welsh economy. It is also fair to say that such corporate interviews are highly useful as a means of empirical investigation in times of great economic and social change (Schoenberger, 1991). In which respect it can be suggested that both processes of European integration specifically, and changes in the mode of capitalist regulation in general, will be contributing to such economic and social change.

Conclusion

The present research makes use of both extensive and intensive forms of empirical research. Earlier, a number of detailed limitations with both the postal survey and case study research were noted. In general, however, the approach adopted was that which was most appropriate given the resources available for the research. On a more general note of reflection on the chosen research strategy, it is clear that the approach adopted is partial in a more fundamental sense. Both components of the original empirical research focus on the corporate organisation of production and how this affects the character of multinational involvement in particular regions. However, as noted and widely argued elsewhere, regional institutional capability may also makes an important contribution to the embeddedness and competitiveness of multinational investments. And in this respect it was also noted that Wales possesses some of the most developed institutional infrastructure of the UK regions. Thus the original research focuses almost exclusively on one side of the equation of industry embeddedness and competitiveness – the corporate dynamics – to the exclusion of the other side – the institutional dynamics. Discussion of other published material examining the contribution of Wales' institutional infrastructure of industry performance is nevertheless taken up in Chapters 9 and 10.

In focusing on a peripheral region such as Wales and in focusing on multinationals then, in theory at least, this study should detect some of the strongest processes of market integration as they impinge on one of the weaker regional economies in the EU. The next chapters report on some original empirical material on the contribution of multinationals to processes of European integration.

CHAPTER 7

The Market Orientation
of Multinationals in Wales

Introduction

In this chapter the markets served by multinational-owned manufacturing establishments in Wales are examined. On the face of things, the Welsh manufacturing operations of multinationals might appear to be adversely affected by processes of market integration in two respects. First, it is arguable that multinational manufacturing operations in Wales serve predominately mass markets and may therefore be particularly vulnerable to strategies of rationalisation and production switching centred on cost reduction. Closely related to this is the idea, derived from product cycle theory, that peripheral regions such as Wales also tend to have a degree of specialisation in the manufacture of mature or standardised products for which demand may be stagnating or declining. Processes of market integration may well exacerbate tendencies toward, on the one hand, closure and rationalisation in mature or standardised industries and, on the other hand, growth in newer or niche industries. Second, the growth potential of manufacturing operations and their competitive position is considered to be related to the geographical spread of markets they serve. One important factor in the instability of inward investment in peripheral regions has been the limited geographical spread of markets served. Arguably, then, there is a connection between the quality of inward investment and the geographical spread of markets being served (e.g. see Roth and Morrison, 1992).

This chapter now goes on to consider the nature and geography of markets served by multinational manufacturing operations in Wales. It then goes on to consider more directly the possible impact of market integration upon the competitive position of multinational manufacturing operations in Wales.

The Branch Plant Syndrome, Product Cycles and Markets

Table 7.1 permits an initial analysis of the sorts of markets being served by Welsh manufacturing operations of multinational companies. Respondents were asked whether their operations served mass or niche markets and whether these were fast growing, growing, stagnant or declining. One limitation here is that no definitions of these categories were provided and respondents were able to indicate any of the categories that were relevant. The first point to note is that equal proportions of establishments consider that they are serving mass and niche markets. There is also a small number which serve both mass and niche markets. This is generally encouraging since peripheral region economies, such as Wales are often considered to be composed primarily of industry producing for mass markets – and hence being composed of rationalised forms of production. It is also encouraging given that it is now widely held that mass markets – and with them the more rigid forms of mass production – are being undermined by the growth of niche markets and flexible forms of production. The assumption in this line of argument is that niche markets tend also to be growing markets. As we saw earlier, there is considerable debate about the causes and extent of any such transition from mass or Fordist forms of production to flexible forms of production. Nevertheless, the existence of some form of crisis within traditional mass production industries – the sort often considered to be the staple of peripheral region industry – seems beyond question. Given all this, the orientation of Welsh multinational-owned manufacturing industry toward niche markets may be a cause for optimism regarding the future stability of investment and employment.

Table 7.1 Type of market served according to ownership

	UK	US	EU	Japan	Other	Total
Mass	10 (37.0)	10 (37.0)	12 (50.0)	7 (63.6)	5 (55.6)	44 (44.9)
Niche	13 (48.2)	14 (51.9)	8 (33.3)	4 (36.4)	4 (44.4)	43 (43.8)
Both	4 (14.8)	3 (11.1)	4 (16.7)	0 (0.0)	0 (0.0)	11 (11.2)

Source: Author's survey

Table 7.2 Type of market served according to vintage

	Pre 1950	1950–59	1960–69	1970–79	1980–89	1990–
Mass	4 (28.6)	4 (33.3)	6 (40.0)	14 (56.0)	9 (47.4)	5 (71.4)
Niche	8 (57.1)	4 (33.3)	8 (53.3)	11 (44.0)	9 (47.4)	2 (28.6)
Both	2 (14.3)	4 (33.3)	1 (6.7)	0 (0.0)	1 (5.3)	0 (0.0)

Source: Author's survey

There are some interesting variations in the sorts of markets being served by manufacturing operations of different ownership. For example, it appears that the majority of both EU-owned and Japanese-owned establishments in Wales are oriented towards mass markets. This contrasts with the UK and US-owned establishments, the majority of which are oriented towards serving niche markets.

Similarly there are some variations in the sorts of markets served by establishments of different vintages. The branch plants established during the 1960s and 1970s are those which are often considered, in the literature, to be those which have been most rationalised and most oriented towards mass markets. In Table 7.2 the data suggest that there is no real evidence of this being the case for multinational manufacturing establishments in Wales. Indeed, if anything, those operations established since 1990 appear to be most oriented towards mass markets. Whilst the older operations appear to be most orientated towards serving niche markets.

According to product cycle theory, at least, a large proportion of peripheral regional manufacturing activity is likely to be composed of the production of mature or standardised products for which demand may be stagnant or even declining. Table 7.3 therefore again provides some encouraging signs regarding the sorts of markets being served by multinational manufacturing operations in Wales. Only around one-third of establishments are involved with producing goods for markets which are stagnant or declining with the remaining two-thirds serving growing or fast growing markets – though only a small minority of establishments appear to have significant growth prospects linked to their serving fast-growing markets.

Table 7.3 also provides evidence of the poor competitive position of UK-owned multinational manufacturing operations in Wales. The majority of these establishments indicated that they were serving stagnant or declining markets. This stands in contrast to overseas-owned manufacturing establishments in Wales. The majority of US, EU and Japanese-owned establishments all indicated that they were serving growing markets. Here at least is some confirmation for the argument that the most rationalised forms of production exist within the UK-owned manufacturing sector in Wales.

As is to be expected, the majority of new multinational investments in Wales (post 1980) are serving growing or fast growing markets (see Table 7.4). A little more surprisingly, the majority of those operations established in the 1970s are also serving growing or fast growing markets. This is surprising given, as noted above, the assumption in the literature that plants of this vintage will be some of the most rationalised and potentially vulnerable. More balanced proportions of operations established before 1970 are oriented towards serving growing and stagnant markets which suggests more mixed future prospects for these operations.

Table 7.3 Growth of markets served according to ownership

	UK	US	EU	Japan	Other	Total
Fast growing	1 (3.0)	3 (10.3)	2 (6.3)	0 (0.0)	0 (0.0)	6 (4.8)
Growing	14 (42.4)	20 (68.0)	22 (68.8)	15 (83.3)	6 (50.0)	77 (62.1)
Stagnant	17 (51.5)	6 (20.7)	8 (25.0)	2 (11.1)	6 (50.0)	39 (31.5)
Declining	3 (9.0)	3 (10.3)	2 (6.3)	1 (5.6)	1 (8.3)	10 (8.0)

NB Percentages may not sum to 100 due to multiple responses.
Source: Author's survey

Table 7.4 Growth of markets served according to vintage

	Pre-1950	1950–59	1960–69	1970–79	1980–89	1990–
Fast growing	2 (11.1)	0 (0.0)	1 (4.3)	1 (3.8)	1 (3.4)	1 (10.0)
Growing	9 (50.0)	8 (47.1)	11 (47.8)	17 (65.4)	19 (65.5)	9 (90.0)
Stagnant	6 (33.3)	7 (41.2)	10 (43.5)	6 (23.1)	6 (20.7)	0 (0.0)
Declining	1 (5.6)	2 (11.8)	1 (4.3)	2 (7.7)	3 (10.3)	0 (0.0)

Source: Author's survey

A number of case studies can serve to illustrate the connection between European-wide restructuring and market conditions. On the one hand, Grundig and Hitachi's transfers of production to, and Exide's expansion in, South Wales are related to the growth and development of the UK market.

Grundig, Llantrisant

Grundig's transfer of production from Germany to Wales is illustrative of rationalisation in a growing but highly competitive consumer electronics market. It illustrates the weak position of EU firms in these highly competitive markets and the importance of both external and internal tariff and non-tariff barriers in to restructuring and product sourcing.

In 1993 Welsh-based Gooding Consumer Electronics (GCE) and Grundig of Germany established a joint venture to sell and market television satellite receivers. Despite the highly competitive nature of the consumer electronics market, GCE firmly believed that it could make a success of its existing sub-contract electronics business in Wales, the joint venture and a television factory in France. Indeed the stated aim at the time was to rival Far East television manufacturers in Europe (Adburgham, 1995a). However, a slump in the market coupled to a lack of forthcoming finance for GCEs television operations prompted the sale of GCEs share of the satellite receiver business to Grundig in 1995 (Adburgham, 1995b).

Whilst the transfer of production from Germany to Wales was in keeping with the company's earlier attempts to be cost competitive with Far East imports and local production, more importantly it made sense given that the UK was the fastest growing and most developed of national markets within the EU. Interestingly, a company source suggested that it was external tariff duties imposed on receivers which are due to rise from 11.5% to 14%, rather than internal barriers to trade, around which the major rationalisation, investment and sourcing decisions within Europe revolve. The same source also suggested that EU decision-making procedures regarding the harmonisation of standards for satellite and terrestrial transmission of data are hampering product development and growth of EU companies. Currently, much of the EU market is served by imports from the Far East though such an increase in tariff duties may encourage both localised production by Far East companies as well as some international subcontracting by EU firms including Grundig.

The closure of Hitachi's video cassette recorder (VCR) factory in Germany and the partial transfer of production to Wales illustrates how a severe, albeit probably temporary, slump in part of a highly competitive European market can prompt corporate restructuring.

Hitachi Consumer Electronics, Hirwaun

Hitachi set up its consumer electronics operations in South Wales in 1979 and initially began producing television sets. Subsequently, it also began making VCRs. Independently of this, Hitachi had also established a VCR plant at Landsberg in Germany to serve the German and other mainland European markets. The company blamed the closure of its German factory on a slump in the markets served by this factory. In 1993, the time the closure was announced, output at the German factory had fallen by two-thirds from levels six years previously and was making the factory unprofitable. Conversely, in the UK, demand for VCRs was still buoyant and had even grown fractionally on previous years (Gribben, 1993).

Exide's plans for large scale closures and selective investment are taking place against generally buoyant market conditions, and a strong market position in the UK.

Exide, Cwmbran

The plans to expand Exide's lead-acid battery operations at Cwmbran are illustrative of the strategic choices regarding investment and rationalisation that accompany European expansion through acquisition.

The European automotive components industry is one which has been undergoing considerable reorganisation. Both new supplier-relations with the major car makers and European integration have contributed to rationalisation in terms of the numbers of components firms, numbers of factories and the size of these factories. With a dominant position in its domestic market, the US firm Exide expanded aggressively into Europe with a number of acquisitions during 1994 and 1995. In 1994 Exide acquired the Spanish firm Tudor, then the third largest battery maker in the EU. Exide also acquired two smaller UK battery makers Gemala and BIG Batteries. Later in 1995 Exide acquired the leading battery maker in the EU, CEAC of France. The company was 'now in a position to realise the benefits of the synergy between our worldwide operations.' (Hawkins, quoted in Griffiths, 1995a). BIG Batteries' main factory at Cwmbran had become one among some 41 European plants then operated by Exide.

On the other hand, the closure of BPs ethylene cracker plant at Baglan Bay in South Wales provides an example of rationalisation in the face of structural overcapacity in the European chemicals industry coupled to long-term shifts in the prices of commodity feedstock (oil and gas).

BP Chemicals, Baglan Bay

Ethylene is the basic building block for many chemicals products and in 1973, as part of BP's diversification into chemicals, the company opened a complex of 12 plants at Baglan Bay. The complex was based around one large ethylene cracker which would supply the other 11 producing a range of other chemicals. In building Baglan Bay, and in diversifying into chemicals, BP's strategy was to provide a captive market for its naphtha oil as a feedstock. At its time of opening, Baglan Bay was one of the largest ethylene crackers in Europe. However, from the start the plant had a troubled history. Almost immediately the cost competitiveness and the rationale for the complex were being undermined by the rise in oil prices during the mid to late 1970s which was prompting a switch by European petrochemicals firms away from naphtha oil to ethane gas as a feedstock for ethylene production when commissioning new plant.

By the early 1980s BP was openly admitting that its diversification into chemicals had been little better than a disaster. By this time the company had shed between one-quarter and one-third of its chemicals business. Large scale rationalisation in the face of overcapacity and the switch to ethane gas had prompted the closure of 18 ethylene plants in Europe between 1979 and 1982. By this time BP Chemicals had begun to talk of converting its old Grangemouth ethylene plant to use the cheaper ethane gas as a feedstock. It was not until 1988, however, that the death knell of the Baglan Bay cracker was sounded with the announcement that there would be a £200m expansion of ethylene production at Grangemouth to double production and use ethane gas. In 1994 BP Chemicals announced the closure of the Baglan Bay ethylene plant. Lawrie Stark, then General Manager, at Baglan Bay commented that 'Employees at the plant have made great efforts to improve productivity and cut costs but recession and industry overcapacity have proved too much for us' (Jones, 1994).

At first glance, the findings presented so far might seem to run counter to the expectation that (Fordist) mass production would be concentrated in the UK and US-owned sector of manufacturing industry in Wales. However, there are three complementary explanations for the patterns revealed in Tables 7.1 to 7.4. First, of itself, the orientation of recent Japanese manufacturing investment in Wales towards mass markets should not be surprising. The presently rather rationalised forms of production at the European subsidiaries of Japanese companies is entirely in keeping with expectations regarding product life cycles (Thomsen, 1993). Thus, Japanese firms have initially begun manufacture of standardised mass-market products and it may be some time before newer products, along with research and development activity are decentralised to EU locations.

Second, it can be suggested that the patterns in Tables 7.1 to 7.4 reflect the withdrawal of UK and US multinationals from mass markets. There may be both positive and negative aspects to such a withdrawal. On the one hand, evidence indicates that in the 1980s and 1990s US manufacturing firms operating in Europe have begun to reverse their long-standing strategies of product standardisation (Boddewyn and Grosse, 1995). On the other hand, mass-market UK and US firms have undoubtedly been outcompeted in an increasing number of mass production industries and have been left to occupy smaller stagnant or declining market niches. This would certainly apply to Japanese firms supplanting many UK, EU and US firms as leaders in mass-market industries, though it does not explain the orientation of EU-owned establishments in Table 7.3.

Third, then, why the orientation of EU-owned establishments towards mass markets given that EU producers have also been severely affected by competition from Japanese firms? The answer may lie partly in the fact that the UK economy has been just about the most open in the first instance to Japanese imports and latterly to Japanese direct manufacturing investment. The contrast between UK-owned and EU-owned establishments may also be a reflection of rationalisation within EU industry, with the larger EU producers winning out – perhaps at the expense of the UK firms. This, in turn, is likely to be a function of both the greater degree of protection afforded by some member states to their domestic firms and the openness of the UK economy to merger and acquisition activity. The automotive components industry provides one of the best examples of such a sharp decline in the fortunes of UK firms relative to EU firms. It is also an industry which is highly relevant in the context of multinational involvement in Welsh manufacturing industry.

It would be wrong, however, to assume that niche markets are based exclusively on new products or else upon growing or rapidly growing consumer demand.

Many niche markets are based on old products and on stagnant or declining consumer demand. One of the case studies of restructuring in Wales with a European dimension illustrates this point well.

Nu-kote International, Deeside

The closure of Nu-kote International's ribbon manufacturing operation in North Wales provides an example of the vulnerability of operations serving declining markets and in which rationalisation and capital concentration are the order of the day.

Nu-kote international was formed as a leveraged buy-out of the typewriter and computer ribbon business of Buroughs Business Machines. Buroughs had opened a ribbon manufacturing operation as one of the first factories on the Deeside industrial estate established on the site of the former steel works at Shotton and Nu-kote inherited this operation. In 1995 Nu-kote, the third largest ribbon producer in the EU and the largest in the US, acquired Pelikan Hardcopy AG the largest ribbon producer in the EU. Pelikan had three production sites in Europe: at Aberdeen in Scotland, near Hanover in Germany and near Zurich in Switzerland. In 1993 Nu-kote announced that it was closing its Deeside factory and transferring production to its newly acquired operation in Scotland. The closure took place against a background of declining demand for ribbons as compared to laser and ink-jet printers and increasing capital concentration and rationalisation among the remaining companies in the market. It is estimated that there is a continuing market for typewriter and printer ribbons for perhaps another ten years.

The orientation of Welsh manufacturing establishments towards niche markets need not be a cause for optimism especially if these niche markets are predominately stagnant or declining niches. Table 7.5 shows that this is indeed the case for a portion of multinational manufacturing operations in Wales. Table 7.5 examines whether establishments are serving mass or niche markets which are growing or declining. Most perturbing here is the fact that nearly half of the

Table 7.5 Type and growth of markets according to ownership

	UK	US	EU	Japan	Other	Total
Mass growing	7 (25.9)	7 (25.9)	12 (42.9)	5 (55.6)	1 (14.3)	32 (32.3)
Mass stagnant & declining	5 (18.5)	4 (14.8)	5 (17.9)	1 (11.1)	3 (42.9)	18 (18.2)
Niche growing	8 (29.6)	11 (40.7)	7 (25.0)	3 (33.3)	2 (28.6)	31 (31.3)
Niche stagnant & declining	7 (25.9)	6 (22.2)	4 (14.3)	0 (0.0)	1 (14.3)	18 (18.2)

NB Percentages may not sum to 100 due to multiple responses
Source: Author's survey

UK-owned establishments serving niche markets are serving stagnant or declining niche markets. The problem is less acute for US-owned establishments.

Table 7.6 Type and growth of markets according to vintage

	Pre-1950	1950–59	1960–69	1970–79	1980–89	1990–
Mass growing	5 (31.3)	4 (20.0)	4 (26.7)	7 (36.8)	5 (35.7)	4 (80.0)
Mass stagnant & declining	1 (6.3)	6 (30.0)	2 (13.3)	3 (15.8)	3 (21.4)	0 (0.0)
Niche growing	6 (37.5)	5 (25.0)	5 (33.3)	6 (31.6)	5 (35.7)	1 (20.0)
Niche stagnant & declining	4 (25.0)	5 (25.0)	4 (26.7)	3 (15.8)	1 (7.1)	0 (0.0)

Source: Author's survey

Table 7.6 shows that those operations serving stagnant or declining niche markets, and hence which are some of the most susceptible to future closure or rationalisation, are predominantly those established during the 1950s and 1960s; though why this should be is not altogether clear. These patterns can be interpreted broadly in a couple of ways. In particular the healthy position of 1970s operations *vis-à-vis* those established earlier needs some explanation. One contributing factor to the relative vitality of 1970s investments may be that the most rationalised and most vulnerable of these operations were shut during the early 1980s leaving the least rationalised and most competitive to survive with the 1980s and 1990s. There is some evidence to suggest that this 'cosmetic' effect in terms of improving the characteristics of the stock of older investments may be quite significant in a number of localities and regions in the UK (Fothergill and Guy, 1992; Phelps, 1993a; Watts, 1991). A second contributory factor to the relative vitality of operations established during the 1970s and after may be the origin of that investment. The first Japanese investments in the UK and Wales took place in the 1970s and there was also somewhat of a growth in German and French investment at this time as well. Thus the orientation of these more recently established

Table 7.7 Type of output according to ownership

	UK	US	EU	Japan	Other	Total
Finished goods	25 (65.8)	22 (61.1)	24 (70.6)	16 (80.0)	11 (78.6)	98 (69.0)
Components	3 (7.9)	4 (11.1)	5 (14.7)	4 (20.0)	1 (7.1)	17 (12.0)
Both	10 (26.3)	10 (27.8)	5 (14.7)	0 (0.0)	2 (14.3)	27 (19.0)

Source: Author's survey

operations may reflect changes in the competitive position of firms in the UK and US in relation to those from Japan, Germany and France.

Table 7.8 Type of output according to vintage

	Pre-1950	1950–59	1960–69	1970–79	1980–89	1990–
Finished goods	10 (58.8)	7 (46.7)	15 (62.5)	24 (75.0)	26 (76.5)	10 (76.9)
Components	2 (11.8)	1 (6.7)	4 (16.7)	2 (6.3)	5 (14.7)	3 (23.1)
Both	5 (29.4)	7 (46.7)	5 (20.8)	6 (18.8)	3 (8.8)	0 (0.0)

Source: Author's survey

A further indication of the extent of rationalised forms of production can be gleaned from the types of manufacturing function performed by establishments in Wales. The branch plant stereotype applies most closely to certain forms of assembly-only or components-only production activities. From Table 7.7 it is apparent that only a minority of establishments are engaged in component-only manufacture as part of a vertical division of labour within their parent company (Massey's part-process branch plants). The majority manufacture finished goods, though the questionnaire did not distinguish whether these establishments were simply engaged in rationalised assembly-only activities (again perhaps as part of a vertical parent company division of labour) or integrated manufacture. Interestingly, and if the integration of component manufacture and final assembly on site is an indication of less rationalised forms of production, a fair proportion (19%) of establishments appeared to be more than branch plants.

Furthermore, a fair proportion of UK-owned establishments appeared to be concerned with the manufacture of components and final assembly. Taken at face value, this tends to contradict the earlier findings contained above and in chapter 5, that the more rationalised forms of manufacture are present in the UK-owned sector of Welsh manufacturing industry. However, it should be remembered that although UK-owned establishments might be relatively integrated in terms of manufacturing functions they might be quite truncated in terms of non-manufacturing functions relative to the foreign-owned sector and indigenous manufacturing operations in Wales. A second interpretation, which is appealing in terms of both our general understanding of the branch-plant syndrome in the UK and in terms of some of the findings presented in this section, is that UK-owned establishments may be quite vertically integrated in terms of their manufacturing operations but may also be serving stagnant or declining markets.

Table 7.8 indicates that a larger proportion of longer established multinational operations appear to have integrated manufacturing than more recently established operations. This could be a direct function of vintage in as much as functional integration at subsidiary operations is related to their age (Haug, Hood and Young,

1983). So too may vertical integration in just the manufacturing functions take place over time as parent companies concentrate production activities at particular sites. However, it may also be that there is no relationship between the extent of integrated manufacture and vintage. Arguably, then, some of the earliest branch plants as well as those into the 1960s have been some of the most self-contained: the high degree of vertical integration on-site ensuring that such operations had few contacts with the local economy. By contrast, recent investment is much less vertically integrated and concerned with final assembly only. Indeed some have gone so far as to suggest that Japanese manufacturing investments have been little more than warehouses (Williams *et al.* 1991) – though this has been qualified in respect of Japanese investments in Wales (Munday *et al.* 1995). Certainly Tables 7.7 and 7.8 tend to suggest that multinationals have gradually streamlined their European operations to create a vertical division of labour with greater specialisation by plants. This would be the case especially for US firms and their European operations.

Geographical Markets

Table 7.9 Percentage of output exported according to ownership

% exports	UK	US	EU	Japan	Other	Total
0	4 (11.1)	1 (3.0)	4 (12.1)	4 (23.5)	1 (7.1)	14 (10.5)
1–25	14 (38.9)	2 (6.0)	19 (57.6)	2 (11.8)	9 (64.3)	46 (34.6)
26–50	12 (33.3)	11 (33.3)	4 (12.1)	3 (17.6)	2 (14.3)	32 (24.0)
51–75	3 (8.3)	14 (42.4)	4 (12.1)	6 (35.3)	1 (7.1)	28 (21.1)
76–100	3 (8.3)	5 (15.2)	2 (6.1)	2 (11.8)	1 (7.1)	13 (9.8)
Average	28.4	55.0	25.2	40.5	23.8	35.3

χ^2=44.92, p<0.0001
F=7.221, p<0.0001
Source: Author's survey

From Table 7.9 it appears that Welsh multinational manufacturing operations have a healthy export orientation. Only a minority of 10% are oriented solely towards the UK market with the remaining 90% engaged in some exporting. The temptation is to assume that those multinational operations serving purely national markets are there because of local markets and may be largely unaffected by processes of European integration. However, in most EU member states there is still considerable scope for rationalisation of essentially nationally-based companies in response to increased competition with European integration as the case of BICC's expansion at Wrexham illustrates. Recent expansion at BICC's Wrexham operations following closures of factories elsewhere in the UK illustrates the process of rationalisation accompanying acquisition in a UK market subject to increasing competition from EU producers.

Table 7.10 Geographical spread of markets according to ownership

	UK	US	EU	Japan	Other	Total
Solely UK	6 (17.1)	1 (3.2)	5 (17.2)	3 (18.8)	2 (15.4)	17 (13.7)
UK & other EU	10 (28.6)	6 (19.4)	10 (34.5)	6 (37.5)	2 (15.4)	34 (27.4)
EU & other European	8 (22.9)	11 (35.5)	6 (20.7)	4 (25.0)	7 (53.8)	36 (29.0)
Worldwide	11 (31.4)	13 (41.9)	8 (27.6)	3 (18.8)	2 (15.4)	37 (29.8)

Source: Author's survey

BICC, Wrexham

In 1989 BICC, the largest cable manufacturer in the UK, acquired Sterling Greengate Cable Co. Ltd from the US firm Raytheon. Sterling Greengate had factories in Warrington and Aldermaston. BICC closed the latter facility and transferred production to its own factories in Leigh and Wrexham. As a result 100 jobs were gained at the Wrexham operations (Thomas, 1992: 247). The acquisition represented part of a strategy on the part of BICC to combat increased competition from major EU producers during the 1980s. In the 1970s and early 1980s BICC, had by its own admission, used its dominant position in the UK market to charge premium prices. Its major EU competitors had as a result increasingly penetrated the UK market with imports rising from 8% of the domestic market in 1980 to 19% in 1988 (Monopolies and Mergers Commission, 1990). Furthermore, the two leading EU Cables manufacturers Alcatel and Pirelli had been expanding into major EU and world companies through acquisition. BICC had belatedly responded to this challenge by acquiring cable manufacturers in Italy, Spain and the US. At the time, the acquisition of Sterling Greengate gave BICC an estimated 9% share of the EU market behind Alcatel (16%) and Pirelli (15%) and was justified since the company 'needed a strong base in the United Kingdom to compete in Europe and other export markets and to provide technical and engineering support for its Worldwide operations' (Monopolies and Mergers Commission, 1990: 31). In the long-term the future of the Wrexham factories is less clear. One of the factories at Wrexham produces mainly mains cables – the technical standards for which have yet to be harmonised to any great degree within the EU. Indeed one representation to the Monopolies and Mergers Commission inquiry suggested that no significant impact of any such harmonisation would to felt for a decade (i.e. by the late 1990s). However,

BICC and other UK manufacturers were concerned about the openness of the UK market compared to other EU markets especially given the privatisation of utilities in the UK.

Overall, the figures in Tables 7.9 and 7.10 tend to confirm the historically good export orientation of inward investment in Wales relative to other peripheral UK regions. The data in Table 7.9 again confound simple associations of the more rationalised forms of production in the UK-owned manufacturing sector in Wales. UK-owned establishments are not the least export oriented of multinational-owned manufacturing operations in Wales. A higher proportion of EU and Japanese-owned operations than UK-owned operations appear to be oriented solely toward the UK market. One possible explanation for this pattern could centre on the build up of secondary component producing operations by Japanese-owned firms and a similar emphasis of EU investment in Wales on component producing sectors (notably the automotive components industry) which are primarily oriented to local/national markets. In this respect there appears to be a bifurcation in the sales orientation of Japanese-owned establishments in Wales with the secondary investment geared towards supplying UK consumer electronics and automotive original equipment manufacturers (OEMs) and the OEMs themselves being highly export oriented and geared towards EU and broader European markets. The build up of such secondary-type investment, especially that related to initial Japanese investments, despite the limited markets served could be viewed positively as a contribution to local multiplier effects, though as we saw earlier these have been the least positive aspect of Japanese investment in Wales. It could also be viewed negatively as the creation of what Amin and Robins (1990) term 'branch industrial complexes' – in which the fragility of the branch plant syndrome is extended over broader complexes of dependent suppliers. US-owned establishments appear to be the most export oriented of multinational investments in Wales. This is perhaps understandable given the generally higher degree of internationalisation evident among US multinationals and the lengthy experience of US multinationals within Europe.

Table 7.10 provides some greater geographical resolution regarding the main markets served by manufacturing establishments in Wales. Interestingly enough there are some discrepancies between the findings contained in Table 7.9 and Table 7.10. The greater numbers and proportions of establishments which appear to be oriented toward solely the UK market in Table 7.10 than in Table 7.9 may be a reflection of the fact that some establishments which have reported very low levels of exports have essentially discounted these for the purposes of supplying the information contained in Table 7.10. Nevertheless, the figures in the two tables are broadly in line and confirm that, in general, multinational manufacturing operations in Wales are quite export oriented. The figures do, however, place UK-owned establishments in a slightly less favourable light. The local orientation of EU-owned establishments is confirmed but that of Japanese-owned establishments questioned.

Beyond providing a corrective to the data contained in Table 7.9, Table 7.10 is also of use in analysing in greater detail the geographical spread of markets served by multinationals in Wales. As we saw earlier in Chapter 4, the existence of market clusters undermines the notion of a single European market. It is inappropriate to make any detailed conclusions regarding the orientation of multinationals in Wales towards certain market clusters which appear to exist within Europe. However, two other observations can be made about the data contained in Table 7.10 which also undermine the idea of a single European market. First, respondents were given the opportunity to specify on the questionnaire whether they served specifically the EU market as a whole. This category has been omitted from Table 7.10 because only one establishment indicated that it served specifically the EU market as a whole. Second, the numbers and proportions of establishments serving EU and other markets and worldwide markets suggests that processes of European integration need to be understood in some broader context of the internationalisation of production.

Regionalisation elsewhere in the world economy, and in North America, in particular, may have an important effect on manufacturing operations serving worldwide markets from locations in the EU irrespective of whether such regionalisation is trade creating or diverting. Irrespective of whether EU production sites become less competitive with lower or higher cost sites in North America as a result of free trade agreements there, they are likely to suffer a loss of export markets which may then subsequently have an effect on capacity utilisation and efficiency. According to one recent survey, 35% of foreign-owned manufacturing operations in Wales had world product mandates (Lewis, 1995). The implication here must be that many of these highly export oriented foreign-owned manufacturing operations in Wales may be affected to some extent. This scenario should, however, be put in some further context since the actual impact on multinationals operating in the EU may be minimal for two main reasons.

First, and drawing on the evidence discussed earlier, the trade diverting effects on regionalisation in North America may be restricted to a few particular industries as is in the case with the EU. We saw earlier how Jacquemin and Sapir's (1988) evidence suggested that European integration had only been at the expense of world integration with respect to a few politically sensitive sectors such as agricultural produce and aerospace equipment. Regionalisation in North America might therefore be expected to have a similarly marginal effect on the competitive position of EU-based production. Second, regionalisation in North America may have little effect on the competitive position of EU-based production since very few operations of multinationals are likely to serve both North America and the EU markets. The majority of those operations in Wales serving worldwide markets are likely to be serving some EU markets together with markets in, for instance, former colonies in Africa and Asia. Traditionally there has been little cross penetration of North American and EU markets by way of trade as far as finished goods are concerned. Rather, US and EU multinationals have engaged in oligopolistic reaction to serve markets directly through localised production. The main impact of regionalisation in North America may therefore be in terms of trade in components – with a greater pressure towards corporate division of labour and integration of production on a continental scale at the expense of that on a global scale. Though to an extent the limitations to any such global division of labour and integration of production have probably long-since been recognised in any case.

In particular, Table 7.10 confirms that the high export orientation of US-owned establishments revealed in Table 7.9 is a reflection of the fact that the majority of these establishments are actually oriented toward a larger market than simply the EU. Indeed, the majority of US-owned establishments are oriented towards supplying worldwide markets. This, in turn, confirms that processes of European integration are taking place within a broader market context especially as far as US-owned operations in Wales are concerned. According to Lewis's (1995) survey, the possession of world product mandates also appears to be most widespread among US-owned manufacturing operations in Wales. Thus, whilst over 15% of US manufacturing operations in Wales claimed to have continental product mandates over 60% claimed to have world product mandates (Lewis, 1995). This does tend to confirm the equivocal implications of regionalisation elsewhere in the world economy for US operations in the EU.

From the patterns in Table 7.10, it seems likely that UK, EU and, to an extent, Japanese-owned establishments may orient themselves towards market clusters given the orientation of these establishments towards local (UK) and other EU national markets and towards EU and other world markets. The orientation of EU-owned establishments toward the UK and other EU markets again raises the prospect that some rationalisation of EU industry (i.e. that in the UK) is taking place. This might, in the first instance, be through cross penetration of national markets, leading perhaps to closures and eventually (though this is still some way off) the formation of European-wide corporate divisions of labour. In some respects, the notion of market clusters may be least relevant to understanding the pattern of sales of US-owned establishments. US-owned establishments appear to be serving mainly worldwide markets – though if regionalisation elsewhere in the world economy continues apace there may be some retrenchment of the sales patterns shown in Table 7.10. Interestingly, then, regionalisation outside of the EU may nevertheless have implications for corporate rationalisation and reorganisation in the EU – especially where investments have been serving worldwide markets.

From Table 7.11 it is apparent that it is the most recently established operations which are the least export oriented. This in turn is likely to represent the bifurcation of recent investment mentioned earlier. Because of the bifurcation of investment with, on the one hand, reasonably large export-oriented investments and, on the other hand, smaller component operations geared toward local markets there is this pattern of exports. The bifurcation is nowhere more evident than in the

Japanese-owned sector whose initial final assembly operations have been followed by a second wave (Munday, 1995) of component plants.

Table 7.11 Percentage of output exported according to vintage

	Pre-1950	1950–59	1960–69	1970–79	1980–89	1990–
0	1(5.9)	2(13.3)	2(8.7)	1(3.3)	3(10.0)	4(33.3)
1–25	5(29.4)	3(20.0)	9(39.1)	13(43.3)	11(36.7)	3(25.0)
26–50	5(29.4)	4(26.7)	9(39.1)	8(26.7)	5(16.7)	0(0.0)
51–75	4(23.5)	5(33.3)	2(8.7)	6(20.0)	7(23.3)	3(25.0)
76–100	2(11.8)	1(6.7)	1(4.3)	2(6.7)	4(13.3)	2(16.7)
Ave	44.12	42.00	30.04	31.90	36.17	32.17

$\chi^2=21.523$
F=0.753
Source: Author's survey

Table 7.12 Geographical spread of markets according to vintage

	Pre-1950	1950–59	1960–69	1970–79	1980–89	1990–
Solely UK	1 (6.7)	2 (14.3)	2 (10.0)	2 (6.7)	3 (10.7)	4 (40.0)
UK & other	3 (20.0)	1 (7.1)	5 (25.0)	10 (33.3)	10 (35.7)	4 (40.0)
EU & other European	3 (20.0)	6 (42.9)	4 (20.0)	9 (30.0)	9 (32.1)	2 (20.0)
Worldwide	8 (53.3)	5 (35.7)	9 (45.0)	9 (30.0)	6 (21.4)	0 (0.0)

Source: Author's survey

Also the greater orientation of recent (1980s) investment towards the EU market is just discernable in Table 7.12. Put another way, investments prior to 1980 appear to be more oriented towards worldwide markets. This is particularly the case when one looks at the oldest (pre-1950) investments of which over half serve worldwide markets. There are a number of possible interpretations of the data here. First, export orientation may be related to age of operations in as much as older investments have gradually extended the geographical scope of their markets or have been allocated greater scope or even world or continental product mandates by parent company organisations as perhaps other sites have been closed or rationalised. Second, the orientation of more recent investments towards local and EU markets may be a reflection of the growing coherence of the EU market both in terms of its widening and more particularly its deepening – which is crucial to plants being able to serve the SEM. Finally, it may also be that for the most recent investments, regionalisation elsewhere (especially North America) is playing some role in the clearer identity of the EU as a market. In other words, parent companies may be gearing their investments towards serving each of the emerging trade blocs and hence investments in the EU are geared towards specifically that market rather than having a broader remit as might have been the case in the past.

This of course then reiterates the point made earlier that regionalisation whilst changing the investment strategies of multinationals, may also prompt some rethink of operations currently serving worldwide markets. Here, then, the future of some of the oldest multinational manufacturing investments in Wales is unclear. One can speculate that they may lose some of their functions/status and employment if parent companies convert them into factories producing not for world markets but just for the EU market when establishing newer (and more productive?) plants to serve the other trade blocs.

Table 7.13 Locations of plants to which components are transferred by ownership

	UK	US	EU	Japan	Other	Total
UK	4 (30.8)	2 (14.3)	2 (20.0)	0 (0.0)	0 (0.0)	8 (18.6)
UK & EU	4 (30.8)	4 (28.6)	5 (50.0)	3 (100.0)	2 (66.7)	18 (41.9)
World	5 (38.5)	8 (57.1)	3 (30.0)	0 (0.0)	1 (33.3)	17 (39.5)

Source: Author's survey

Table 7.14 Locations of plants to which components are transferred by vintage

	Pre-1950	1950–1959	1960–1969	1970–1979	1980–1989	1990–
UK	2 (28.6)	3 (37.5)	1 (11.1)	1 (12.5)	1 (14.3)	0 (0.0)
UK & EU	3 (42.9)	1 (12.5)	4 (44.4)	4 (50.0)	3 (42.6)	2 (66.6)
World	2 (28.6)	4 (50.0)	4 (44.4)	3 (37.5)	3 (42.6)	1 (33.3)

Source: Author's survey

A number of respondent establishments produced components for use in other parent company factories. They were asked where they sent their output. There are a number of Welsh-based establishments which supply other parent company plants in the UK, suggesting a geographically-limited intra-corporate division of labour. However, this is not just a feature of UK-owned establishments in Wales (see Table 7.13). A smaller number of US and EU-owned establishments may be

part of such UK-wide corporate divisions of labour. The bulk of component-producing establishments send their output to parent company factories distributed
throughout the EU and the rest of the world. For UK, EU and Japanese-owned
establishments, European-wide divisions of labour are important. These patterns
probably reflect the fact that many branch plants which were part of part-process
forms of organisation within UK companies have been closed during the 1970s
and 1980s, leaving component-producing factories which are part of wider, more
viable, international corporate divisions of labour. US-owned establishments in
Wales are likely to have been a part of international divisions of labour for much
longer, given the tendency toward global integration within US multinationals –
car production being the prime example.

Table 7.14 indicates where operations of different vintages send their component output to other parent company operations in the EU. The small numbers of
observations prevent any hard and fast conclusions here. There is just the tentative
suggestion in the data that recent investments (post-1960) tend to be part of more
international corporate vertical divisions of labour than older investments (pre-
1959).

The Single European Market and Restructuring

Earlier, the Commission's own analyses of the impact of the SEM initiative upon
particular industries and member state economies was described in a little detail.
Employment statistics are not available at the regional level for the industrial
classification upon which those analyses were based. Consequently, no replicative
analysis at a regional level could be undertaken to consider the impact of the SEM
upon the Welsh economy. All that can be done by way of an initial discussion of
the likely impact of the SEM on the multinational sector in the Welsh economy is
to compare the main UK Standard Industrial Classification 1980 (SIC) industries
in which Welsh multinational manufacturing operations are clustered with the
main NACE industries affected by the creation of the SEM.

The Commission's analyses focus on the barriers to trade facing, and the
economies of scale associated with, different industries. A fuller discussion of the
latter will be made in Chapter 8. Some of the basic findings regarding the main
types of barriers to trade and their significance to different industries are contained
in the Commission's *The Economics of 1992* (CEC, 1988). For instance, technical
barriers to trade were judged to be of great importance in the following industries:
electrical engineering, mechanical engineering, pharmaceutical, food and tobacco,
and precision and mechanical equipment. The former two are sufficiently broad
to cover a considerable portion of multinational manufacturing operations in
Wales. However, the Commission also noted, for instance, that technical barriers
were not significant with respect to consumer electronics – an industry in which
there is considerable, primarily Japanese, multinational involvement in Wales.
Wales does have a number of multinationals operating in the chemicals industries,

though not a particularly high concentration of these are in the pharmaceutical industries. Multinational manufacturing operations in Wales are also important in industries such as footwear and clothing, wood and furniture and metal articles, however, technical barriers are only considered to be of medium importance for these industries. On the basis of this necessarily rather cursory examination of the barriers affecting different industries, there would appear to be few grounds for the overly pessimistic view that 'Wales is not well placed to gain from the Single European Market...' (Wales TUC, 1990). Instead it would appear that the creation of the SEM, and specifically the removal of remaining barriers to trade, will have little effect on the competitiveness of multinational manufacturing operations in Wales.

More recently the Commission has produced a more refined analysis of the industrial and national impact of the SEM initiative (CEC, 1990). This involves the identification of industries sensitive to the creation of the SEM defined on the basis of levels of price dispersion and the importance of barriers to trade. Forty industries were defined as sensitive and these were grouped into three categories. It is the last of these categories, 'sectors with moderate non-tariff barriers' which includes white goods, consumer electronics, and textiles and clothing and in which we are most interested in. Essentially, this slightly more refined analysis again confirms that the SEM initiative is likely to have little or moderate effect on the competitive position of multinational manufacturing operations in Wales.

Information from the survey of multinational manufacturing operations in Wales can provide a more direct indication of the impact of the SEM initiative. Table 6.13 suggests that for virtually two-thirds of multinational manufacturing operations in Wales removal of barriers to trade have had little or no impact on their competitive position. Overall, removal of barriers appears to have created as many 'opportunities' as 'threats' given that equal proportions of establishments have experienced more competition and have been able to compete more effectively as a result. Removal of barriers figured in a major way in the restructuring plans of only one of the case study companies.

Wella, Pontyclun

The Ondawel manufacturing subsidiary of Wella AG was the first German manufacturing investment in Wales – having been established in 1938. The Ondawel factory made a range of shampoos for the UK market. Wella's closure of the factory and the transfer of production and product sourcing to mainland European locations was the outcome of a very clear company strategy to concentrate production in core plants with the creation of the SEM (Wella AG, 1995).

A company spokeswoman described how 'following a review of its manufacturing strategies, it [the company] is concentrating production in fewer locations. It will result in the transfer of production from Ondawel to other locations in Europe.' (Jones, 1993b). Production lines were transferred from

Wales to Germany, Italy, France and South America. In actual fact the company had been following a recently formulated strategy of closing the large number of factories it previously operated in many EU member states and concentrating production in a few core product-specialist plants on mainland Europe. Production has now been concentrated with just five factories – two in Germany, one in each of France and Italy and one in Istanbul. Between five and six plants had been shut in the last three years alone and the total number of plants operated in Europe by Wella has fallen from 15 to 5. Staff at the company suggested that this rapid restructuring of operations in Europe was directly linked to the most recent stage of European integration – the creation of the SEM – and the elimination of non-tariff barriers in particular.

Certainly the findings here tend to confirm Buckley and Artisien's (1988) suggestion that the SEM will be slow to dissolve the need for multinationals to have a presence in national markets. They suggest that

> 'The size and speed of tariff reductions and other attempts at harmonisation will have an impact upon the timing of rationalisation moves by multinationals. Inertia in the location of facilities will only be overcome by large and permanent changes in intervention.' (Buckley and Artisien, 1988)

Such instances of large and permanent changes in intervention precipitating restructuring are often quite conspicuous. Warner-Lambert's decision to shift part of its production from its Parke-Davis subsidiary operations in Wales to continental Europe reflects the conjunction of a strategy of reorganisation in an industry with overcapacity and the impact on the UK market caused by a change in Government policy.

Parke-Davis, Pontypool

Parke-Davis's factory at Pontypool manufactured a range of pharmaceutical products for the UK and for export. For some little time before the rationalisation of operations at Pontypool, Warner-Lambert had been reorganising its worldwide pharmaceutical operations to take advantage not just of the Single European Market but also moves toward regionalisation elsewhere. The company described how 'We restructured the management of our pharmaceuticals and consumer product businesses along global lines, taking advantage of new trading blocs' (Warner-Lambert, 1991: 1). In its 1993 annual report the company described how it was undertaking 'the worldwide rationalisation of manufacturing and distribution facilities to take advantage of the elimination of trade barriers primarily in Europe, North America and the Andean region...[with] a worldwide staff reduction programme of approximately 2700 positions... As a result of this programme, the company has already closed twelve manufacturing facilities, mainly in Europe and South America...' (Warner-Lambert, 1993: 28). Indeed, as one company spokesman suggested, 'the pharmaceutical industry in Europe has been suffering from overcapacity and there was a very real chance that Pontypool would see a complete closure of its manufacturing plant' (Stoker, quoted in Jones, 1993a). The rationalisation of the Pontypool facility fits within this general context of corporate reorganisation but was also the product of specific UK Government policy relating to the funding of the National Health Service (NHS) which affected the viability of the UK market. In order to keep a check on the rising cost of the NHS, the UK Government expanded the number of pharmaceuticals products not available on prescription to include some of those manufactured by Parke-Davis. This was one of a number of such closures and cancellations of new plants at the time. (Abrahams, 1993)

More generally, the results contained in Table 7.15 could be interpreted at face value to suggest that the impact of the SEM has been and will continue to be minimal. However, the results contained in Table 7.15 and in the Commission's industry analysis are static – capturing the 'once and for all' immediate effects of the creation of the SEM. The dynamic effects are rather harder to judge and to capture in empirical analysis. A second interpretation might therefore be that, given that it can take time before competition reaches sufficient pitch to prompt action and given that Table 7.15 provides a snapshot just one and a half years past the 1992 deadline, the modest impact of the SEM at this stage is all that might reasonably be expected.

Table 7.15 Impact of the SEM on competitiveness according to ownership

	UK	US	EU	Japan	Other	Total
Able to compete	2 (5.3)	1 (2.8)	7 (21.2)	4 (21.0)	2 (15.4)	16 (11.5)
More competition	5 (13.2)	3 (8.3)	3 (9.0)	2 (10.5)	1 (7.7)	14 (10.0)
Both of the above	3 (7.9)	6 (16.7)	7 (21.2)	3 (15.8)	1 (7.7)	20 (14.4)
Little or no effect	28 (73.7)	26 (72.2)	16 (48.5)	10 (52.6)	9 (69.2)	89 (64.0)

Source: Author's survey

Table 7.15 also reveals some differing experiences of competitive pressures between groups of establishments under different ownership. The numbers of observations are, however, small and the tentative conclusions drawn here should be treated with extreme caution. For example, it appears that a greater number and proportion of UK-owned manufacturing operations have experienced more competition than have been able to compete more effectively than is the case for overseas-owned establishments. EU and Japanese-owned establishments feel on balance better able to compete as a result of the removal of barriers – though here other factors may play a part, including vintage effects and, in the case of Japanese-owned establishments, simply the fact of 'being there'. The rather neutral impact of the SEM on US firms appears to confirm the finding that, as yet, the removal of remaining barriers to trade has had little effect on US manufacturers operating in the EU (Boddewyn and Grosse, 1995).

Table 7.16 Impact of the SEM on competitiveness according to vintage

	Pre-1950	1950–59	1960–69	1970–79	1980–89	1990–
Able to compete	0 (0.0)	1 (6.7)	3 (12.5)	3 (9.7)	4 (11.8)	3 (27.3)
More competition	2 (11.8)	2 (13.3)	2 (16.1)	5 (16.1)	2 (5.9)	1 (9.0)
Both of the above	5 (29.4)	2 (13.3)	3 (12.5)	5 (16.1)	3 (8.8)	1 (9.0)
Little or no effect	10 (58.8)	10 (67.7)	16 (66.7)	18 (58.0)	25 (73.5)	6 (54.5)

Source: Author's survey

Table 7.16 provides data on the impact of the SEM on different vintages of multinational manufacturing operations in Wales. There is just a hint that the fortunes of older operations of pre-1979 (and especially pre-1959) vintage are different from those of more recent vintage (post-1980). A greater proportion of the former appear to be facing more competition as a result of the SEM whilst a greater proportion of the latter appear better able to compete as a result of the SEM.

Table 7.17 Impact of the SEM measures on multinationals in Wales

Technical Standards	Physical barriers	Others	Combination
5 (9.8)	15 (29.4)	14 (27.5)	17 (33.3)

Source: Author's survey

Finally, Table 7.17 gives some indication of the main sources of change in competitive position related to the creation of the SEM. Harmonisation of technical standards has had an impact on competitiveness for only a handful of establishments. Removal of physical barriers to trade such as customs checks and administration were more important but for the majority of establishments it was the removal of a combination of barriers which had an impact on competitiveness.

Conclusion

In general the research findings presented in this chapter are readily interpretable in terms of the known history and characteristics of inward investment into Wales together with an understanding of changes in competitive advantage and the origin of foreign direct investment at an international scale.

There is some encouragement to be drawn from the fact that multinational manufacturing operations in Wales are not simply concerned with serving mass or stagnant or declining markets. However, it does appear that US and especially UK-owned manufacturing operations are the most vulnerable given that they tend, in the main, to be serving stagnant and declining mass and niche markets. In other respects, UK-owned manufacturing operations do not appear to measure up entirely to the branch plant stereotype. The data suggested, for instance, that the UK-owned establishments were quite 'internationalised' in terms of the spread of markets they served. A fair proportion of UK-owned establishments also seemed to be integrated in terms of manufacturing functions they performed. The case studies suggested that rationalisation, investment and transfers of production involving Welsh operations of multinationals took place against a variety of market contexts; though no rationalisation of, or transfers of production from, Welsh operations took place in the context of growing or fast growing markets.

There would appear to be no such thing as the Single European Market – at least not in terms of the way in which multinationals serve international markets through manufacturing investments. The majority of multinational investment, if the Welsh case is anything to judge by, is tied up with serving a combination of local markets and other parts of the European – not necessarily the EU market. At the other end of the spectrum a fair proportion of manufacturing investment in the EU may be serving a much larger market than simply the EU. For this investment the implications of regionalisation elsewhere in the world economy are not at all clear.

As yet the SEM appears to have had little impact one way or the other on the competitive position of the multinational sector of Welsh manufacturing industry. In other words the static effects of the removal of remaining barriers to trade may be relatively minor. However, the dynamic effects of ongoing increasing levels of competition may not yet have reached a pitch sufficient to start prompting rationalisation or reinvestment strategies by multinationals. Certainly the case studies illustrate that there has been a modest but steady stream of rationalisation and investment and transfer decisions which have involved reorganisation and rationalisation of production on a European-wide basis. Some of the cases also illustrate that it may take some time before loss of market share and competition from overseas firms prompts strategic reaction. It is also clear from the case studies that there may still be considerable scope for rationalisation within the territory of individual member states let alone across the whole EU territory.

CHAPTER 8

The Scale and Competitive Position of Multinationals in Wales

Introduction

An understanding of the impact of processes of European integration and corporate restructuring upon multinational manufacturing operations in Wales needs to take account not only of the sorts of markets being served by establishments but also the performance of establishments in producing for these markets. For example, it may be that whilst Welsh operations of multinationals are quite well placed in terms of serving growing mass and niche markets they may be relatively uncompetitive compared either to other parent company plants or the plants of competitor firms. Given the importance of multinationals to the Welsh economy and given the focus of this study, a key issue to be explored in this chapter is that of the extent to which Welsh manufacturing operations are effectively in competition with other parent company plants. For multinationals, in the short to medium term at least, competitive pressures in particular markets often manifest themselves not in terms of the decision to remain or withdraw from the market but in terms of decisions about where to source products from. In turn, these product sourcing decisions have implications in terms of investment and rationalisation for company plants with similar production responsibilities.

The simplest and most extreme scenario regarding restructuring in multinationals can serve to illustrate the sorts of intra-corporate competition alluded to above. It is arguable, for instance, that processes of European integration will bring about the concentration of production in fewer, often larger, cost competitive plants under the aegis of multinationals. In this respect Welsh and UK-based plants of multinationals are possibly some of the smaller least capital intensive operations within their respective parent company organisations and may therefore be some of the most likely candidates for rationalisation. With this sort of scenario in mind, the Welsh TUC has used the Census of Production to examine the size distribution of manufacturing local units in Wales. They suggest that the metal manufacturing, vehicles and components and electrical and electronic engineering sectors are the most competitive in Wales. The Welsh Affairs Committee had earlier argued that

'Wales will be affected in the same way as other peripheral areas of Europe as American and European companies concentrate production in fewer plants to exploit economies of scale. Some sectors of the economy will be more affected than others; increased competition and the resultant shake-out will occur in those sectors which at present are nationally oriented and fragmented, for example telecommunications, food products and building products.' (Welsh Affairs Committee, quoted in Wales TUC, 1989: 7)

The Welsh TUC's (1989) study also suggests that the mechanical engineering sector in Wales – being dominated by smaller sized operations – is vulnerable to rationalisation.

However, as was argued earlier in chapter 4, the efficiency and profitability of plants is more than simply a question of size (in output or employment terms) but also a question of capacity utilisation and the combination of capital and labour. As Baden-Fuller and Stopford (1988) in a study of the European domestic appliance industry note, some of the largest plants are also some of the least efficient and vice versa. In examining the extent to which Welsh manufacturing establishments compete with other parent company sites as well as the main dimensions of comparative plant performance this chapter will, then, be concerned with qualifying the extreme scenario presented above.

The process of rationalisation within Europe is periodically and graphically illustrated in cases such as Hoover's relocation of production from France to Scotland. Given their paucity such cases tend to be conspicuous and controversial. In the main they tend to raise issues to do with 'social dumping' and the exploitation of variations in labour costs. Such switching might be viewed as the tip of the iceberg of rational intra-corporate competition through which multinationals secure productivity gains *in situ* without closures and transfers (Ramsay, 1995). EU-wide regional and national variations in productivity are much less than those in labour costs – reflecting the different nature of production and capital-labour combinations in different EU locations which multinationals recognise and can exploit. Thus, the rational tendency for multinationals to compare plant performance across the EU highlights the diversity of factors contributing to the diversity plant performance and hence the possible motives for rationalisation.

Multiplant Operations in the EU

Other studies have demonstrated that multiplant operations are quite common in general and in Europe in particular (Scherer, *et al.* 1975). Data from the survey of multinational-owned manufacturing operations in Wales provides further confirmation of the prevalence of multiplant operations in Europe.

To begin with, Table 8.1 provides information on the numbers and proportions of Welsh manufacturing plants which produce at least some of the same range of products as other parent company production sites. Just over half of the respondents indicated that their parent company had production sites which produced at least some of the same product range and therefore, to an extent, competed with their Welsh plants. As was to be expected the majority of UK-owned establishments were in potential competition with other company sites. At this stage we can suggest that the extent of this competition is likely to be quite limited geographically – the majority of these UK-owned plants in Wales competing with company plants elsewhere in the UK.

Table 8.1 Welsh plants with similar parent company plants in the EU according to ownership

	UK	US	EU	Japan	Other	Total
Similar production sites	23(60.5)	13(37.2)	27(79.4)	6(30.0)	6(42.9)	75(52.8)

χ^2=19.32, p<0.001
Source: Author's survey

Similarly, it was to be expected that a large proportion of EU-owned plants in Wales are potentially in competition with other company production sites – though here the extent of inter-plant competition is likely to be less limited geographically. It may also be that the recent vintage of these EU-investments in Wales, means that they compare favourably with plants elsewhere, though as we saw earlier the main mode of entry of EU-investment was through acquisition which may have little impact on the vintage of capital. Given their recent arrival in the EU and given the limited production networks which have developed in Japanese companies in Europe it is to be expected that only a minority of Japanese-owned plants in Wales have at least partially comparable company sites elsewhere in the EU. On first glance the fact that only 37% of US-owned plants in Wales produce at least part of the same product range as other company plants in the EU is a little surprising given the long history and geographical spread of US multinational operations in the EU. However, one explanation of this quite low figure is that during their often lengthy presence in European countries US firms have gradually created quite streamlined European corporate divisions of labour; moving away from localised (market oriented) investment strategies toward centralised (production oriented) strategies involving vertical divisions of labour based upon a high degree of specialisation on a plant-by-plant basis.

Table 8.2 shows that there is no straightforward connection between the date of establishment of operations and whether their parent companies have similar production sites elsewhere in the EU. For example, the majority of parent companies with Welsh operations established between 1960 and 1979 *do not* have similar production sites elsewhere in Europe. This contrasts with the majority of parent companies with Welsh operations established before 1960 and after 1979 which *do* have similar production sites elsewhere in Europe. There are a number of possible interpretations of these data. The greater proportions of recently established operations (since 1980) with similar production sites elsewhere in Europe might be interpreted as one manifestation of the arrival of global-localised corporate structures. If so the existence of competitor operations may reflect the attempt to serve local markets within Europe through a number of production sites. More straightforwardly, however, it may reflect more mundane issues of the mode of entry of recent multinational investments in Wales. Since the major mode of entry in the foreign-owned manufacturing sector is acquisition, the existence of competitor sites to recently established operations may reflect the integration of these operations into, as yet, unrationalised corporate networks of pan-European production locations.

Table 8.2 Welsh plants with similar parent company plants in the EU according to vintage

	Pre-1950	1950–59	1960–69	1970–79	1980–89	1990–
Similar production sites	13(76.5)	10(66.7)	10 (41.7)	17(53.1)	12(35.3)	7(53.8)

$\chi^2 = 10.18$
Source: Author's survey

Table 8.3 Extent of multiplant operations in the EU according to ownership

	UK	US	EU	Japan	Other	Total
1 site	8(36.4)	5(38.5)	9(33.3)	2(40.0)	1(16.7)	25(34.2)
2 sites	6(27.3)	3(20.0)	11(40.7)	1(20.0)	2(33.3)	23(31.5)
3 or more sites	8(36.4)	5(38.5)	7(25.9)	2(40.0)	3(50.0)	25(34.2)

Source: Author's survey

Table 8.4 Extent of multiplant operations in the EU according to vintage

	Pre-1950	1950–59	1960–69	1970–79	1980–89	1990–
1 site	4 (33.3)	2 (20.0)	2 (20.0)	4 (25.0)	5 (41.7)	5 (71.4)
2 sites	5 (41.7)	4 (40.0)	2 (20.0)	6 (37.5)	3 (25.0)	1 (14.3)
3 or more sites	3 (25.0)	4 (40.0)	6 (60.0)	6 (37.5)	4 (33.3)	1 (14.3)

Source: Author's survey

Table 8.3 suggests that such inter-plant competition, where it occurs, may be geographically extensive with production operations in Wales thrown into potential intra-corporate competition with plants in a wide range of EU regions with varying conditions for production and institutional support for industry. Given their long history of investment in Europe, US firms have developed much more geographically extensive divisions of labour and hence Welsh-based US-owned plants are in potential competition with plants in a wide range of EU locations. As suggested earlier, UK-owned plants in Wales compete with other company plants primarily elsewhere in the UK.

In the past, such localised inter-plant competition may have heightened the fragility of inward investments into peripheral regions. It may also be fair to say, however, that as UK companies have internationalised their operations such duplication of production capacity within the UK may become ripe for rationalisation not only for this reason in itself but also because the range of alternative production locations and perhaps the spread of different plant performance may have been increased (leading to heightened inter-plant competition).

Table 8.4 suggests that the extent of intra-corporate competition, where it occurs, may be quite considerable. Roughly two-thirds of establishments which have similar production sites elsewhere in the UK or EU have more than one such counterpart, whilst a third may be in potential competition with three or more parent company plants in Europe alone. Thus, Table 8.4 highlights the potential extent of inter-plant competition which Welsh based manufacturing establishments may find themselves. There appear to be few variations in the extent of potential competition according to plant ownership except to say that such competition appears to be greatest for UK and EU-owned plants which is to be expected given the results in Table 8.1.

Table 8.5 Geographical extent of multiplant operations in the EU according to ownership

	UK	US	EU	Japan	Other	Total
UK only	12 (57.1)	1 (7.7)	4 (15.4)	3 (60.0)	1 (16.7)	21 (29.6)
UK & one other EU	3 (14.3)	5 (38.5)	14 (53.8)	1 (20.0)	1 (16.7)	24 (33.8)
UK & two or more EU	6 (28.6)	7 (53.8)	8 (30.8)	1 (20.0)	4 (66.7)	26 (36.6)

Source: Author's survey

There appears to be a more straightforward relationship between the age of an operation and the numbers and geographical spread of similar production sites elsewhere in the parent company organisation (Tables 8.5 and 8.6). Thus, older factories may be doubly vulnerable in that the extent of potential inter-plant competition is greater than for newer factories and given that they are thrown into such competition with other parent company production sites in a wider range of locations with varying conditions for production.

**Table 8.6 Geographical extent of multiplant operations
in the EU according to vintage**

	Pre-1950	1950–59	1960–69	1970–79	1980–89	1990–
UK only	4 (33.3)	1 (11.1)	2 (22.2)	3 (18.8)	6 (50.0)	3 (42.9)
UK & one other EU	6 (50.0)	3 (33.3)	1 (11.1)	6 (37.5)	3 (25.0)	4 (57.1)
UK & two or more EU	2 (16.7)	5 (55.6)	6 (66.7)	7 (43.8)	3 (25.0)	0 (0.0)

Source: Author's survey

If Welsh plants are of a younger vintage than other company plants producing the same products then they may, other things being equal, be less likely candidates for rationalisation. As mentioned earlier in chapter 5, using date of establishment of a production facility as an indicator of vintage is fraught with problems – not least the fact that reinvestment, which tends to undermine this assumption, has been on the increase. In as much as date of establishment gives an idea of the vintage of Welsh production operations in comparison to their counterparts elsewhere in the EU, Table 8.7 provides some basic indications of the comparative vintage of Welsh manufacturing operations. The figures, rather surprisingly indicate that UK-owned operations in Wales are some of the newest within their corporate spheres and should therefore be less at risk than the sites with which they may be in competition. Given that UK firms have been internationalising during the recent decades, the Welsh based operations appear to be quite secure given their relative 'newness'. It could be that this is not the case in other UK regions. Equally surprisingly, given the recent origin of EU investments in Wales, EU-owned establishments are among the oldest of similar parent company plants elsewhere in the EU. This is likely to be a reflection of the fact that the dominant mode of entry of EU firms into Welsh manufacturing industry has been through acquisition of quite long-standing production operations. Nevertheless, the older

Table 8.7 Comparative age of Welsh plants according to ownership

	UK	US	EU	Japan	Other	Total
Youngest	6 (54.5)	3 (37.5)	5 (27.8)	0 (0.0)	1 (20.0)	15 (33.3)
Oldest	2 (18.2)	1 (12.5)	8 (28.6)	1 (33.3)	2 (40.0)	14 (31.1)
Same	3 (27.3)	4 (50.0)	5 (27.8)	2 (66.7)	2 (40.0)	16 (35.6)

Source: Author's survey

vintage of EU-investments in Wales could be a cause for concern given the tendency for rationalisation following acquisition.

As we have seen, a fair proportion of multinational-owned manufacturing operations in Wales are in potential competition with other company plants elsewhere in the EU. We can also consider the likely future extent of inter-plant competition by examining whether parent companies have plans to open new plants in the next five years. In fact, very few parent companies with plants in Wales were planning to open new plants producing similar products to those at their Welsh operations. Increased inter-plant competition from new plant opening may therefore be minimal. However, the data here gives no idea about the impact of merger and acquisition strategies on the competitive position of Welsh manufacturing operations. In other words the competitive position of Welsh operations is unlikely to be seriously undermined through future new plant openings but may currently and in the future be affected to a greater degree by decisions regarding repeat investments (positive) and rationalisation (negative) following acquisition.

Table 8.8 Parent companies with EU-wide strategies for production according to ownership

	UK	US	EU	Japan	Other	Total
Specialisation	9 (47.4)	5 (50.0)	3 (15.0)	3 (60.0)	2 (50.0)	22 (37.9)
Integration	4 (21.0)	4 (40.0)	9 (45.0)	0 (0.0)	0 (0.0)	17 (29.3)
Both of the above	6 (31.6)	1 (10.0)	8 (40.0)	2 (40.0)	2 (50.0)	19 (32.8)

Source: Author's survey

Table 8.9 Parent companies with EU-wide strategies for production according to vintage

	Pre-1950	1950–59	1960–69	1970–79	1980–89	1990–
Specialisation	2 (20.0)	2 (28.6)	6 (75.0)	6 (42.9)	3 (30.0)	2 (33.3)
Integration	3 (30.0)	4 (57.1)	1 (12.5)	1 (7.1)	4 (40.0)	3 (50.0)
Both of the above	5 (50.0)	1 (14.3)	1 (12.5)	7 (50.0)	3 (30.0)	1 (16.7)

Source: Author's survey

The sorts of strategies being adopted by parent companies operating in the EU can put the competitiveness of individual plants in a different light. The general strategies being pursued by firms can give an indication of the general state of intra-corporate competition. Respondents were asked whether their parent companies had strategies for European production whereby individual plants became more specialised or whereby there was greater integration between individual sites, or both. Specialisation can, depending on which markets a plant serves, provide greater autonomy and security. Strategies involving specialisation *and* integration to form the classic part-process organisational structure Massey has spoken of may also promote security but at the expense of autonomy and functional capacity. Table 8.8 shows that around a third of establishments suggested that their parent company strategies for Europe included elements of both specialisation and integration. Nearly a quarter (24%) of establishments with comparable production sites in Europe indicated that their parent company had no strategies for European production involving elements of integration or specialisation. The data also suggest that there is considerable scope for specialisation and integration among UK and EU-owned operations in particular. From Table 8.9, it appears as though the operations of the 1960s and 1970s may be becoming more specialised. The implications of this are not altogether clear since in Chapter 6 (Table 6.6) it was noted that operations of these vintages serving niche markets were evenly split between those serving growing and declining niches. It appears as though 1970s investments will benefit from a greater degree of specialisation and integration into wider corporate networks of production.

Two of the case study companies provide examples of how rationalisation decisions may not strictly reflect individual plant performance but the economies accruing to a group of plants. In the case of Wella, a clear corporate strategy appears to have undermined the position of individual factories.

Wella, Pontyclun

As we saw earlier, the closure of Wella's Ondawel factory in Wales was part of an explicit and radical restructuring of he company's European operations. A number of factors lie behind the closure of the Welsh factory, though explicit inter-plant competition *per se* does not appear to have been important.

First, the main reason for concentrating production on mainland Europe was to take advantage of the lower cost of material inputs in Germany, France and Italy. Raw materials in the form of chemicals and packaging and containers in the form of plastics were both cheaper from mainland European sources than UK sources. The concentration of production in fewer factories on mainland Europe no doubt enhanced such pecuniary scale economies. Second, although the Welsh factory was broadly similar in size and productivity to he factories operated in Europe (including both those which had been closed and the French factory at which production was being concentrated), nevertheless the accumulation of rationalisation decisions eventually left the Welsh factory as one of the smallest remaining factories. There is also some suggestion that the Welsh factory suffered from a high overhead cost structure in comparison to the existing factories. Thus, a concern with the comparative productivity of the factory does appear to have figured in Wella's decision to shut the factory in Wales. Finally, the company was interested in building up production at its French factory which, although smaller than the Welsh factory at the time, was also near the German border and nearer head office. The suggestion here is that there were some managerial/coordination economies to be made with a transfer of production from Wales to France.

The case of Nu-kote's closure of its Welsh factory illustrates not just issues of comparative size but also the issue of capacity utilisation and economies in distribution.

Nu-kote International, Deeside

As we saw earlier, Nu-kote International's closure of its Welsh factory and transfer of production to Scotland took place against the background of a declining market soon to disappear altogether. Thus in general and according to a company spokesman 'It is just the economy of scale dictated by the world market, that as a group we cannot produce the same product in different locations cost effectively' (Roberts, 1995).

In detail a number of factors figured in the decision to close the company's welsh factory. First, the Deeside factory was the smallest of the company's European operations; employing 180 compared to roughly 450 at the Scottish operation. According to company sources, the Welsh factory despite being smaller was as, if not more, efficient than the Scottish operation, had a wider product range and exactly the same production technology. Crucially, the Scottish operation had spare capacity in which the transferred production lines could be accommodated. Second the Nu-kote case also illustrates the economies of European-wide distribution and their, connection with production reorganisation. Nu-kote's Welsh factory shipped its products direct to customers whereas the three other European operations, including the one in Scotland acquired from Pelikan AG, shipped their products to a central European distribution centre in Germany. In closing its Welsh factory, then, the company stood to gain further economies in the distribution of its products.

Comparative Scale and Performance

Having established that a fair proportion of multinational-owned manufacturing operations in Wales have their counterparts producing similar products elsewhere in the UK or the EU we can try to ascertain the comparative performance and capabilities of Welsh plants.

The postal survey sought to gain information on the performance of Welsh operations in comparison to other similar parent company sites in the EU. Respondents were asked to rank the performance of their operations compared to other parent company sites producing at least some of the same output on a scale of 1 to 5, where the score 1 pertained to a much lower/worse comparison and 5 pertained to instances where the Welsh plant compared much more favourably. Only those establishments which had indicated that their parent company had other plants elsewhere in the UK or EU which produced at least part of the same product range were included in this part of the analysis. In other words the inter-plant comparisons relate to Welsh plants for which their respective parent companies have at least one similar plant (defined in terms of overlap of products) in the EU. The detailed approach in this set of questions is similar to that used by Hood and Young (1983) though their study had the considerable advantage of being conducted on a face-to-face basis.

There are of course a number of methodological problems in such plant comparisons. First, and as already alluded to, postal surveys are an inferior means of capturing the required data than face-to-face interviews in which ambiguities regarding what is being compared with what can be ironed-out. Second, and as Hood and Young (1983: 122–123) note, abilities to make such comparisons are dependent upon reporting structures and the availability of information within parent company organisations. Third, and closely related to this is whether the respondents at the Welsh establishments have the appropriate knowledge. All that could be done here was to send questionnaires to individuals with a good overview of the Welsh establishment as well as some knowledge of other company operations in Europe; these being mainly plant managers or managing directors. Fourth, such comparisons are between plants which at worst may have very little in common apart from the fact that they produce some of the same product range. These reservations with the data obtained by way of the questionnaire survey mean that the results presented and discussed below must be treated with a good deal of caution. Statistical tests are presented along with the data on comparative plant performance though these are not intended as proof of, for instance, differences according to ownership or vintage but are used to help detect possible general tendencies in the make-up of multinational involvement in Welsh manufacturing industry.

Two main statistical tests were used to examine the data on comparative plant performance; analysis of variance and chi-squared. First, then, the rank scores can be used to produce mean rank scores according to various categories of, for instance, ownership and vintage. These mean scores and distribution of rank scores for each ownership or vintage category can be compared using an analysis of variance test. This procedure rests on the assumption that the actual scale of rank scores can be treated, for the purpose of this analysis, as an interval scale. An analysis of variance test compares the degree of variation (the sum of the squared differences from the mean) *within* groups of observations, with the degree of variation (the sum of squared differences from an overall or 'grand' mean) *between* groups of observations (Blalock, 1979). The larger the variation within groups of observations the greater the likelihood that the groups of observations represent distinct populations with separate means; in this case the greater the likelihood that different 'ownership' categories or 'vintages' of operation have distinctly different performance compared to company operations elsewhere in the EU. Naturally the test can be highly sensitive to, in this case, how the categories of ownership and vintage were defined. Five categories of ownership and six of vintage are initially defined and tests run for this categorisation. Tests were also run on a reduced number of categories. In this case, only the three main ownership categories of UK, US and EU-owned operations were compared whilst for the purpose of examining the connection between plant performance and vintage, the initial five categories were collapsed into two to allow comparisons between 'old' and 'new' operations.

Second, chi-squared tests can be computed. Again, the test is sensitive to the number of categories in each scale and more particularly the expected cell count. So here again tests were also run on a reduced number of ownership and vintage categories as for the analysis of variance tests described above.

Table 8.10 shows the mean rank score for the performance of Welsh operations in comparison to other company sites according to ownership. The vast majority of respondents rated their Welsh plant's performance as being similar to that of company sites elsewhere in the EU. This has a further implication in that there were barely any statistically significant differences on comparative plant perform- ance according to ownership or vintage – as revealed by either analysis of variance or chi-squared tests. There is also a further contributory element to this central tendency. Welsh operations are here being compared to other similar parent

Table 8.10 Comparative performance and functions of Welsh operations according to ownership

	UK	US	EU	Japan	Other	Total	F	χ^2
Output	3.09	2.69	2.76	2.80	2.50	2.90	0.76	8.37
Process technology	3.05	2.77	3.04	3.20	3.00	3.00	0.54	8.61
Product range	3.36	3.08	3.44	2.60	3.67	3.31	1.65	15.99
Productivity	3.24	3.15	3.12	3.00	2.67	3.11	0.58	18.33
Decision-making	3.05	3.00	3.16	3.20	3.00	3.09	0.30	4.42
Research & development	3.00	2.69	2.60	3.40	3.33	2.86	1.08	11.30
Product adaptation	3.10	2.92	3.12	3.20	3.67	3.13	1.17	10.25
Engineering	2.90	2.90	2.92	3.40	3.33	3.00	1.01	7.72

NB F and χ^2 statistics given for tests run on five ownership categories
* significant at the 95% confidence limit, ** significant at the 99% confidence limit
Source: Author's survey

company sites. In other words, Welsh operations are being compared to a range of other parent company sites in the EU and not, for instance, the best or worst of these sites. As such, probably the most accurate interpretation of the data is that Welsh operations are being compared to some sort of 'average' of other similar parent company sites in the EU. Thus an initial point to note is that there is considerable similarity in the comparative performance of multinational-owned manufacturing operations in Wales and their counterparts elsewhere in the UK or the EU. To an extent this is to be expected as other studies provide evidence of such similarities between comparable plants. Hood and Young's study for example found 'considerable similarities in the technological intensity of plants within multiplant groups in Europe' (Hood and Young, 1983: 123).

Overall, the results are quite encouraging. Welsh manufacturing establishments compare favourably with similar parent company plants in the EU with respect to their process technology, product range, levels of productivity, degree of decision-making autonomy and capabilities with respect to product adaption. Welsh operations compare less favourably with respect to output levels (i.e. size), research and development activity and engineering capabilities. These results can be interpreted in a couple of ways. First, Welsh operations appear to be generally smaller but more productive than similar parent company sites. On the surface of things this could be taken to suggest that Welsh plants are reasonably well-placed in any emerging era of flexible forms of production. However, it is doubtful even given the healthy comparative performance with regard to most of the other performance criteria listed in Table 8.10 that Welsh plants have the 'quality' needed to justify their being considered exemplars of flexible production techniques. Alternatively the slightly smaller size of Welsh establishments compared to similar parent company production sites could mean that Welsh plants are vulnerable to any corporate rationalisation strategies which focus on consolidating production and exploiting economies of scale.

On the one hand, one case study illustrates the importance of labour costs and flexibility – as opposed to simply volume of production – as factors in the productivity differences between production locations and as part determinants of rationalisation decisions.

Grundig, Llantrisant

We saw earlier that Grundig had transferred production of satellite receiver related operations from Miesau, Germany to Wales. This transfer of production appears to be a logical move given the development of the UK market, the small scale nature of production in Germany and the general company strategy of shifting production to lower cost locations both within and outside the EU.

The growth and sophistication of the UK market was perhaps the major reason behind the consolidation of Grundig's production into a single plant in Wales. Certainly the move made sense given that the German factory, whose output was mainly given over to production of electrical components for TVs, was much smaller (120,000 units) and less productive (after allowing for wage differences) than that in Wales (300,000 units) at the time of its closure.

The closure of the German factory and the take-up of the German market by the South Wales plant is also in keeping with a corporate strategy of cost reduction. In the late 1980s and early 1990s Grundig had been rationalising in the face of intense competition from Far East consumer electronics manufacturers. On the one hand, it had begun to rationalise a number of consumer electronics factories in Europe, including job cuts at two television factories in Germany and the closure of one in Spain as well as merging its video cassette recorder operations with those of Philips. On the other hand it was also attempting shift consumer electronics production out of Germany to lower cost locations such as Portugal and Malaysia (Parkes, 1992). The clear suggestion in press reports is that higher labour costs and long-term currency movements favoured Wales as a location at which to combine the output of the two factories (Adburgham, 1995b). In this respect, a company source suggested that cost differences between Germany and the UK the two countries were compounded by differences in the flexibility with which labour can be used in the two countries.

On the other hand, a number of the case studies do tend to confirm that rationalisation and reorganisation decisions do, to an extent, revolve around considerations of plant size and economies of scale – though in each case there are also other subsidiary factors in the equation. Perhaps the best example of the importance of economies of scale to the competitiveness of a plant is provided by BP Chemicals' Baglan Bay ethylene plant.

BP Chemicals, Baglan Bay

We saw earlier how BP Chemicals' closure of its Baglan Bay cracker took place against a backcloth of industry overcapacity as well as a misplaced corporate strategy in relation to long-term feedstock prices. In detail, the closure appears to have been based on some sort of inter-plant comparison of profitability and long-term prospects which, in the case of Baglan Bay, had been undermined by a number of investment and divestment decisions since its opening.

Four years prior to the closure of Baglan Bay, BP Chemicals was describing how 'We are continuing to focus our investments on those business sectors where we enjoy a combination of strengths – a leading technology, access to cost competitive feedstock and an established market position' (BP, 1990: 21). There appears to have been some explicit intra- and inter-corporate comparison of plants since in 1991 'Major restructuring and reorganisations have started, based upon the results of benchmarking all sites against the best performers in their class' (BP, 1991: 6). With the expansion of production of ethylene at Grangemouth announced in 1988 Baglan Bay would become the smallest ethylene plant within BP Chemicals' European operations. At 330,000 tonnes, Baglan Bay's output was just less than that of the company's more cost effective plant at Lavera in France (335,000 tonnes) and considerably smaller than the company's joint venture at Darmagen in Germany (740,000 tonnes) and the new plant at Grangemouth (600,000 tonnes). Not only was the Baglan Bay plant alone among the company's plants in using naphtha oil as a feedstock, it was also isolated from BPs oil and gas pipelines (which ran from Kinneil to Grangemouth) and from BP Chemicals' remaining downstream plants (during the 1980s BP Chemicals had divested or closed many of the 11 other plants in the original Baglan Bay complex). The company put an altruistic gloss on what was a rational commercial decision to close its Baglan Bay plant when describing how 'Since the early 1990s, BP Chemicals has been reshaping and upgrading its asset base. In April 1994, it closed the loss-making ethylene cracker at Baglan Bay in Wales – a move to help reduce Europe's structural overcapacity in ethylene.' (BP 1994: 24).

Exide's choice of its newly acquired Cwmbran factory for expansion into one of a few European 'superplants' appears at least partly based on existing plant size and market position.

Exide, Cwmbran

As we saw earlier, Exide's aggressive expansion into Europe through acquisition had left it with an imperative to rationalise the excessively large number of battery making factories in Europe. Early speculation suggested that up to two-thirds of the 41 factories then operated by the firm would need to be shut (Griffiths, 1995b). The aim of the company was clear – to integrate the operations of its acquired companies, keeping the best and closing the worst (Griffiths, 1995b). To this end, the Cwmbran factory was chosen as the site for a £6m investment to turn it into a 'superplant' modelled on those operated by Exide in the US (Jones, 1995). A number of factors appear to have contributed to the selection of Cwmbran for expansion. Sources at Cwmbran suggested that the strong position in the UK market gained with the two acquired companies provided a sound base for expansion. There is also a suggestion that labour costs may have been a factor since it was also noted that the Welsh location fitted well with Exide's aims of translating its cost-competitive mass production in the US to the EU. Finally, and related to this aim of cost-competitive mass production, it must be noted that the Cwmbran factory was one of the largest of all those newly acquired by Exide.

Transfers of production to BICC's Wrexham plants do seem to be quite clearly related to economies of scale and specialisation.

BICC, Wrexham

BICC's transfer of production from its acquired Aldermaston factory to factories in Wrexham and Leigh, was as we saw earlier, an attempt to rationalise production among its domestic operations in the face of intensified competition from EU producers.

The closure of Aldermaston and the transfers of production were part of an explicit strategy as part of the acquisition of Sterling Greengate. This initial rationalisation appears to have been based on a number of factors including comparative profitability, product range, physical constraints and labour costs and turnover at the company's factories. The two plants acquired from Sterling Greengate (at Aldermaston and Warrington) were the smallest (in output terms) in the expanded BICC cable group. The company's two Welsh factories appear effectively to have been above consideration of rationalisation given that they were the two largest and most profitable factories in the group. Of the newly acquired factories, Warrington's output was devoted entirely to the production of mains cables and was consequently quite profitable. The Aldermaston factory, however, manufactured an extremely wide range of cables for a wide customer base and was loss-making – though there is the suggestion that higher wages and labour turnover (compared to their other factory locations) may have contributed to losses. BICC's own factory at Leigh had recently become loss-making and hence the company saw the transfers of production as a way of enhancing scale economies and profitability in Wrexham and restoring profitability at its Leigh factory (Monopolies and Mergers Commission, 1990).

Table 8.10 provides a breakdown of the comparative performance and capabilities of Welsh manufacturing establishments according to ownership. Tests did not reveal any statistically significant differences in comparative plant performance according to ownership. Indeed, with respect to comparative engineering capabilities both analysis of variance and chi-squared tests suggests that the similarities between the three main ownership categories (UK, US and EU) are so close as to be suspicious. Bearing this in mind some tentative observations can be made regarding variations in comparative plant performance among manufacturing establishments of different ownership. UK-owned Welsh manufacturing establishments compare slightly favourably with other similar parent company plants across virtually the entire range of performance indicators. The results here could be taken to be a reflection of the fact that UK multinationals are still naturally oriented towards the UK as a production location. Hence, the favourable performance of UK-owned establishments may ostensibly be in relation to other parent company plants located in the UK. An examination of the data does provide some support for this idea. Chi-squared tests were used to examine whether there was a difference in comparative performance between UK-owned plants which were comparing themselves against UK-based sites and those comparing themselves against sites located in the UK and elsewhere in the EU. No statistically significant differences were revealed though the plant performance of UK-owned Welsh manufacturing establishments appeared more variable and less unambiguously positive in comparison to other company sites in the UK and elsewhere in the EU. In other words, the greater the geographical spread of similar parent company sites within Europe the more variable the comparative performance of UK-owned establishments in Wales. This in turn therefore suggests that whilst UK-owned Welsh manufacturing operations may be relatively secure in relation to strategies of rationalisation focused on domestic operations they may be less secure in relation to strategies involving rationalisation on an EU-wide basis.

Of all the ownership categories, US-owned Welsh plants compare the least favourably with their parent company competitor plants. US-owned Welsh operations appear to be somewhat smaller on average than their counterparts and to lack innovative capacity in terms of research and development and adaptation of products and processes; though they are on average as productive as similar parent company plants elsewhere in the UK or EU and also have similar levels of decision-making capacity. The most likely interpretation of these results is that they reflect the sort of comparative strategies adopted by US companies operating in Europe. US firms have made the greatest strides in terms of creating a division of labour within Europe and within this division of labour UK plants may simply be performing a specialised role. In other words, although on the surface the UK-based operations of US firms compare unfavourably with similar parent company plants in the EU, they nevertheless are comparable in efficiency terms. It may therefore be that UK operations are performing some of the less techno-logically sophisticated more labour intensive forms of production within European-wide corporate divisions of labour and despite their deficiencies are relatively secure because of this. Against this, however, it can be recalled that considerable rationalisation and closure has been occurring in the US-owned sector of overseas industry in Wales (Chapter 5). Such volatility, if apparent in the EU more generally may have negative implications for the US-owned operations in Wales given their smaller size and lack of innovative capacity.

The performance of EU-owned plants also compares unfavourably with similar parent company plants elsewhere in the EU. Here again Welsh operations are relatively lacking in innovative capabilities. We saw earlier that EU-owned establishments are among the oldest among similar parent company plants in the EU. As such the poor performance coupled with the age of EU-owned operations in Wales does provide some cause for concern. In the short-term such poor perform-ance might be tolerated as acquisition provides an immediate means of entry into the UK market for EU firms, but in the long-term and if the poor comparative performance persists then EU-owned operations may be vulnerable to rationalisa-tion given their age.

Japanese-owned Welsh operations appear to compare favourably with any similar plants which exist in the EU. The results here are a little difficult to interpret, since Japanese firms have yet to develop an extensive presence in Europe let alone extensive production networks. Much of Japanese direct manufacturing investment has been in the UK and as such there is very little to compare with UK plants. The fact that Welsh plants compare unfavourably in terms of size is a little surprising given the length of time such plants have been established. Perhaps more surprisingly is the finding that Japanese-owned operations in Wales compare favourably in terms of non-manufacturing functions such as research and development and decision-making autonomy given that there is little doubt that Japanese manufacturing investment in the UK as a whole is, as yet, of a rather rationalised form. The results here may well be a function of the sectoral composition of Japanese investment in Wales – concentrated as it is in the consumer electronics field. Limited design and development work has been devolved to some Welsh plants and this in itself may have been enough to produce the favourable comparison with similar, perhaps more labour-intensive, operations in other peripheral EU regions.

The rank scores obtained for individual criteria of plant performance can be combined into aggregate scores relating to performance over a number of related criteria. Three such composite scores were obtained relating to the comparative performance of plants in terms of:

1. production activities (output levels, productivity, product range and process technology)
2. non-production activities (decision-making autonomy, research and development, product adaptation and comparative engineering)
3. all the listed criteria of plant performance.

Given the high degree of central tendency in the results, the creation of such composite rank scores might be expected to reveal a little more variation in plant performance according to ownership and vintage. In fact, an analysis of variance test suggests that the central tendency in the results is so marked that the similarities between plants of different ownership in terms of non-production functions are great enough to be suspicious. None of the composite rank scores produce statistically significant differences according to the ownership of plants.

Newly established manufacturing operations of multinationals in Wales have an above average comparative performance with the exception of research and development activities (see Table 8.11). It should also be noted however that both old and new operations have below average capabilities compared to the similar parent company production sites in the EU – confirming the general lack of research and development activity among multinationals in Wales. The fact that new operations compare more favourably in terms of their performance and other functional capabilities than their older counterparts with other parent company production sites could be an indication of new investments being qualitatively different from old. Of particular interest is the fact that old operations compare

Table 8.11 Comparative performance and functions of Welsh operations according to vintage

	Pre-1950	1950 -59	1960 -69	1970 -79	1980 -89	1990-	F	χ^2
Output	3.00	2.60	2.80	3.00	2.92	3.29	0.57	16.82
Process technology	2.90	2.80	3.33	2.94	2.83	2.83	1.23	12.00
Product range	3.80	3.10	3.00	3.38	3.17	3.17	1.45	15.95
Productivity	3.00	3.20	3.10	3.20	3.17	3.17	0.08	18.38
Decision-making	2.82	3.20	3.11	3.19	3.00	3.00	1.06	9.55
Research & development	2.73	2.90	2.80	3.06	2.83	2.83	0.17	20.42
Product adaptation	3.09	3.00	3.10	3.38	3.00	3.00	0.72	11.74
Engineering	2.90	3.00	3.10	2.94	3.17	3.17	0.44	10.51

NB F and χ^2 statistics given for tests run on five ownership categories
* significant at the 95% confidence limit, ** significant at the 99% confidence limit
Source: Author's survey

less favourably with new operations with their respective similar parent company production sites in the EU with respect to output levels and process technology. This is interesting since whilst we might expect this result for process technology it is frequently argued and evident in the data that recent rounds of investment have become progressively smaller in output terms. The other difference of note – though none of the differences are statistically significant – between old and new is in terms of engineering capabilities with regard to which new operations appear to compare more favourably than old operations relative to the parent company sites. Again we can speculate that the greater degree of functional integration among new operations has led to a greater emphasis on certain functions such as purchasing and engineering and having these more fully integrated with aspects of day to day manufacturing. The poorer comparative capabilities of new operations are to be expected given that establishments usually gain functions such as research and development over time (e.g. see Haug, Hood and Young, 1983).

Conclusion

The survey material presented above provides further evidence of the extent of multiplant operations in Europe. A large proportion of Welsh manufacturing operations are part of multiplant operations within their respective parent companies. As a consequence of this, it is reasonable to expect that a proportion of these

Welsh plants are, in turn, effectively in competition with other parent company plants for the allocation of new product or market responsibilities, important administration or research and development functions, or indeed their very survival if rationalisation is the order of the day.

Naturally there are variations in the extent of multiplant operations and their geographical spread and hence the extent and intensity of any inter-plant rivalry which may exist. US firms have the most extensive multiplant operations in Europe but ironically because of this and their long standing attempts to integrate production on a European-wide basis there may be little inter-plant rivalry which impacts negatively on Welsh operations. Inter-plant rivalries may be greater among the multiplant operations of UK and EU firms which have yet to rationalise European-wide production to the same degree as US firms. The fact that a third of establishments surveyed had parent companies which were attempting strategies of specialisation and integration raises the prospect of intensified inter-plant competition in the short-term but greater security for multiplant operations in the long-term.

There were considerable similarities in the performance of Welsh manufacturing operations compared to their counterparts elsewhere in the UK or the EU. Plants tended to differ slightly more in terms of their production-related performance than in terms of their non-production capabilities. This in turn suggests that rationalisation decisions concerning multiplant operations may hinge on quite minor differences in plant performance or indeed may not be strictly related to plant performance at all. The case studies made it clear that long established and highly productive operations can be closed as part of more general corporate strategies. In one recent study of the emergence of pan-European corporate strategies the authors claim that increasing use is being made of quantitative techniques such as linear programming to determine appropriate plant closures – on the basis of minimum disruption to product sourcing (Collins and Schmenner, 1995). Here, then, plant performance may not strictly be the determining factor in plant closures but rather the impact of closing any particular factory – irrespective of performance – on a company's ability to source products from a network or group of factories. The decision to shut factories and or transfer production might be rational on a corporate level and yet appear less rational at the level of the factories concerned (Ramsay, 1995).

CHAPTER 9

The Local Embeddedness
of Multinationals in Wales

Introduction

A final consideration regarding the impact of processes of market integration and rationalisation within the EU and their impact specifically on Welsh manufacturing industry is that of local embeddedness. The term 'mobile investment' is suggestive of the idea that multinational manufacturing investments are footloose and not tied to particular localities or regions. However, the vast bulk of multinational investment is, to an extent, tied to particular localities or regions. Many multilo-cational and multinational firms invest large amounts of time, money and human resources in establishing and maintaining production at particular locations. There will be some non-recoverable sunk costs associated with production in a particular place even for the most rationalised forms of branch plant production. To the extent that firms become attached to, or embedded in, particular production locations in this way, there will be costs involved in rationalisation, no matter how unsuccessful the particular operation is. There is ample evidence to suggest that corporate rationalisation strategies are (at least partly) cognisant of such costs of withdrawing from particular production locations (Clark, 1994).

Thus, the present research attempted to address some aspects of local em-beddedness in order to understand the extent to which and in what way they play a role in mediating process of rationalisation associated with market integration. As noted earlier in Chapter 4, there are two main directions from which one can approach the issue of embeddedness. First, there are the private or corporate dynamics; through which companies' organisational structures permit a degree of integration with the local economy. Second, there are the social or collective dynamics through which private capital is attracted to a location due to the sharing of numerous costs or else these being to an extent borne by the public sector. Inevitably the present study allows only a perfunctory and partial analysis of the issue of embeddedness. The chapter opens with a discussion of the extent to which multinational manufacturing operations are integrated into the Welsh economy by way of backward material linkages (i.e. purchases of materials and components from Welsh-based suppliers). It goes on to consider the locational attraction and factor endowments of Wales relative to other EU regions and then finally the institutional infrastructure of Wales relative to other EU regions.

Local Purchasing Linkages

One important indicator of the degree of embeddedness of industry in a particular economy is the extent to which firms buy their various production inputs locally. This is only one indicator, others might be levels of expenditure on training, on equipment and more especially dedicated plant. Nevertheless the extent of local linkage is important not only directly but in terms of possible indirect employment and other less tangible benefits associated with transactions with local suppliers.

Table 9.1 Percentage of material inputs, by value,
from Wales according to ownership

	UK	US	EU	Japan	Other	Total
0	1 (2.8)	3 (8.8)	1 (3.3)	1 (6.3)	1 (7.2)	7 (5.3)
1–25	29 (80.6)	27 (76.5)	28 (86.7)	11 (68.8)	12 (85.7)	107 (80.5)
26–50	5 (13.9)	4 (11.8)	2 (6.7)	4 (25.0)	0 (0.0)	15 (11.3)
51–75	1 (2.8)	0 (0.0)	0 (0.0)	0 (0.0)	0 (0.0)	1 1 (0.7)
76–100	0 (0.0)	1 (2.9)	2 (6.7)	0 (0.0)	1 (7.2)	4 (3.0)
Average	13.78	12.62	13.90	18.00	14.64	13.95

F= 0.344
χ^2=13.48
Source: Author's survey

Table 9.2 Percentage of material inputs, by value,
from Wales according to vintage

	Pre-1950	1950–59	1960–69	1970–79	1980–89	1990–
0	0 (0.0)	0 (0.0)	0 (0.0)	2 (6.5)	2 (6.3)	2 (20.0)
1–25	16 (94.1)	11 (91.7)	18 (75.0)	24 (77.4)	26 (81.3)	7 (70.0)
26–50	0 (0.0)	1 (8.3)	6 (25.0)	4 (12.9)	4 (12.5)	0 (0.0)
51–75	0 (0.0)	0 (0.0)	0 (0.0)	0 (0.0)	0 (0.0)	0 (0.0)
76–100	1 (5.9)	0 (0.0)	0 (0.0)	1 (3.2)	0 (0.0)	1 (10.0)
Average	14.71	16.46	15.13	15.97	11.50	14.00

F = 0.277
χ^2=19.99
Source: Author's survey

Respondents were asked what proportion, by value, of their material inputs and component inputs come from Wales, the rest of the UK and overseas. The results are shown in Tables 9.1 to 9.4. The vast majority of multinational manufacturing establishments in Wales source below 25% of their material and component inputs from Welsh-based suppliers. Table 9.1 also shows that, overall, at 14%, levels of local sourcing are low, but probably expected. The figures here confirm those derived from other studies of Welsh manufacturing industry. Welsh manufacturing operations of UK headquartered firms sourced on average 26.4% of their inputs locally compared to 15.9% for foreign-owned manufacturing establishments (Simpson, 1987). Morris *et al.*'s (1993: 46) figures confirm that, at 15% by value, levels of local sourcing by Japanese plants in Wales are similar to those of the foreign-owned manufacturing sector more generally. In recently produced input-output tables for the Welsh economy, foreign-owned manufacturing establishments in Divisions 2, 3 and 4 (i.e. metals and minerals, metal goods, engineering and vehicles industries and other manufacturing industries respectively) spent on average 16.3%, 9.1% and 7.4% of their total non-wage expenditures on inputs from Wales (Hill and Roberts, 1995).

The extreme lack of local embeddedness in terms of localised backward linkages is apparent among several of the case study companies. Nu-kote International's operations at Deeside would be an extreme example.

Nu-kote International, Deeside

Nu-kote's closure of its North Wales factory highlights the extreme lack of integration of some multinational manufacturing operations as well as the drawbacks with attempting to attract and retain multinational investment solely through financial assistance.

At the time of closure Nu-kote's Welsh operations were the subject of a 'live' offer of further financial assistance from the WDA. Presumably the financial assistance on offer was insufficient to offset the economies of rationalisation of manufacture and distribution. Certainly, there was precious little else to tie the company's Welsh factory to the local economy. Virtually nothing in terms of the value of material inputs to the factory came from the local or Welsh economy. Indeed, the company purchased virtually all its material inputs – fabrics, films and plastic mouldings – globally. And whilst sources at the company suggested that important use of local Training and Enterprise Councils was made in terms of training schemes and whilst there was some research and development activity (product adaptation) on-site, the sunk costs embodied in localised labour skills appear to be relatively insignificant against the need for, and economies associated with, rationalisation.

In relation to many other multinational manufacturing investments in Wales, Exide's factory at Cwmbran might be described as being moderately and selectively embedded in the Welsh economy.

Exide, Cwmbran

On the one hand, we saw earlier how labour costs in Wales appear to have figured in the selection of Cwmbran for expansion rather than closure. Company sources suggested that, whilst nearly one-quarter of the total £6m investment made at the Cwmbran factory was provided by the Welsh Office, as yet, the operations had not benefited from any further involvement with the WDA and other local organisations in terms of business support. Also, despite being a centre for major expansion within the company's European operations, and despite being the administrative, purchasing and distribution centre for the company's UK operations, the key function of research and development remains at Exide's other UK factory at Dagenham. On the other hand, one company source estimated that as much as 95% of material inputs to Cwmbran come from the UK much of which is sourced from within Wales.

A number of other studies have indicated that it is UK multiplant firms, rather than foreign-owned manufacturing operations which source least from their respective local economies (see Table 9.1). UK-owned establishments in Wales certainly do have low levels of local sourcing but it is US-owned operations which have the lowest levels of local sourcing. A likely reason for this is that the potential for local sourcing may be constrained due to large scale intra-corporate sourcing of materials and components or else corporate strategies of consolidating purchases with preferred suppliers (see Phelps 1993b for evidence of processes of consolidation).

It has been suggested that the vertically disintegrated forms of production pioneered by the Japanese in their domestic economy are being transplanted into North America and Europe. The implication is that such vertically disintegrated forms of production offer greater possibilities for local sourcing by individual manufacturing operations. This may or may not be a contributory factor in the relatively high levels of local sourcing which are also a reflection of the pressure brought to bear on Japanese operations in the EU by way of anti-dumping actions and rulings on the origin of goods as well as voluntary agreements with member state governments.

Table 9.2 shows that it is the more recently established operations of multinationals and in particular those established during the 1980s which have the lowest levels of local sourcing – though the differences between vintages are not statistically significant. Furthermore, the differences between recent and older investments are small enough to be discounted as part of other effects such as differences in sectoral composition between vintages and the process of 'linkage adjustment' which may yet to have fully taken place. Perhaps the only other pattern of note in Table 9.2 is that the vast majority of all vintages of operations source between 1 and 25%, by value, of their inputs locally but that there are a few of those established during the 1960s, 1970s and 1980s which have higher levels of sourcing (i.e. 26–50%).

Table 9.3 shows the levels of overseas sourcing of material inputs. Overall, levels of international sourcing are quite high but there are also some interesting variations according to ownership of plants. UK-owned establishments have some of the lowest levels of overseas sourcing of material inputs which may reflect the tendency for UK firms to confer considerable autonomy on overseas operations and as a result leave potential international divisions of labour and sourcing opportunities unexploited. Interestingly Japanese-owned establishments have the highest level of overseas sourcing. This is certainly a reflection of either high levels of intra-corporate sourcing of key components from domestic or Far East plants or else the limited geographical availability of cost and quality competitive components. Given that Japanese-owned establishments also had the highest levels of local sourcing, there appears to be an unusual bifurcation in this input sourcing pattern.

**Table 9.3 Percentage of material inputs, by value,
from overseas according to ownership**

	UK	US	EU	Japan	Other	Total
0	3 (8.3)	2 (5.6)	2 (6.7)	0 (0.0)	1 (7.1)	8 (5.9)
1–25	18 (50.0)	16 (44.4)	13 (39.4)	4 (23.5)	7 (50.0)	57 (42.2)
26–50	8 (22.2)	6 (16.7)	8 (26.7)	6 (35.3)	4 (28.6)	32 (23.7)
51–75	7 (19.4)	8 (22.2)	6 (18.2)	6 (35.3)	2 (14.3)	17 (13.3)
76–100	0 (0.0)	4 (11.1)	4 (12.1)	1 (5.9)	0 (0.0)	14 (10.9)
Ave	27.25	36.31	38.67	41.76	25.50	34.40

$F = 1.699$
$\chi^2 = 13.56$
Source: Author's survey

Table 9.4 confirms that there is a bifurcation of sourcing patterns among recently established operations (post-1980). These have the highest levels of sourcing from overseas and and as we saw above had the lowest levels of local sourcing. Again this pattern might be readily explained by sectoral differences in the composition of different vintages and 'linkage adjustment'. Overall, then, the patterns of sourcing revealed in Table 9.4 (and 9.2) seem to suggest little relationship between vintage and sourcing patterns.

Geographical variations in material input costs and international sourcing strategies can have a bearing on decisions regarding rationalisation and investment in Europe as the case of Wella illustrates.

Table 9.4 Percentage of material inputs, by value, from overseas according to vintage

	Pre-1950	1950–59	1960–69	1970–79	1980–89	1990–
0	0 (0.0)	1 (7.7)	2 (8.3)	3 (9.7)	0 (0.0)	2 (20.0)
1–25	9 (52.9)	4 (30.8)	14 (58.3)	12 (38.7)	14 (42.4)	2 (20.0)
26–50	3 (17.6)	3 (23.1)	3 (12.5)	10 (32.3)	7 (21.2)	2 (20.0)
51–75	4 (23.5)	3 (23.1)	4 (16.7)	5 (16.1)	9 (27.3)	4 (40.0)
76–100	1 (5.9)	2 (15.4)	1 (4.2)	1 (3.2)	3 (9.0)	0 (0.0)
Ave	31.41	38.57	26.38	32.42	38.42	36.6

$F = 0.746$
$\chi^2 = 18.63$
Source: Author's survey

Wella, Pontyclun

Wella's Pontyclun factory is probably typical of the majority of multinational investments in Wales in terms of the degree of integration into the local economy. Certainly the Pontyclun manufacturing operations enjoyed the usual connections with organisations such as the Welsh Development Agency and local Training and Enterprise Councils without these having any significant bearing on competitiveness. Indeed, if anything, the Wella case highlights the fact that embeddedness, in this case primarily in terms of material linkages, does not necessarily make a positive contribution to plant competitiveness.

It is estimated by company sources that around 10%, by value, of material inputs to the Welsh factory came from Welsh sources – mainly in the form of plastics from local suppliers. A further 10% of materials – in the form of chemicals – came from UK-based suppliers outside Wales. However, these 'local' sources of inputs were considered not to be price competitive compared to mainland European suppliers. Since a major consideration in the company's rationalisation strategy hinged on reducing material input costs, to some extent the Welsh factory's 'local' linkages hindered its competitiveness. The company also encountered problems in transferring production lines from its Wales to its factory in France where, initially at least, the lines proved only half as efficient as they had been in Wales. On the face of things, this might be taken as an indication of the non-transferability of certain sunk-costs related to skills and learning economies developed in Wales over a long time. However, company staff categorically refuted this interpretation suggesting instead that the poor condition of the production lines coupled with problematic relations with mainland European equipment suppliers had been the cause of the problems.

Sunk costs in the form of locationally-fixed expenditures on plant and equipment can engender locational inertia and hence affect both the extent and pace of rationalisation notably in process industries such as petro-chemicals. BP Chemicals' ethylene 'cracker' and chemicals complex at Baglan Bay illustrates this.

BP Chemicals, Baglan Bay

The closure of BP Chemicals' Baglan Bay ethylene cracker demonstrates some of the huge sunk costs involved in rationalisation. Chemicals plants provide some of the best examples of the connection between internal economies of scale and local embeddedness. Chemicals plants conform most closely to the 'cathedrals in the desert' branch plant stereotype being locally embedded by virtue of the large place-specific capital investments and their highly self contained nature. The internal economies associated with Baglan Bay complex began to break down as BP Chemicals closed and divested itself of various elements of its chemicals business downstream of ethylene production. Baglan Bay, isolated from BP Chemicals' other sites, was crucially dependent upon the other 11 plants in the complex. However, the company closed a number of these during the 1980s – so undermining the viability of the plant whose other markets were rather limited.

Locational Attractions of Wales

Organisational or corporate dynamics are part of the equation of local embeddedness. The other part of the equation consists of the various locational advantages or factor endowments of Wales as well as the extent and efficacy of institutional infrastructure which exists to enhance firms' competitiveness and embeddedness. This chapter now turns to an examination of the factor endowments and institutional capacity of Wales as perceived by multinational operations of different vintages. To an extent the empirical material presented in the following two sections highlights the quandary over how it may be possible to upgrade cost minimising investment by way of an improved institutional infrastructure in Wales.

Respondents were asked to rank the advantages of Wales as a location in comparison to other EU regions. Table 9.5 shows the mean ranking obtained for a number of locational characteristics broken-down by ownership. Once again there is a high degree of central tendency in the results suggesting that the perceived locational advantages may be quite precisely related to the type and requirements of individual investments rather than there being marked systematic difference between EU regions. Central tendency here is also related to the fact that respondents were asked to compare Wales to other EU regions in general and not to similar peripheral regions. Hence, the data contained in Tables 9.5 to 9.6 might be more accurately interpreted as a comparison of Wales' factor and

institutional endowments in relation to the average situation in the EU. Nevertheless an analysis of variance test reveals that there are some statistically significant
differences in the ranking of the locational advantages of Wales according to
ownership.

Table 9.5 Comparative locational attractions of Wales according to ownership

	UK	US	EU	Japan	Other	Total	F	χ^2
Availability of suppliers	2.39	2.60	2.44	3.05	2.54	2.56	3.77**	27.70
Labour availability	3.31	3.56	3.62	3.67	3.38	3.51	1.32	18.09
Labour costs	3.63	3.65	4.09	3.89	3.85	3.81	3.01*	16.33
FACTOR	9.31	9.82	10.15	10.67	9.77	9.88	3.46**	n.a.

NB F and χ^2 statistics given for tests run on five ownership categories
* significant at 95% confidence limit, ** significant at 99% confidence limit
Source: Author's survey

Across all ownership groups Wales compares favourably with other EU regions in
terms of labour availability and labour costs (Table 9.5). Wales compares less
favourably with other EU regions in terms of the availability of suppliers for all
ownership groups with the exception of Japanese-owned operations. An analysis
of variance test for the three main ownerships groupings (UK, US and EU) does
not reveal any statistically significant differences in the ranking of the availability
of suppliers in Wales according to ownership. This suggests that the real differences
in the evaluation of the availability of suppliers in Wales compared to other EU
regions is between Japanese-owned operations and the rest. Why should Japanese-
owned operations consider Wales to have a comparative advantage in terms of the
availability of suppliers? After all, Japanese manufacturing firms in general have
made it quite clear that there have been problems with the availability and quality
of supplies in Europe and in the UK in particular. It is unlikely that Wales is any
better in this respect. The reasons for this positive evaluation of the availability of
supplies in Wales by Japanese-owned manufacturing operations may lie in the
nature of the purchasing process of these firms. There are, in turn, several aspects
to any such explanation. First, the key, high value, inputs of Japanese operations
in Wales may come from the far east in any case. Second, the philosophy of *Kaizen*
and the practice of just-in-time manufacture combine to place a premium on input
quality, reliability and delivery. Where supplies are truly unavailable locally
Japanese-owned suppliers have been imported or transplanted. Otherwise, Japanese-owned operations have been content to work closely with the available
suppliers to bring them up to the required standards. In other words, Japanese-

owned operations may have little problem with the availability of suppliers in Wales because of these close working relationships with imported or existing suppliers. US, UK and EU firms may have problems because of their traditionally arms length, non-collaborative relations with suppliers which have left them little means of improving the local supplier base.

There also appear to be statistically significant (at the 95% confidence level) differences in the ranking of the cost of labour in Wales relative to other EU regions. Here EU-owned operations rank the comparative labour cost advantages of Wales the highest. This may simply be a reflection of the fact that the majority of these EU-owned operations originate from German or French companies which face relatively high domestic wage rates. Wales has by no means the lowest labour costs of EU regions but some of the lowest in the major markets of the EU. For market-based investment in the northern EU economies Wales probably represents a low labour cost location.

Table 9.6 Comparative locational attractions of Wales according to vintage

	Pre-1950	1950–59	1960–69	1970–79	1980–89	1990–	F	χ^2
Availability of suppliers	2.47	2.50	2.23	2.65	2.75	2.62	1.50	17.44
Labour availability	3.47	3.23	3.40	3.55	3.65	3.83	1.35	15.90
Labour costs	3.82	3.69	3.64	3.64	3.80	4.08	0.92	13.08

NB F and χ^2 statistics given for tests run on six vintage categories
* significant at 95% confidence limit, ** significant at 99% confidence limit
Source: Author's survey

Table 9.6 examines the factor endowments of Wales compared to other EU regions as perceived by different vintages of multinational operations in Wales. In general the below average ranking suggests that Wales compares poorly with other EU regions in terms of the availability of suppliers. This poor estimation of the supplier-base in Wales is apparent for all vintages of multinational investment. However, there appears to be a greater range of opinions of Wales's position among respondents from recently established operations (1970s, 1980s and 1990s) – with small numbers even suggesting that the supply infrastructure in Wales is greater than in the other EU regions. Two complementary possible explanations of this pattern suggest themselves. First, older operations – primarily UK, US and EU-owned investments – may be less oriented toward local sources of supply given the past emphasis placed on global or corporate input sourcing strategies. As a result of this, purchasing functions and management at these operations may be relatively unaware of, or indifferent to, potential local suppliers. Second, newly established operations, by virtue of the fact that they have recently completed appraisals of possible locations in Europe and by virtue of their greater interest in local supply sources, may have a greater knowledge of, and interest in, the supplier-base in Wales and in other EU regions.

Traditionally, Wales, as a peripheral region, has attracted cost-minimising multinational investment on the basis of relatively abundant labour and low wage rates. Table 9.6 confirms that these remain important attractions of Wales compared to other EU regions, in that, in general, all vintages of multinational operations in Wales perceive the Principality to compare favourably with other EU regions in respect of labour, availability and cost. The data also confirm the importance of these locational attractions to the most recent multinational investments. Indeed a greater proportion of these newly established operations (1980s and 1990s) than older operations perceive Wales to compare favourably with other EU regions with respect to such labour issues. At least in terms of its motives, if not in terms of its character, then, recent multinational manufacturing investment is little different from that of the past. Indeed, this picture may hold for most peripheral regions in the EU since as Amin *et al.* (1994) note that 'with the exception of labour quality and skills, regional attributes emphasised today remain very similar to those which attracted cost/price minimising mobile investment into the LFRs [less favoured regions] during the 1960s and 1970s...' (Amin *et al.* 1994: 21). Two recent examples of transfers of production into Wales from Germany illustrate this point exactly.

Hitachi Consumer Electronics, Hirwaun

Whilst the closure of Hitachi's German plant was, as we saw earlier, related to a slump in mainland European markets there is also a sense in which it may have been part of some sort of corporate strategy. The company's 1994 annual report describes how '...the company reorganised its global production organisation through such measures as closing a VCR plant in Germany and integrating its operations into those of a UK plant, a move that followed the shutdown of a similar facility in the United States in late 1992.' (Hitachi, 1994). In the North American case, the company had shifted television and VCR production out of the US to Mexico and Malaysia (Hitachi, 1993). Whilst the slump in the mainland European market may have precipitated the closure decision, there is some evidence to suggest that the reorganisation of production in Europe has much to do with an attempt to cut costs in a highly cost competitive market. In closing its German factory, Hitachi transferred some production to Wales but also reverted to sourcing some of its range (presumably the more expensive models) of VCRs from Japan and Malaysia. In the circumstances, the main but not the exclusive advantage of switching production to Wales was in terms of the relative costs of production. The company estimated that labour costs in Wales were between 13% and 17% lower than those in Germany (Gribben, 1993). Differences in the strength of currencies will have exacerbated such cost differences. With 1000 employees (compared to 330 at the Landsberg plant) and a greater product range, however, there was also some sense in consolidating production in Wales since presumably there is greater flexibility to redeploy assembly workers between production lines.

The Grundig case also illustrates the importance of labour costs as an attraction of Wales to manufacturing investment in the EU – though as we saw earlier, the relative cost of labour was only one of a number of factors contributing to a relocation of production from Germany to Wales. In addition to labour costs there is some suggestion that there are some economies to be gained in terms of the availability and knowledge of local labour which has resulted from the build up of Japanese electronics firms in South Wales.

Grundig, Llantrisant

Certainly Grundig's operations are fairly typical in terms of the degree of integration of electronics firms into the Welsh economy. A company source suggested that around 12.5% of the value of material inputs came from Wales including metal and plastics parts, fastenings and packaging. Similarly, as yet, no local organisations had had any significant bearing on the competitiveness or embeddedness of the manufacturing operations. The company had not, for instance, received any financial assistance from the WDA. However, labour availability and expertise were also mentioned as a significant advantage of being located in Wales. When the company was established it attempted to combine the best of Japanese and European business practices drawing upon a core team of employees all with experience of working for Japanese companies in Wales. In addition to this a company source suggested that the ready pool of labour with experience of electronics assembly work meant that training costs were lower than they might otherwise be.

The rank scores for the three indicators of comparative locational attraction in terms of availability of suppliers and labour and labour costs can be added together to form a composite rank score relating to factor endowment (FACTOR in Table 9.5). This composite rank score once again suggests that there are differences in the evaluation of Wales as a location according to ownership. EU and Japanese-owned operations rate Wales more highly as a location in terms of its comparative factor endowments than UK and US-owned establishments (the differences being statistically significant at the 95% confidence level). For Welsh manufacturing operations of all ownership categories Wales compares favourably with other EU regions in terms of its factor endowments.

Institutional Infrastructure in Wales

The sorts of institutions and policy initiatives to help encourage the competitive advantage and local embeddedness of local industry vary from region to region in the EU. Within the UK context it seems clear that Wales, through the Welsh

Development Agency among other organisations, has developed a 'significant institutional infrastructure' and some of the most successful and innovative policies aimed at enhancing industry competitiveness (e.g. Cooke, 1992; Rees and Morgan, 1991). However, less is known about whether this institutional infrastructure exerts any effect on manufacturing industry or how it is regarded among manu- facturing firms in Wales. However, in comparison to other peripheral, let alone core, regions with institutions proactive in the sphere of industrial and technology policy Wales's position may be less favourable. The questionnaire survey sought to try and gain some indication of how the institutional infrastructure in Wales compares to that in other EU regions.

From a survey of agency support for inward investors and other firms, Young and Hood (1995) have identified several levels of aftercare from the strategic to the operational. The institutional capacity in Wales is relatively well-developed on a number of fronts. At the strategic level there are the sectoral priorities regarding the attraction of inward investment. In Wales the focus has been on quite a range of sectors (including research and development) but with some success in a few (especially financial services, automotive components and information technology) Below this there are a number of operational elements worth noting.

Under the Eurolink programme Wales has become a 'closely integrated fifth member of the original "four motors for Europe"' (Cooke, 1992: 377). Here Welsh-based firms are partnered with similar firms in Baden Wurttemberg and Rhone Alps to exchange technology etc. (Cooke, 1992). There is also considerable support for innovation both through DTI and EU schemes administered by the Welsh Office and the WDA and through the WDA's support of a number of academic centres of excellence and technology centres across Wales (Cooke and Morgan, 1992). The success of these centres has been mixed. For instance the electronic data interchange (EDI) centre for Wales, whilst successful in increasing awareness of EDI among Welsh-based firms, has had little scope to assist firms with the implementation of EDI. The Welsh Garment Centre which has been involved with providing technology, training and consultancy services is threat- ened with a limited life (Henderson, 1994). As yet the impact of such public sector based support for innovation is still minor compared to intra- and inter-firm sources of innovation (Cooke and Morgan, 1992; Phelps, 1995) and has had little discernible effect on rates of innovation.

Another example of the build-up of institutional capacity in Wales relates to supplier development. Under the WDA's 'source Wales' initiative local suppliers are assisted with the adoption of the likes of electronic data interchange (EDI) and statistical process control (SPC). The WDA also prospects on their behalf for local and international business. The WDA has also been instrumental in encouraging major inward investors to initiate supplier associations and encourage Welsh-based suppliers to join these and other associations outside Wales. Here at least there seems some consensus among participants regarding the success of such supplier associations in generating benefits in terms of the transfer of best practice and

technology (Henderson, 1994). Whilst there are quite large-scale sourcing opportunities identified under the initiative (£80m in 1994–95), naturally only a fraction
of these have been translated into actual orders for Welsh-based suppliers. Progress
in Wales seems broadly in line with that in other similar schemes (e.g. see Tomaney,
1995 on the Irish Development Agencies 'National Linkage Programme').

Only more recently has the WDA become involved, along with local Training
and Enterprise Councils and further education colleges, in training issues and as
yet its activity here has been limited to a number of pilot projects. These pilot
projects or 'collaborative training consortia' have been initiated in the automotive
components and information technology industries; the idea being that firms in
these industries could pool their training needs and make specific training courses
at local colleges viable. In reality, the training needs of firms within these sectors
at any one time have not coincided creating problems in terms of the viability of
courses and hence restricting the amount of collaborative training undertaken thus
far (Henderson, 1994).

For one set of commentators this institutional infrastructure has played a key
role in the renaissance of Wales as a manufacturing location. Morgan has suggested
that in Wales 'these institutions constitute the core of a relatively well-developed
growth coalition' (Morgan, 1992: 164). There undoubtedly exists the institutional
basis for public sector led growth coalitions in Wales. At present, and as far as
inward investment attraction is concerned, there is the essentially public sector
based 'Team Wales' partnership between the WDA, local authorities, Training and
Enterprise Councils, Enterprise Agencies etc. However, as yet private sector
involvement in such a potential growth coalition in Wales is virtually non-existent
in the sense of large manufacturing companies being involved in aspects of
economic strategy formulation either at a local or nationwide level. The involvement of firms, chiefly major inward investors, in the low-level politics involved
with the local delivery of services is, however, considerable. The best example here
being that of the training programmes mentioned above. The implications of this
are not necessarily positive since the attentions and resources of local institutions
may have been captured by a few key firms leaving the large part of the
multinational-owned manufacturing sector in Wales uncatered for.

Cooke, Price and Morgan (1995) identify a renaissance in the Welsh economy.
During the 1980s, manufacturing employment in Wales has been stable against
continued decline across the UK as a whole. This they take as evidence of the
Welsh economy 'becoming more of a manufacturing economy than it was, or than
the UK is now' (Cooke, Price and Morgan, 1995: 109). They go further, when
reviewing trends in the share of manufacturing and services in GDP in Wales and
the UK, implying that the Welsh economy has moved into higher value-added
manufacturing activities (Cooke, Price and Morgan, 1995: 109–112). These
interpretations of the recent performance of the Welsh economy have been
contested (Lovering, 1996). Equally questionable is the claim that 'the institution
building and judicious intervention that have been possible in Wales in the

interstices of Thatcherism and its aftermath, have created a far more robust regional economy than prevailed hitherto' (Cooke, Price and Morgan, 1995: 106).

Table 9.7 Comparative institutional infrastructure of Wales according to ownership

	UK	US	EU	Japan	Other	Total	F	χ^2
Supplier development	2.67	2.83	2.85	3.26	3.17	2.90	3.49**	18.60
General training	3.12	3.12	3.09	3.26	2.85	3.10	0.88	14.46
Specific training	2.88	3.06	3.00	3.00	2.67	2.95	0.96	15.54
Site Selection	3.41	3.55	3.45	3.42	3.00	3.42	1.14	17.20
Financial assistance	3.44	3.42	3.53	3.42	3.00	3.42	0.82	20.26
Innovation support	3.19	3.31	3.29	3.58	3.10	3.30	1.20	11.69
INFRASTRUCTURE	18.92	19.54	19.27	19.89	17.70	19.21	1.23	n.a.

NB F and χ^2 statistics given for tests run as five ownership categories
* significant at 95% confidence limit, ** significant at 99% confidence limit
Source: Author's survey

Table 9.7 shows the rank scores obtained for the comparative strength of Wales in terms of a number of policy areas. For UK, US and EU-owned establishments, Wales compares unfavourably with the EU regions in terms of policy initiatives to encourage the development of suppliers. However, for Japanese-owned establishments Wales compares favourably with other EU regions in terms of policies geared toward the development of supplier firms. An analysis of variance test suggests that these differences in perception are statistically significant at the 99% confidence level. A closer examination of the data also suggests that the main element in such variations according to ownership is between UK and Japanese multinationals. There are a number of possible explanations for this pattern. First, it may be that the differing assessment of Wales's supplier development infrastructure reflects the differences in approach in relationships with suppliers as noted earlier. That is, because Japanese-owned operations are more concerned with supplier development than UK and US firms they have a greater awareness and appreciation of the initiatives that exist. Alternatively, because UK and US firms are currently adopting successful Japanese manufacturing techniques, including elements of supplier development, they may be looking for more support in this area. There is no doubt that Wales, in fact, has some of the most developed policies to assist the development of suppliers within the UK. Through the 'source Wales' initiative the WDA has fostered a number of supplier associations, has managed on a minor scale to substitute local for non-local sources of supply to major manufacturers and has assisted local suppliers to diversify their customer base particularly their exports to other EU regions with which there are close relationships (Cooke, 1992). The low ranking of Wales's supplier development initiatives by UK-owned establishments in Wales is therefore surprising given the region's acknowledged strength in this field within the UK and given UK multinationals limited experience of other EU regions. It may also serve to highlight the lack of resources devoted to this issue in relation to the problem.

Training is another field in which there may be long-term benefits in terms of embeddedness as a result of providing assistance to inward investors. Here the available studies would suggest that there is considerable scope for improving the assistance provided to inward investors (Rees and Thomas, 1994; Price, Cooke and Morgan, 1994). Indeed these commentators have singled out training as perhaps the key area of support infrastructure in need of future development. Thus,

> 'If Wales is to capture the second and third rounds of inward investment, it is imperative that local branch-plant managers – who are engaged in fierce competition with other locations within the same company – are able to point to factors, such as the [vocational education and training] VET infrastructure, which help to sustain the competitive advantage of the plant over time'. (Morgan and Rees, 1995: 19)

Whilst Wales compares favourably with other EU regions in terms of general training provision it compares less favourably in terms of training assistance tailored towards specific company needs.

Wales also appears to compare favourably with other EU regions in terms of assistance with site selection and financial initiatives. This positive comparison with other EU regions regarding such assistance holds for operations of different ownership and is perhaps understandable given that these have been the traditional strengths of the WDA. Two case studies provide evidence of the continued salience of financial assistance to the attraction of multinational investment in Wales. Fenner Plc's expansion and relocation to a new factory in Maerdy illustrates very clearly the continued importance of financial incentives as an attraction of Wales compared to other EU locations.

Fenner, Maerdy

During 1995 Hull-based Fenner Plc, a diversified engineering company, made a number of acquisitions including W A Thatcher Ltd at Maerdy which made components for the car industry. In 1996 Fenner announced that it would be closing factories in, and transferring production from, Hull and Peterborough and expanding production at a new factory in Maerdy in Wales. 300 jobs were to be lost at Hull and another 145 at Peterborough whilst employment at Maerdy was planned to increase from 145 to 540. At the time, the move was highly controversial given that £13m of the total £25m investment was being funded in one way or another through the WDA.

Clearly, the concern was that financial incentives had been used to lure jobs from the North of England to Wales. In contrast, the company claimed that there had been very substantial competition from overseas agencies for the project with sites in France and Ireland being considered (Adburgham and Parker, 1996). Despite the company denying that low wages in Wales had been a factor in the decision to shift production (Davies, 1996), the move does appear to be consistent with a strategy to shift production to lower cost locations. The company had earlier transferred some production from Hull to another company site in China.

The partial transfer of production from Parke-Davis's operations in Pontypool illustrates the importance of financial incentives in attracting investment to Wales but also the vulnerability of such investment once market circumstances change.

Parke-Davis, Pontypool

We saw earlier that the partial closure of Parke-Davis's operations at Pontypool were connected with a worldwide reorganisation of company operations coupled to changes in the regulation of the UK health-care market. The working out of the company's rationalisation of manufacturing in Europe during the 1980s and 1990s reveals, however, the underlying poor cost-competitive position of the UK operations.

The closure resulted in the loss of 300 jobs and the transfer of product lines to the US, France and Germany. Earlier decisions regarding consolidation of manufacturing operations may provide a clue as to why the Pontypool operations were rationalised and production shifted to mainland Europe. Back in 1985 Warner-Lambert closed its Eastleigh factory in Hampshire and transferred production to Pontypool. At the time the company said that 'It would have made a lot of sense to move the lot to Europe. What tipped the balance was the generous assistance from the Welsh Office' (quoted in Jackson and Reeves, 1985). Thus, although 'Our Pontypool plant is now one of the largest and most complex in the whole of Warner-Lambert worldwide' (Butler, quoted in Smith, 1988) it was clearly not in a very cost-competitive position *vis-à-vis* other company plants in Europe – its viability being dependent on limited list drugs and financial assistance.

Similarly irrespective of ownership respondents to the survey considered Wales to compare favourably with other EU regions in terms of institutional support for innovation. This good ranking of initiatives for innovation support compared to supplier development is somewhat surprising as the WDA's activities are perhaps no more successful or high-profile than those on other EU regions.

The rank scores obtained for individual criteria pertaining to institutional infrastructure were combined into a composite index of policy infrastructure (INFRASTRUCTURE in Table 9.7). However, tests did not reveal any statistically significant differences in the assessment of Wales's institutional infrastructure according to ownership.

We can also examine perceptions of comparative institutional capacity in Wales as perceived by different vintages of multinational operations in Wales (see Table 8.8). It has been suggested that, compared to earlier vintages of investment, the recent Europe-oriented rationalised multinational investments in the UK are more sensitive to local institutional support or aftercare. Thus 'A notable feature of this wave of investment is its sensitivity to local infrastructure and sourcing capability...' (Hood and Young, 1988: 97). In part this may derive from the changing character and role of recent multinational operations (e.g. Hood and Young, 1988; Young, Hood and Peters, 1994). However, it may also be due to the greater competition between EU regions in terms of the provision of such after-care infrastructure alongside traditional financial incentives (Amin *et al.* 1994). Certainly, from the perspective of those involved with the development of institutional support for inward investment in Wales, this observation – about the sensitivity of recent investment to localised institutional infrastructure – fits rather uncomfortably with the continuing emphasis on cost minimisation of recent multinational investment in the UK and Wales (reported in Chapter 5 and immediately above).

Table 9.8 Comparative institutional infrastructure of Wales according to vintage

	Pre- 1950	1950– 59	1960– 69	1970– 79	1980– 89	1990–	F	χ^2
Supplier development	2.94	2.80	2.75	2.90	2.63	2.85	0.56	14.16
General training	3.12	3.15	2.95	3.17	3.13	3.30	0.65	13.69
Specific training	3.06	2.85	2.76	3.00	2.97	3.31	1.09	13.46
Site selection	3.31	3.27	3.29	3.47	3.44	3.85	1.34	20.95
Financial assistance	3.31	3.38	3.76	3.33	3.27	3.69	1.78	20.06
Innovation support	3.13	3.38	3.40	3.30	3.36	3.38	0.34	9.95

NB F and χ^2 statistics given for tests run as five ownership categories
* significant at 95% confidence limit, ** significant at 99% confidence limit
Source: Author's survey

However, the data from the postal survey reveal few variations in perception of the comparative institutional capacity of Wales according to vintage of multinationals operating in Wales. For instance, Table 9.8 shows that the comparative institutional support in terms of financial assistance appears to be ranked highest by respondents for those operations established in the 1960s and 1970s. Financial assistance may have figured quite prominently in the investment decision of these operations at a time when regional policy was at its most active. Hence, perceptions of Wales may be coloured by this. The generally poor perceptions of the comparative institutional support for supplier development in Wales was noted above. The poor perception of Wales in this respect is repeated across all vintages of multinational investments with the exception of the most recent investments of the 1980s and 1990s. These recently established operations appear to have a more favourable perception of the supplier development initiatives taken in Wales than do their older counterparts. Again, this may have much to do with the generally greater awareness of, and commitment to, issues of supplier development among new multinational investments. Here at least, then, there is some confirmation for Hood and Young's (1988) contention about the evolving nature of multinational investments.

In general, across the range of vintages of multinational investment in Wales, there is indifference regarding the comparative institutional support in Wales for either general or specific training. There are also no differences in perception according to vintage of the institutional support for innovation in Wales which tends to be on balance positive.

Overall it can be said that despite the recent effort put into developing various elements of an institutional infrastructure in support of inward investment, the level of such institutional support in Wales is not considered especially superior to that in other EU regions. Certainly, heightened inter-regional competition for mobile investment in the EU appears to increasingly have incorporated such elements alongside the traditional emphasis on financial incentives. This would certainly put the celebrated Welsh institutional infrastructure in a less favourable light. It would also tend to undermine the rather complacent view of the problem for the Welsh economy being one of 'consolidation of gains and overcoming the residual difficulties and inequities associated with the demise of a previous mode of production' (Cooke, Price and Morgan, 1995: 132). However, the results above may also reflect a more general lack of interest in institutional support for innovation and supplier development etc. among multinationals investing in Europe (see Amin *et al.* 1994). Seen in this light, such institutional infrastructure geared to capturing 'quality' mobile manufacturing investment may be irrelevant. Rather the quality of general supply-side resources appears to be much more important than specific schemes of assistance (Amin *et al.* 1994: 51–52). Thus, more recently, and despite the existing institutional infrastructure in support of inward investment, commentators in Wales have begun to sound the alarm bells regarding basic education and vocational skills among the working population and among the young in particular (Morgan and Rees, 1995). The problems of peripheral regions in the UK are symptomatic of those of the UK in general which, as a 'societal-specific system', has neglected the development of certain non-academic skills (Rubery, 1994). The commentaries on Wales's 'skills deficit' are composed with awareness that, in the UK at least, the improvement of such skills would require regions to 'go it alone' to some extent.

Conclusion

Processes of rationalisation accompanying market integration in Europe are mediated to an extent by the local embeddedness of industry. Rationalisation is far from costless – time, money and resources invested in producing in a particular place can be lost and hence there is a degree of inertia in corporate structures and strategies in general and multiplant operations in particular. This is even true to an extent with the many weakly embedded investments examined in the case studies. The material presented in this chapter represents a rather partial empirical investigation of embeddedness. This is true of the survey material in particular which focused only on local linkages and the comparative assessments of the locational attractions of Wales. Other aspects of local embeddedness such as levels of investment and reinvestment in plant and equipment were not investigated.

The levels of local linkage exhibited by multinational manufacturing operations in Wales were low but perhaps expected. In general, both the survey material and the case studies suggested that localised linkages were sufficiently weak as to have had no bearing on processes of restructuring. There has been much concern over the quality of Japanese manufacturing investment in the UK and particularly about the levels of local sourcing of material inputs. However, the survey data presented above suggests that, if anything, Japanese-owned manufacturing operations in Wales have higher levels of local sourcing than UK and US-owned operations which have been subject to much less scrutiny and criticism. In the short-term, then, there may be considerable scope for increasing local sourcing among UK and US-owned establishments – especially as they are attempting to adopt the type of supplier relations characteristic of Japanese firms. This in itself might make a valuable contribution to economic development in Wales. In the long-term there may be considerable impediments to improving levels of local sourcing since respondents to the survey considered that Wales compared unfavourably with other EU regions with respect to the availability, and policies to assist the development of suppliers. As yet, then, the WDA's attempts to encourage local sourcing may have had little effect despite their being some of the most well-developed such policies in the UK. At present the WDA's efforts have been focused on a few large firms and would need to be extended to other companies. Some re-focusing of inward investment attraction towards specific gaps in supply industry structure might also be needed.

Wales certainly compares favourably with other EU regions in terms of labour costs and availability – the factors which historically have been important in attracting inward investment. However, Wales also compared favourably with other EU regions with respect to a range of forms of policy assistance. It is this policy infrastructure alongside general supply-side features, such as labour skills, which needs to be developed in Wales is to attract more than simply the cost-minimising investment which has been the staple of recent inward investment projects in Wales. The development of this institutional infrastructure sits a little uncomfortably with the traditional and continued attraction of Wales to inward investors. There is a real difficulty in breaking out of the cycle of attracting cost-minimising investment because of the low level of resources devoted to supporting and developing inward investors and indigenous industry across the various institutions. Indeed at present there are limited possibilities for the WDA, for example, to concentrate more of its resources on such activities since, with the gradual reduction of grant-in-aid from Government, it is locked into a cycle of advance factory development, sales and lease to raise revenue to continue as an organisation (see Thomas, 1996). Thus, whilst there may have been a subtle shift in the marketing of Wales as a location, the main activities of the WDA continue to be in terms of site and property development.

CHAPTER 10

Conclusions

This chapter begins by drawing some conclusions regarding the impact of European integration upon multinational-owned manufacturing industry in Wales. It then moves on to consider three more general themes in a little more detail. First, this chapter returns to the question of whether ownership and vintage are useful to an understanding of the character and response of multinationals to processes of European integration. Second, it develops one issue to emerge from the empirical material presented in Chapter 7; namely, the connection between economic integration at the intra-national, European and world scales. Finally, this chapter considers the very topical and important policy issue of the possibilities for encouraging multinational embeddedness and competitiveness in the peripheral region context.

Multinationals and European Integration: The Welsh Experience

We saw earlier how there was a degree of pessimism about the impact of the SEM on the Welsh economy. However, the data presented in the preceding chapters suggests that the creation of the SEM has had very little positive or negative effect on multinational manufacturing operations in Wales. The case studies highlighted that there were probably as many transfers of production into Wales as closures and transfers out of Wales over the last five or six years. Furthermore, the case studies illustrated that the effects of removing remaining non-tariff barriers appear to be less important in shaping restructuring decisions than, for example, relative wage levels, movements in exchange rates and government policies.

The size structure and other characteristics of multinational manufacturing operations in Wales does not appear to be particularly adverse. Welsh plants tend to be smaller but just as productive as similar parent company plants elsewhere in the EU. The case studies tended to highlight the fact that size (and therefore presumably economies of scale) was only one among a number of factors figuring in the rationalisation and investment decisions of multinationals. Indeed, corporate rationalisation strategies in relation to the SEM appeared to create a tension between the interests and performance of individual plants on the one hand and a group or collection of company plants on the other. Perhaps in one important respect the poor competitive position of Welsh manufacturing industry was highlighted. The stock of multinational manufacturing investments in Wales compared unfavourably in terms of research and development activity with other similar parent company operations elsewhere in the EU.

The embeddedness or potential embeddedness of multinational in Wales was a negligible factor in shaping the rationalisation and investment decisions of multinationals. The survey material indicated that the vast majority of multinational manufacturing operations in Wales were only very weakly integrated in terms of backward material linkages. The case studies confirmed that such low levels of local linkage were insufficient to engender any locational inertia within corporate strategies. Furthermore, whilst the reasons for closure and transfer decisions seem quite idiosyncratic, the reasons for Wales benefiting from transfers seem quite consistently to centre on relative labour costs and financial assistance. In other words, the stream of transfers (and new investments) into Wales were not gained by virtue of the quality of institutional support for firms but by virtue if the longer-standing attractions of Wales and competencies of its institutions.

Thus, Wales continues to attract cost minimising manufacturing investments. This continued attraction of Wales appears to hold both within the UK, across the EU and even across the world, as recently and spectacularly demonstrated by Ronson International's decision to shift production of lighters from its Korean to its Welsh factory (Walsh, 1996). The continued attraction of Wales to such cost-minimising investment by multinationals sits uncomfortably with the attempt to provide comprehensive institutional support to raise the quality of multinational investments in Wales. This is seen, for example, in the fact that, despite this emphasis on institutional support and despite the reputation of Welsh institutions in some spheres of such support, it is still the traditional attractions of Wales – labour costs and availability and financial incentives – which multinationals perceive to compare most favourably with other EU regions. The problem this poses for institutions concerned with the attraction and development of manufacturing investment in Wales are severe and will be returned to in the final section of this chapter in a more general discussion of the possibilities for embeddedness.

Ownership, Vintage and European Integration

Earlier in this book, ownership and vintage were established as two important possible determinants of the character of multinational manufacturing operations and their responses to European integration. The empirical material presented in the preceding three chapters does lend some selective support for the idea that ownership has some bearing on the way in which multinationals have responded to further European integration but less support for the idea that vintage exerts a similar effect.

Certainly, the comparative business systems literature (e.g. Whitley, 1992a,b) would suggest that multinationals of different countries of origin exert a qualitative as well as a quantitative effect on the stock of multinational manufacturing investments in a host economy. The quantitative effect of multinationals of different ownership on the Welsh economy is clear to see – with the changing origins of manufacturing investment at a world level exerting an effect at the level of the Welsh economy. Thus, a number of the empirical patterns observed in the preceding three chapters are interpretable in terms of the changing origin and competitive position of multinational investment. The qualitative impact most stressed by the competitive business systems literate is only more selectively apparent in the data. There are perhaps three main examples of this. First, some qualitative differences between US operations and the rest appear in the form of the geographical spread of markets served and in terms of the organisation of production in the EU. US-owned establishments tended to have highly internationalised patterns of sales which in part may be due to the large number of the operations having been given continental and world product mandates. US-owned operations are also rather unique among multinational operations in Wales in often being part of quite complex European-wide corporate divisions of labour. Second, there are the Japanese-owned operations whose distinctive contribution, in comparison to UK, US and EU firms, has been a 'demonstration effect' of best practice to indigenous and multinational supplier firms in Wales. Thus, Japanese operations in Wales had rather unique perceptions of the supply-base and supplier development initiatives in Wales. This, it was noted, is likely to be a product of Japanese firms' own efforts at supplier development. Third, the unique contribution of UK firms in a qualitative sense appears to be that they are, in most respects, residual. Of the various ownership categories, UK-owned operations appear fairly consistently to be the residual worst performers in relation to types and spread of markets served, in terms of plant characteristics and functions and in terms of their embeddedness in the Welsh economy. Though it is not always fair to say that they conform to some notion of the stereotypical branch-plant, they are nevertheless perhaps the most poorly placed with respect to further European integration.

There appears to be less support in the Welsh case for the vintage of multinational manufacturing investments being determinant of the character of these investments and their response to further European integration. As noted earlier, the vintage effect is difficult to judge. Certainly, in quantitative terms, the impact of qualitatively new investments on the stock of multinational manufacturing operations in host regions in the UK is likely to be small, given that the dominant components of change, in the foreign-owned sector have been acquisition and *in situ* growth and contraction (Stone and Peck, 1996). In fact, as Encarnation and Mason (1994) note, the vintage and ownership effects observed by many commentators often elide in the case of Japanese manufacturing investment which is both recent and arguably qualitatively different from previous rounds of investment. As we saw earlier, the character of Japanese manufacturing investment is readily interpretable in terms of product cycle theory (Thomsen, 1993) and it is debateable whether it is likely to become any different from previous rounds of investment in the long-term. Where there does appear to be a difference between new and previous investments it appears restricted to a handful of high-profile investments – such as Sony, Bosch etc. Here, it is arguable that these investments are different but limited in number precisely because there is a limit to how far the institutional infrastructure can usefully be spread. In other words, given the current level of resources directed to institutional support for the likes of training, research and development and technology transfer and supplier development, it is only likely that a handful of such high quality investments will be forthcoming since these effectively capture what resources are available. This raises an important policy question in terms of the tension between attracting a large quantity of cost-minimising investment or, given the current resources devoted to institutional support for industry development, a much smaller quantity of high quality investments.

Multinationals and National, European and World Integration

The focus of much of the literature and empirical material covered in this book has been on the intra-regional effects of regional economic integration. However, this ignores the extent to which processes of European integration are bound up with on the one hand, intra-national restructuring and, on the other hand, processes of worldwide integration.

One fact which has tended to be overlooked in analyses of the SEM is that an important and continuing element of restructuring in relation to the SEM is intra-national in scope. Certainly, the Commission in its analysis of the impact of the SEM has tended to focus on the growth of restructuring through community-wide mergers and acquisitions. However, as noted earlier, mergers and acquisitions of national scope continue to be important within the EU. Furthermore, much rationalisation which is national in scope and unconnected to mergers and acquisitions has some relation to processes of European integration. As the case studies demonstrated, intra-national rationalisation can be; a response to pressures from European competitors (as in the case of BICC); the result of strategies of sourcing within the EU (as with Nu-kote International); the result of the search for a more competitive location including locations on mainland Europe (as in the case of Fenner).

One further implication of the research presented earlier in Chapter 7 is that intra-regional processes of economic integration cannot be separated from broader processes of world integration. Arguably, then, there is a need to consider the interaction of intra- and inter-regional economic integration. Currently the basis and nature of multinational-led integration through trade and investment within trade blocs is rather different from the integration between blocs. For example, integration by way of investment between blocs is driven by issues of market access whilst that within trade blocs is driven by strategies of simple and complex integration to use the UNCTAD terminology. Thus, trade is a much more powerful integrative feature within trade blocs than between trade blocs (Campbell, 1994).

In general terms, much depends on the extent to which regionalisation in the world economy is natural as opposed to strategic (protectionist) in origin. To date, economic integration in each of the three main trade blocs is in large measure natural. As such regional economic integration need not be at the expense of world integration. If this is the case, there may be few significant trade or investment diverting effects of such regionalisation and there may be little impact on the evolution of multinational manufacturing company strategies. If, however, there is an important element of protectionism inherent in the contemporary regional-isation, then the strategies of multinationals may be affected. So Ruigrok and van Tulder (1996) note that the strategies of 'glocalisation' increasingly prevalent among multinationals are essentially politically rather than business orientated.

In particular the discussion in Chapter 7 raised the prospect that those multinational operations in the EU (or other trade blocs) currently serving world markets may be affected by inter-bloc rivalries. One interpretation here is that regionalisation may cause some retrenchment within multinationals which are integrated on a worldwide basis and having single factories with World Product Mandates (WPMs). This is certainly a trend which Ruigrok and van Tulder (1996) see as some multinationals take a step back from truly global strategies whilst others more fully develop strategies of glocalisation. They see the greater preva-lence of such regional corporate divisions of labour as a product of both the threat of exclusion from markets and opportunities for firms to influence regulatory bodies. Put in its simplest terms, those factories with WPMs operating in any of the trade blocs may suffer some loss of status as companies switch to having a number of factories each with Continental Product Mandates (CPMs). This regionalisation may represent a renewed challenge to multinational operations with WPMs. As far as the EU is concerned this process of retrenchment seemed to be particularly applicable to US firms in the EU where there might be a renewed impetus for these firms to rationalise plants with WPMs in favour of similar operations in the NAFTA area.

A second interpretation is that regional economic integration may also heighten inter-regional competition among multinationals and, as a result, more integrated forms of production. It may engender a greater cross-penetration of regional markets by rival multinationals which, to date, has been quite limited. Such cross-penetration of markets through oligopolistic reaction has tended to be rather limited due to US dominance and the weak position of European multinationals. One implication of European integration is that emergent Euro-champions will be in a much better position to challenge US firms in North America whilst neither US or EU firms can ignore Japanese presence in North America and the EU and will need to establish a greater presence in the Far East. Thus, the authors of one recent study consider that 'the impetus for further development of integrated production systems is most likely to flow from external competition in global markets and the continuing international development of companies in industries with substantial economies of scale' (Millington and Bayliss, 1996: 147).

Finally, the discussion so far has concentrated on the dynamics of intra- and inter-regional economic integration in terms of investment and trade in finished products. There may be more important implications of regional economic integration or world economic integration in terms of the flows of intermediate goods (components), labour and finance. Regional economic integration may curtail international transfer of components, labour and finance with a greater emphasis on intra-regional flows. In other words a greater self-reliance at a regional scale in terms of component production and local sources of finance and managerial and technical skills.

The Regional Possibilities for Multinational Embeddedness

During the 1970s and early 1980s it was common place for academic interpretations of the activities of multinationals to chronicle the disengagement of such companies from their traditional centres of activity in both domestic and host economies and to stress the ability of such firms to transcend regional and national economic boundaries. In the last decade there has been a greater recognition of the fact that multinationals still remain embedded in, and derive their competitive advantage from, these traditional centres of activity. As yet, though, there remains little understanding of how multinationals interact with indigenous industry in such locations. Traditionally multinationals have been seen as key forces behind the erosion and dissolution of external economies upon which smaller indigenous enterprise is based. More recently, the complementarity of multinational and indigenous firms in the agglomeration of production and virtuous circles of growth in trade and concentration of production has been recognised (see, for example, Cantwell, 1988).

This whole issue is rendered more complex by the fact that there are a number of ways in which firms can become embedded in particular locations (Phelps, 1997). We saw earlier that, to an extent, firms are embedded in particular locations due to demand-side considerations or the need to have a presence in certain markets. For multinationals, regional integration is very gradually lessening the need for such presence. However, from a supply-side perspective there are still competitive advantages to be derived from being attached to particular locations. In general, little of the multinational manufacturing activity in Wales is embedded to any significant degree. However, the way in which, for example BP Chemicals' complex at Baglan Bay was embedded is different to the way in which Exide's operations are.

On a theoretical front the variety of ways in which multinationals can be embedded in particular locations serves to illustrate both the variety of ways in which multinationals in any given region will actually be embedded and the variety of possible points of leverage for policy. However, much of the academic and policy-related literature on the subject of industry competitiveness and embeddedness has been focused on successful regions and has been rather partial in nature – focusing on institutions *or* technological externalities *or* the social and cultural bases to embeddedness in particular localities. Future research should therefore address the multiplicity of ways in which industry is, and can become, embedded and derive some sort of competitive advantage from a particular location and hence the variety of forms of intervention which may be relevant. Such a broader understanding of embeddedness is important in the peripheral region context where uncritical attempts to reproduce the 'models' of economic development exemplified by successful regions in Europe are unlikely to be enough.

The multiplicity of ways in which multinational investment can become embedded in a host economy offers a range of policy options at a local or regional level. Indeed, currently the weight of academic thought on issues of industry embeddedness and competitiveness suggests that this is perhaps the most appropriate scale at which industrial policy could and should be formulated (e.g. Ohmae, 1993). The Commission has argued that

> 'Regions should set-off their relative strengths and weaknesses against that of their main competitors. They should then develop strategies and policies to attract the particular types of activity and sector which they have a reasonable chance of securing.' (CEC, 1993;118)

There is a sense in which the different ways in which different types of multinationals investment can become locally embedded present an opportunity for localities and regions to differentiate their inward investment strategies and support in such a way. The evidence on Wales presented above and on peripheral regions reported elsewhere (Amin *et al.* 1994) suggests that such regions are, however, locked in to a cycle of attracting certain types of investment which it may be difficult to reverse in the medium term. Thus,

> 'the traditional cost/price-based locational advantages of the LFRs continue to remain high on the list of potential investors, investors appear to require a restricted set of new factors from LFRs, normally associated with "quality" investment... The most prominent appears to be "human capital" factors such as training, higher education, housing and skills and infrastructure needs...' (Amin *et al.* 1994: 24)

In other words, some of the strategies and policies which the Commission sees as being a means of differentiating regions within the EU are in fact additional to, and not substitutes for, existing attractions of regions. Regions everywhere in the EU are likely to be upgrading their institutional infrastructure to try to attract inward investment. The problem is that there is little to suggest that schemes to encourage supplier development and technology transfer and the like have any discernable effect on either the quality of investment attracted to a region or the competitiveness and embeddedness of existing investments in regions (Amin *et al.* 1994).

Certainly the evidence from Wales suggests that, as yet, the region's celebrated institutional infrastructure and policies aimed at inward investors has had a limited impact on the nature and embeddedness of their investments. What does appear to have happened is some form of institutional capture by a few high profile companies in Wales – as appears to have happened in other peripheral UK regions, such as the North East (e.g. see Crowther and Garrahan, 1988; Peck, 1996). This applies whether it is site and infrastructure assembly, supplier development, training, technology transfer schemes and financial assistance – witness the huge sums of the current and future grant aid budget tied up in the recently announced Lucky Goldstar investment in Wales (Wilkinson, 1996). It is not clear whether there currently is, or will ever be, the scale of resources devoted to schemes such a 'Source Wales' or technology transfer initiatives to make up for otherwise considerable supply-side inadequacies in the Welsh economy and so stimulate competitiveness and embeddedness across the range of multinational investments in Wales. Certainly, and for the foreseeable future, the WDA – the central body among those coordinating and delivering services to multinationals – is locked into a cycle of property development and sale and leasing to survive and as a result is not able to devote sufficient resources to business services. The potential for such institutional capture coupled to changes in the dominant mode of entry of inward investment in the UK raises issues of accountability. Indeed it may occur precisely because of the lack of monitoring and the 'murkiness' of institutional activities and expenditures in support of inward investment. A recent National Audit Office report noted that there was no systematic monitoring of monies spent in the cause of creating and safeguarding jobs in Wales (Thomas, 1996). The need for some kind of monitoring is also apparent given the tendency for regional bodies to put together packages of assistance to inward investors in which there are numerous and important sweeteners – such as assistance with training, customisation of site infrastructure etc. – which are additional to the direct grant aid.

Furthermore the crucial determining factors in terms of attracting 'quality' mobile investment, as noted by Amin *et al.* (1994), are those which are largely beyond the control of local or regional bodies. Thus, the 'critical and political parameters affecting the health of local economies are still set at the national and increasingly the international level' (Rhodes, 1995: 347). The likes of education and training systems are essentially a matter of national policy. And, whilst regional bodies, such as those in Wales, may be aware of the inadequacy of educational and training systems and standards in the UK as far as the needs of multinational investments are concerned, there may be relatively little that they can do to alleviate this inadequacy. The WDA's attempts to start up collaborative training consortia essentially highlighted the problems of trying to tackle such basic supply-side issues at a regional level. Thus, it appears to be very difficult for peripheral regions such as Wales to attract anything other than the cost-minimising multinational investment that they have attracted to date. Viewed pessimistically the sorts of after-care being produced by the likes of the WDA in Wales represent a more sophisticated place-marketing to the same prospective customers, it is simply that the expectations of multinationals whether in respect of quality or cost-minimising investments has risen. On a more general note, some of these limitations with the Welsh institutional infrastructure do tend to confirm Peck and Tickell's (1994) scepticism regarding the capacities of local or regional level governance to exert much influence on multinational restructuring.

Finally, what of the prospects for creating economically competitive, export-oriented clusters of industry in peripheral regions? This is not a question which appears to have troubled many academics and policy-makers with a special interest in peripheral region development. Industry clusters have become perhaps the prime notion underlying peripheral region development strategies following the work of Porter (1990) and a huge literature documenting and re-affirming the success of agglomerated forms of production. Implicitly or explicitly, the notion of clusters appears to underlie strategies of regional development in, for example, Ireland (Tomaney, 1995) and Wales (Morgan B., 1993). Each of these regions has some of the most developed institutional infrastructure in the British Isles and this undoubtedly is a factor in their interest in the notion of industry clusters since 'if a region wants to self-regenerate or appreciably improve its industrial performance it must develop an integrated and sophisticated governance structure' (Teague, 1994: 282). Yet there are formidable difficulties in creating an appropriate governance structure capable of engendering and sustaining such industry clusters even in regions with a degree of governmental autonomy and existing institutional infrastructure. Teague's discussion of Northern Ireland provides a sobering tale of the difficulties of creating such industry clusters in a physically peripheral region. He argues that 'peripherality establishes formidable barriers in the way of market access and competitiveness' (Teague, 1994: 286). Thus, in Teague's view physical peripherality obstructs both access to markets and formation of the agglomeration economies upon which successful clusters of industry are based.

Teague's view of peripherality may be overly pessimistic. The discussion of market clusters in Chapter 4 alluded to the possibilities for multinationals to serve particular groups of national markets from physically peripheral regions. Strictly speaking, then, physical peripherality creates few problems of market access. Arguably, though, it does prevent the creation of agglomeration economies which would subsequently benefit from such export markets in the manner outlined by Storper (1992) and Krugman (cited in Martin and Sunley, 1995). A number of studies have suggested that small firms increasingly are able to thrive away from existing centres of economic activity (Keeble and Tyler, 1995; Vaessen and Keeble, 1995) and even in physically peripheral locations (Oakey and Cooper, 1989). A large element of this rural-urban shift in small firm formation and growth appears to centre on the 'borrowed size' (Alonso, 1973) of certain areas.[1] What all this suggests is that certain peripheral regions may have a better chance of creating and sustaining successful industry clusters than others. Wales, or more correctly, North East and South Wales might be a case in point. To date, South Wales has tended attract cost-minimising investment. Yet its potential accessibility to much of South West England, suggests that there are possibilities to alter its industrial and skills make-up. In a sense the idea of borrowed size underlies perceptions among inward investors of Wales 'as an integral part of the Southern half of Great Britain.' (Cambridge Econometrics, 1990, quoted in Thomas, 1991: 39). This is not just a question of physical accessibility *per se* as the recently announced Lucky Goldstar investment in Wales illustrates. Despite the £120m grant aid associated with the project, it is reported that Goldstar had important reservations about locating its semiconductor plant in Wales, chief among which was the growing skills shortage in Wales. Apparently,

> 'This obstacle was overcome by emphasising the geographical location of Newport next to two Severn bridges and near the intersection of the M4 and M5, which makes movement into and out of England, especially Bristol, London and Birmingham, relatively painless.' (Wilkinson, 1996)

What this illustrates is that there are some limited possibilities for the 'borrowing' of certain skills and expertise from nearby urban areas – notably along the M4 corridor. The ability to 'borrow size' in this way might represent one initial input into the upgrading of industry in the region. In turn this raises issues regarding the connection of policies aimed at particular industries or categories of jobs and transport infrastructure and policy.

---

1   The term 'borrowed size' refers to the phenomenon 'whereby a small city or metropolitan area exhibits some of the characteristics of a larger one if it is near other population concentrations' (Alonso, 1973: 200). One important element of borrowed size derives from the progressive geographical expansion of labour markets (Phelps, 1992a).

Bibliography

Abrahams, P. (1993) 'Health cuts cost jobs and trade, say drugs companies.' *Financial Times*, 14 August, p.22.

Adams, M. (1983) 'Some aspects of foreign direct investment in Wales.' *Cambria* 75–86.

Adams, D., Russell, L. and Taylor-Russell, C. (1994) *Land For Industrial Development.* E & F N Spon, London.

Adburgham, R. (1995a) 'Wales laments a success gone sour.' *Financial Times*, 10 July, p.8.

Adburgham, R. (1995b) 'Grundig moves output to Wales.' *Financial Times*, 17 August, p.6.

Adburgham, R. and Parker, G. (1996) 'Row as £13m grant lures motor parts company to Wales.' *Financial Times*, 8 March, p.18.

Albrechts, L. and Swyngedouw, E. (1989) 'The challenges for regional policy under a flexible regime of accumulation.' In L. Albrechts, F. Moulaert, P. Roberts and E. Swyngedouw (eds) *Regional Policy at the Crossroads: European Perspectives.* Jessica Kingsley, London.

Alonso, W. (1973) 'Urban zero population growth.' *Daedalus 102*, 191–206.

Amin, A., Bradley, D., Gentle, C., Howells, J. and Tomaney, J. (1994) 'Regional incentives and the quality of mobile investment in the less favoured regions of the EC.' *Progress in Planning 41*, 1–112.

Amin, A., Charles, D. and Howells, J. (1992) 'Corporate restructuring and cohesion in the new Europe.' *Regional Studies 26*, 319–331.

Amin, A. and Malmberg, A. (1992) 'Competing structural and institutional influences on the geography of production in Europe.' *Environment & Planning A 24*, 401–416.

Amin, A. and Robins, K. (1990) 'The re-emergence of regional economies? The mythical geography of flexible accumulation.' *Environment & Planning D, Society & Space 8*, 7–34.

Amin, A. and Thrift, N. (1994) 'Living in the global.' In A. Amin and N. Thrift (eds) *Globalization, Institutions and Regional Development in Europe.* Oxford University Press, Oxford.

Amin, A. and Thrift, N. (1995) 'Institutional issues for the European regions: from markets and plans to socioeconomics and powers of association.' *Economy & Society 24*, 41–66.

BP (1990) *BP Annual Reports and Accounts.* British Petroleum Plc, London.

BP (1991) *BP Financial and Operating Information 1987–1991.* British Petroleum Plc, London.

BP (1994) *Annual Reports and Accounts.* British Petroleum Plc, London.

Bachtler, J., Clement, K. and Raines, P. (1993) 'European integration and foreign investment: the regional implications.' In L. Lundqvist and L.O. Persson (eds) *Visions and Strategies in European Integration: a North European Perspective.* Springer Verlag, London.

Baden-Fuller, C. and Stopford, J. (1988) 'Regional level competition in a mature industry: the case of European domestic appliances.' In J. Dunning and P. Robson (eds) *Multinationals and the European Community.* Blackwell, Oxford.

Bailey, D., Harte, G. and Sugden, R. (1994) *Transnationals and Governments: Recent Policies in Japan, France, Germany, the United States and Britain.* Routledge, London.

Balasubramanyam, V.N. and Greenaway, D. (1992) 'Economic integration and foreign direct investment: Japanese investment in the EC.' *Journal of Common Market Studies 30,* 175–194.

Barnes, I. and Barnes, P.M. (1995) *The Enlarged European Union.* Longman, London.

Blalock, H. (1979) *Social Statistics.* McGraw-Hill, London.

Boddewyn, J.J. and Grosse, R. (1995) 'American marketing in the European Union: standardization's uneven progress (1973–1993).' *European Journal of Marketing 29,* 23–42.

Bostock, F. and Jones, G. (1994) 'Foreign multinationals in British Manufacturing, 1850–1962.' *Business History 36,* (1): 89–126.

Britton, J. (1976) 'The influence of corporate organisation and ownership on the linkages of industrial plants: a Canadian enquiry.' *Economic Geography 52,* 311–324.

Britton, J. and Gilmour, I. (1978) *The Weakest Link – A Technological Perspective on Canadian Industrial Development.* Background Study 43, Science Council of Canada.

Brusco, S. (1982) 'The Emilian model: productive decentralisation and social integration.' *Cambridge Journal of Economics 6,* 167–184.

Buckley, P.J. and Artisien, P. (1988) 'Policy issues of intra-EC direct investment: British, French and German multinationals in Greece, Portugal and Spain, with special reference to employment effects.' In J.H. Dunning and P. Robson (eds) *Multinationals and the European Community.* Blackwells, Oxford.

Campbell, D. (1994) 'Foreign investment, labour immobility and the quality of employment.' *International Labour Review 133,* 185–204.

Cantwell, J. (1988) 'The reorganization of European industries after integration: selected evidence on the role of multinational enterprise activities.' In J. Dunning and P. Robson (eds) *Multinationals and the European Community.* Blackwells, Oxford.

Cantwell, J. (1995) 'The globalisation of technology: what remains of the product cycle model?' *Cambridge Journal of Economics 19,* 155–174.

CEC (1988) 'The economics of 1992.' *European Economy 35.*

CEC (1990) 'The impact of the internal market by industrial sector: the challenge for the member states.' *European Economy Special Edition.*

CEC (1991) *Europe 2000: Outlook for the Development of the Community's Territory.* Commission of the European Communities, Brussels.

CEC (1993) 'New location factors for mobile investment in Europe.' *Regional Development Studies 6.* Commission of the European Communities, Brussels.

CEC (1994a) 'Competition and integration: Community merger control policy.' *European Economy 57.*

CEC (1994b) *The Community Internal Market: 1993 Report.* Commission of the European Communities, Brussels.

Charles, D., Monk, P. and Sciberras, E. (1989) *Technology and Competition in the International Telecommunications Industry.* Pinter, London.

Cheshire, P.C. (1995) 'European integration and regional responses.' In M. Rhodes (ed) *The Regions and the New Europe: Patterns in Core and Periphery Development.* Manchester University Press, Manchester.

Chisholm, M. (1995) *Britain on the Edge of Europe.* Routledge, London.

Clark, C., Wilson, R. and Bradley, J. (1969) 'Industrial location and economic potential in Western Europe.' *Regional Studies 3,* 197–212.

Clark, G. (1994) 'Strategy and structure: corporate restructuring and the scope and characteristics of sunk costs.' *Environment & Planning A 26*, 9–32.

Clark, G. and Wrigley, N. (1995) 'Sunk costs: a framework for economic geography.' *Transactions of the Institute of British Geographers NS 20*, 204–223.

Clarke, M. and Beaney, P. (1993) 'Between autonomy and dependence: corporate strategy, plant status, local agglomeration in the Scottish electronics industry.' *Environment & Planning A 25*, 213–232.

Collins, K. and Schmenner, R. (1995) 'Taking manufacturing advantage of Europe's single market.' *European Management Journal 13*, 257–268.

Cooke, P. (1992) 'Regional innovation systems: competitive regulation in the new Europe.' *Geoforum 23*, 365–382.

Cooke, P. and Morgan, K. (1992) *Regional Innovation Centres in Europe: The Experience of the Basque Country, Emilia Romagna and Wales*. Regional Industrial Research Report, Department of City and Regional Planning, University of Wales College of Cardiff.

Cooke, P. and Morgan. K. (1993) 'The network paradigm: new departures in corporate and regional development.' *Environment & Planning D, Society & Space 11*, 543–564.

Cooke, P., Price, A. and Morgan, K. (1995) 'Regulating regional economies: Wales and Baden-Wurttemburg in Transition.' In M. Rhodes (ed) *The Regions and the New Europe: Patterns in Core and Periphery Development*. Manchester University Press, Manchester.

Cooke, P. and Wells, P. (1992) *Global Localisation*. UCL Press, London.

Cox, K. and Mair, A. (1988) 'Locality and community in the politics of local economic development.' *Annals of the Association of American Geographers 78*, 307–325.

Cox, K. and Mair, A. (1991) 'From localised social structures to localities as agents.' *Environment and Planning A 23*, 197–213.

Crowther, P. and Garrahan, P. (1988) 'Corporate power and the local economy.' *Industrial Relations Journal 19*, 51–59.

Cutler, T., Williams, K., Williams, J. and Haslam, C. (1989) *1992: The Struggle For Europe*. Berg, Oxford.

Davies, G. (1978) *West German Direct Investment in Wales: a Promising Start*. Development Corporation for Wales, Cardiff.

Davies, G. and Thomas, I. (1976) *Overseas Investment in Wales: the Welcome Invasion*. Swansea.

Davies, J. (1996) '£25m plant tribute to workforce.' *Western Mail*, 8 March, p.15.

Dicken, P. (1988) 'The changing geography of Japanese foreign direct investment in manufacturing industry: a global perspective.' *Environment & Planning A 20*, 633–653.

Dicken, P. (1992) *Global Shift*. Paul Chapman Publishers, London.

Dicken, P. (1994) 'Global – local tensions: firms and states in the global space economy.' *Economic Geography 70*, 101–128.

Dicken, P. and Lloyd, P. (1976) 'Geographical perspectives on United States investment in the United Kingdom.' *Environment & Planning A 8*, 685–705.

Dicken, P. and Lloyd, P. (1980) 'Patterns and processes of change in the spatial distribution of foreign-controlled manufacturing employment in the United Kingdom, 1963 to 1975.' *Environment & Planning A 12*, 1405–1426.

Dicken, P. and Oberg, S. (1996) 'The global context: Europe in a world of dynamic economic and population change.' *European Urban and Regional Research 3*, 101–120.

Dore, R. (1986) 'Goodwill and the spirit of market capitalism.' *British Journal of Sociology 34*, 459–482.

Dun and Bradstreet Ltd (1994) *Who Owns Whom*. Holmer's Farm Way, High Wycombe, Buckinghamshire HP12 4UL.

Dunford, M. (1994) 'Winners and losers: the new map of economic inequality in the European Union.' *European Urban & Regional Studies 1*, 95–114.

Dunning, J.H. (1958) *American Investment in British Manufacturing Industry*. George Allen, London.

Dunning, J. (1979) 'Explaining changing patterns of international production: in defence of the eclectic theory.' *Oxford Bulletin of Economics and Statistics 41*, 269–295.

Dunning, J. and Robson, P. (1988) 'Multinational corporate integration and regional economic integration.' In J. Dunning and P. Robson (eds) *Multinationals and the European Community*. Blackwells, Oxford.

Encarnation, D. and Mason, M. (1994) 'Does ownership matter? Answers and implications for Europe and America.' In M. Mason and D. Encarnation (eds) *Does Ownership Matter? Japanese Multinationals in Europe*. Clarendon Press, Oxford.

O'Farrell, P.N. and O'Loughlin, B. (1981) 'New industry input linkages in Ireland: an econometric analysis.' *Environment and Planning A 13*, 285–308.

Fothergill, S. and Guy, N. (1992) *Retreat from the Regions: Corporate Change and the Closure of Factories*. Jessica Kingsley, London.

Franko, L. (1976) *The European Multinational: A Renewed Challenge to American and British Big Business*. Harper and Row, London.

Frobel, F., Heinrichs, J. and Kreye, O. (1980) *The New International Division of Labour*. Cambridge University Press, Cambridge.

Geroski, P. (1989) 'The choice between diversity and scale.' In J. Kay (ed) *1992: Myths and Realities*. London Business School, London.

Gertler, M. (1988) 'The limits to flexibility: comments on the post-Fordist version of productivity and its geography.' *Transactions of the Istitute of British Geographers NS 14*, 109–112.

Gertler, M. (1989) 'Resurrecting flexibility? A reply to Schoenberger.' *Transactions of the Institute of British Geographers NS 14*, 109–112.

Gertler, M. (1992) 'Flexibility revisited: districts, nation-states, and the forces of production.' *Transactions of the Institute of British Geographers NS 17*, 259–278.

Gertler, M. and Schoenberger, E. (1992) 'Industrial restructuring and continental trade blocs: the European Community and North America.' *Environment & Planning A 24*, 2–10.

Gibb, R. (1994) 'Regionalism in the world economy.' In R. Gibb and W. Michalak (eds) *Continental Trading Blocs: The Growth of Regionalism in The World Economy*. John Wiley, Chichester.

Gibb, R. and Michalak, W. (1994) 'Conclusion: regionalism in perspective.' In R. Gibb and W. Michalak (eds) *Continental Trading Blocs: The Growth of Regionalism in The World Economy*. John Wiley, Chichester.

Glasmeier, A. (1988) 'Factors governing the development of high tech industry agglomerations: a tale of three cities.' *Regional Studies 22*, 287–302.

Glyn, A., Hughes, A., Lipietz, A. and Singh, A. (1990) 'The rise and fall of the golden age.' In S.A. Marglin and J.B. Schor (eds) *The Golden Age of Capitalism: Reinterpreting the Postwar Experience*. Clarendon Press, Oxford.

Gold, B. (1981) 'Changing perspectives on size, scale and returns: an interpretive survey.' *Journal of Economic Literature 19*, 5–33.

Goodhart, D. (1993) 'Social dumping – hardly an open and shut case.' *Financial Times*, 4 February, p.2.

Granovetter, M. (1985) 'Economic action and social structure: the problem of embeddedness.' *American Journal of Sociology 91*, 481–510.

Gribben, R. (1993) 'Hitachi plant closure attacked.' *Daily Telegraph*, 23 September, p.22.

Griffiths, J. (1995a) 'Exide seals deal for control of leading acid battery maker.' *Financial Times*, 9 March, p.36.

Griffiths, J. (1995b) 'Exide to shut many factories in Europe.' *Financial Times*, 26 September, p.18.

Guido, G. (1991) 'Implementing a pan European marketing strategy.' *Long Range Planning 24*, 23–33.

Harding, A. (1991) 'The rise of urban growth coalitions UK-style.' *Environment and Planning C, Government and Policy 9*, 295–317.

Harvey, D. (1982) *The Limits to Capital*. Blackwell, Oxford.

Harvey, D. (1985) *The Urbanisation of Capital*. Blackwell, Oxford.

Haug, P., Hood, N. and Young, S. (1983) 'R&D intensity in the affiliates of US owned electronics companies manufacturing in Scotland.' *Regional Studies 17*, 383–392.

Hayter, R. (1982) 'Truncation, the international firm and regional policy.' *Area 14*, 277–282.

Heitger, B. and Stehn, J. (1990) 'Japanese direct investments in the EC – response to the internal market 1993?' *Journal of Common Market Studies 29*, 1–16.

Henderson, D. (1994) *Supporting Regional Innovation: An Evaluation of the WDA Strategy*. Unpublished MSc Dissertation, Department of City and Regional Planning, University of Wales College of Cardiff.

Hill, S. and Roberts, A. (1993) 'Why Wales? The competitive advantage.' *Welsh Economic Review, Special Issue: Inward Investment in Wales*, 18–22.

Hill, S. and Roberts, A. (1995) 'Inward investment, local linkages and regional development.' Paper presented to the 26th *Annual Conference of the Regional Science Association International British and Irish Section*, Cardiff, September 12–15.

Hill, S. and Munday, M. (1991) 'The determinants of inward investment: a Welsh analysis.' *Applied Economics 23*, 1761–1769.

Hine, R. (1985) *The Political Economy of European Trade*. Harvester Wheatsheaf, Brighton.

Hirst, P. and Thompson, G. (1992) 'The problem of "globalization": international economic relations, national economic management and the formation of trading blocs.' *Economy & Society 21*, 355–396.

Hirst, P. and Thompson, G. (1994) 'Globalization, foreign direct investment and international economic governance.' *Organization 1*, 277–303.

Hirst, P. and Thompson, G. (1995) 'Globalization and the future of the nation state.' *Economy & Society 24*, 408–442.

Hitachi (1993) *Annual Report*. Hitachi, Tokyo.

Hitachi (1994) *Annual Report*. Hitachi, Tokyo.

Hodder, R. (1994) 'The West Pacific rim.' In Gibb and Michalak (eds) *Continental Trading Blocs: The Growth of Regionalism in The World Economy*. John Wiley, Chichester.

Holmes, P. (1989) 'Economies of scale, expectations and Europe 1992.' *The World Economy 12*, 525–537.

Hood, N. and Young, S. (1976) 'US investment in Scotland – aspects of the branch factory syndrome.' *Scottish Journal of Political Economy 33*, 279–294.

Hood, N. and Young, S. (1983) *Multinational Investment Strategies in the British Isles*. HMSO, London.

Hood, N. and Young, S. (1988) 'Inward investment and the EC: UK evidence on corporate integration strategies.' In J. Dunning and P. Robson (eds) *Multinationals and the European Community.* Blackwell, Oxford.

Hymer, S. (1979) 'The multinational corporation and the law of uneven development.' In R. Cohen *et al.* (eds) *The Multinational Corporation.* Cambridge University Press, Cambridge.

Ietto-Gillies, G. (1993) 'Transnational corporations and UK competitiveness: Does ownership matter?' In K. Hughes (ed) *The Future of UK Competitiveness and the Role of Industrial Policy.* Policy Studies Institute, London.

Jackson, A. and Reeves, R. (1985) 'US drug company to close factory.' *Financial Times,* 28 November, p.8.

Jacquemin, A. and Sapir, A. (1988) 'European integration or world integration.' *Weltwirtschaftliches Archiv 124,* 127–139.

Jessop, B. (1994) 'Post-Fordism and the State.' In A. Amin (ed) *Post-Fordism: A Reader.* Blackwells, Oxford.

Jones, N. (1993a) 'Valley gloom as 390 jobs set to be axed.' *Western Mail* 3 March, p.15.

Jones, N. (1993b) 'Wella moves back to its roots.' *Western Mail,* 10 December, p.13.

Jones, N. (1994) 'Stunned workers fear worse is to come.' *Western Mail,* 13 January, p.3.

Jones, N. (1995) 'Exide to create 200 jobs.' *Western Mail,* 19 June, p.12.

Kay, J. (1989) 'Myths and realities.' In J. Kay (ed) *1992: Myths and Realities.* London Business School, London.

Keeble, D., Owens, P. and Thompson, C. (1982) 'Regional accessibility and economic potential in the European Community.' *Regional Studies 16,* 419–431.

Keeble, D., Offord, J. and Walker, S. (1988) *Peripheral Regions in a Community of Twelve Member States.* Office for Official Publications of the European Communities, Luxembourg.

Keeble, D. and Tyler, P. (1995) 'Enterprising behaviour and the urban-rural shift.' *Urban Studies 32,* 975–997.

Kozul-Wright, R. (1995) 'Transnational corporations and the nation state' 135–171. In J. Michie and J. Grieve-Smith (eds) *Managing the Global Economy.* O.U.P., Oxford.

Krugman, P. (1996) *Pop Internationalism.* MIT Press, Cambridge, Mass.

Krum, J.R. (1991) 'Europe 1992: strategic marketing issues for American multinationals.' *European Business Journal 3,* 39–47.

Lever, W. (1995) 'The European regional dimension.' In W. Lever and A. Bailly (eds) *The Spatial Impact of Economic Changes in Europe.* Avebury, Aldershot.

Lewis, D. (1995) *Entrenched Investments? Foreign Owned Companies, Aftercare Policies and Regional Development in Wales.* Unpublished MSc Dissertation, Department of City and Regional Planning, University of Wales College of Cardiff.

Lipietz, A. (1987) *Mirages and Miracles: The Crises of Global Fordism.* Verso, London.

Lovering, J. (1996) 'New myths of the Welsh economy.' *Planet 116,* 6–16.

McAleese, D. and McDonald, D. (1978) 'Employment growth and the development of linkages in foreign-owned and domestic manufacturing enterprises.' *Oxford Bulletin of Economics and Statistics 40,* 321–340.

McDermott, P. (1976) 'Ownership, organisation and regional dependence in the Scottish electronics industry.' *Regional Studies 10,* 319–335.

Mair, A. (1993) 'New growth poles? Just-in-time manufacturing and local economic strategy.' *Regional Studies 27,* 207–221.

Marshall, J.N. (1979) 'Ownership, organisation and industrial linkage: a case study in the northern region of England.' *Regional Studies 13*, 531–557.

Martin, R. and Sunley, P. (1995) 'Paul Krugman's geographical economics and its implications for regional development theory: a critical assessment.' Paper presented to the *Annual Conference of the Institute of British Geographers*, Newcastle-upon-Tyne, January.

Massey, D. (1979) 'In what sense a regional problem?' *Regional Studies 13*, 233–243.

Massey, D. (1984) *Spatial Divisions of Labour*. MacMillan, London.

Mayes, D. (1978) 'The effects of economic integration on trade.' *Journal of Common Market Studies 17*, 1–25.

Middlemas, K. (1995) *Orchestrating Europe: The Informal Politics of European Union 1973–95*. Fontana Press, London.

Millington, A. and Bayliss, B. (1996) 'Corporate integration and market liberalisation in the EU.' *European Management Journal 14*, 139–150.

Milne, S. (1990) 'New forms of manufacturing and their spatial implications.' *Environment & Planning A 22*, 211–232.

Molle, W. and Morsink, R. (1991) 'Intra-European direct investment.' In B. Burgenmeier and J. Mucchielli (eds) *Multinationals and Europe 1992*. Routledge, London.

Molotch, H. (1976) 'The city as a growth machine: toward a political economy of place.' *American Journal of Sociology 82*, 309–331.

Monopolies and Mergers Commission (1990) *BICC Plc and Sterling Greengate Cable Company Ltd: A Report on the Merger Situation*. HMSO, London.

Morgan, B. (1993) 'Inward investment: the economic impact.' *Welsh Economic Review, Special Issue: Inward Investment in Wales*, 13–17.

Morgan, K. (1991) 'Competition and collaboration in the electronics industry: what are the prospects for Britain.' *Environment and Planning A 23*, 1459–1482.

Morgan, K. (1992) 'Innovating by networking: new models of corporate and regional development.' In M. Dunford and G. Kafkalas (1992) *Cities and Regions in the New Europe: the Global-Local Interplay and Spatial Strategies*. Belhaven Press, London.

Morgan, K. (1996) *The Regional Animateur: Taking Stock of the Welsh Development Agency*. Papers in Planning Research No., Department of City and Regional Planning, University of Wales College of Cardiff.

Morgan, K. and Rees, G. (1995) *Vocational Skills and Economic Development: Building a Robust Training System in Wales*. Occasional Papers in Planning Research, Department of City and Regional Planning, University of Wales College of Cardiff.

Morgan, K. and Sayer, A. (1985) 'A "modern" industry in a "mature" region: the remaking of management-labour relations.' *International Journal of Urban & Regional Research 9*, 383–404.

Morris, J. (1987) 'Industrial restructuring, foreign direct investment, and uneven development: the case of Wales.' *Environment & Planning A 19*, 205–224.

Morris, J. *et al.* (1993) 'Flexible internationalisation in the electronics industry: implications for regional economies.' *Environment & Planning C, Government & Policy 10*, 407–421.

Morris, J., Munday, M. and Wilkinson, B. (1993) *Working For the Japanese: the Economic and Social Consequences of Japanese Investment in Wales*. Athlone Press, London.

Munday, M. (1990) *Japanese Manufacturing Investment in Wales*. University of Wales Press, Cardiff.

Munday, M. (1995) 'The regional consequences of the Japanese second wave: a case study.' *Local Economy 10*, (1), 4–20.

Munday, M., Morris, J. and Wilkinson, B. (1995) 'Factories or Warehouses? A Welsh Perspective on Japanese Transplant Manufacturing.' *Regional Studies 29*, 1–18.

National Industrial Development Council of Wales and Monmouthshire (1937) *Second Industrial Survey of South Wales, Volume 3*. University Press Board, Cardiff.

Oakey, R.P. and Cooper, S.Y. (1989) 'High technology industry, agglomeration and the potential for peripherally sited small firms.' *Regional Studies 23*, 347–360.

Oakey, R., Thwaites, A. and Nash, P. (1982) 'Technological change and regional development: some evidence on regional variations in product and process innovation.' *Environment & Planning A 14*, 995–1036.

Ohmae, K. (1993) 'The rise of the region state.' *Foreign Affairs 72*, 78–87.

Owens, P. (1980) 'Direct foreign investment – some spatial implications for the source economy.' *Tijdschrift voor Economische en Sociale Geografie 71*, 50–62.

Ozawa, T. (1991) 'Japanese multinationals and 1992.' In B. Burgenmeier and J. Muchielli (eds) *Multinationals and Europe 1992: Strategies For the Future*. Routledge, London.

Panditharatna, A. and Phelps, N. (1995) 'A new industry in an older industrial region: skills, technology and linkages.' *Local Economy 9*, 341–353.

Parkes, C. (1992) 'Grundig to shed 3,000 German jobs.' *Financial Times*, 7 July, p.3.

Peck, F. (1996) 'Regional development and the production of space: the role of infrastructure in the attraction of new inward investment.' *Environment & Planning A 28*, 327–339.

Peck, F. and Stone, I. (1993) 'Japanese inward investment in the northeast of England: reassessing "Japanisation".' *Environment and Planning C, Government and Policy 11*, 55–67.

Peck, J. and Tickell, A. (1994) 'Searching for a new institutional fix: the after-Fordist crisis and the global-local disorder.' In A. Amin (ed) *Post-Fordism: A Reader*. Blackwells, Oxford.

Perrons, D. (1981) 'The role of Ireland in the New International Division of Labour: a proposed framework for regional analysis.' *Regional Studies 15*, 81–100.

Petri, P.A. (1994) 'The regional clustering of foreign direct investment and trade.' *Transnational Corporations 3*, (3), 1–24.

Phelps, N.A. (1992a) 'External economies, agglomeration and flexible accumulation.' *Transactions of the Institute of British Geographers NS 17*, 35–46.

Phelps, N.A. (1992b) 'From local economic dependence to local economic development? The case of the Scottish electronics industry.' *Papers in Planning Research* No.136, Department of City and Regional Planning, University of Wales College of Cardiff.

Phelps, N.A. (1993a) 'Branch plants and the evolving spatial division of labour: a study of material linkage change in the northern region of England.' *Regional Studies 27*, 87–102.

Phelps, N.A. (1993b) 'Contemporary industrial restructuring and linkage change in an older industrial region: examples from the northeast of England.' *Environment & Planning A 25*, 863–882.

Phelps, N.A. (1995) 'Regional variations in rates and sources of innovation: evidence from the electronics industry in South Wales and Hampshire-Berkshire.' *Area 27*, (4), 347–357.

Phelps, N.A. (1997) 'Industry embeddedness: a review of literature with illustrations from Wales.' Papers in Planning Research No.162, Department of City and Regional Planning, University of Wales College of Cardiff.

Piore, M. and Sabel, C. (1984) *The Second Industrial Divide*. Basic Books, New York.

Porter, M. (1990) *The Competitive Advantage of Nations*. MacMillan, London.

Potter, J. (1995) 'Branch plant economies and flexible specialisation: evidence from Devon and Cornwall.' *Tijdschrift voor Economische en Sociale Geografie 86*, 162–176.

Pounce, R. (1981) *Industrial Movement in the United Kingdom, 1966–75.* HMSO, London.

Pred, A. (1976) *City Systems in Advanced Economies.* Hutchinson, London.

Price, A., Cooke, P. and Morgan, K. (1994) *The Welsh Renaissance: Inward Investment and Industrial Innovation.* Regional Industrial Research Report No. 14, Centre for Advanced Studies, University of Wales College of Cardiff.

Ramsay, H. (1995) 'Le defi Europeen: multinational restructuring, labour and EU policy.' In A. Amin and J. Tomaney (eds) *Behind the Myth of the European Union: Prospects for Cohesion.* Routledge, London.

Rees, G. and Morgan, K. (1991) 'Industrial restructuring, innovation systems and the regional state: South Wales in the 1990s.' In G. Day and G. Rees (eds) *Regions, Nations and European Integration: Remaking the Celtic Periphery.* University of Wales Press, Cardiff.

Rees, G. and Thomas, M. (1994) 'Inward investment, labour market adjustment and skills development: recent experience in South Wales.' *Local Economy 9,* 48–61.

Rhodes, M. (1995) 'Conclusion: the viability of regional strategies.' In M. Rhodes (ed) *The Regions and the New Europe: Patterns in Core and Periphery Development.* Manchester university Press, Manchester.

Rimmer, P.J. (1994) 'Regional economic integration in Pacific Asia.' *Environment & Planning A 26,* 1731–1759.

Roberts, E. (1995) 'Factory to close down.' Western Mail, 1 April, p.15.

Robson, P. (1987) *The Economics of International Integration.* Allen & Unwin, London.

Roth, K. and Morrison, A.J. (1992) 'Implementing global strategy: characteristics of global subsidiary mandates.' *Journal of International Business Studies 23,* 715–735.

Rozenblat, C. and Pumain, D. (1993) 'The location of multinational firms in the European Urban System.' *Urban Studies 30,* 1691–1709.

Rubery, J. (1994) 'The British production regime: a societal-specific system?' *Economy and Society 23,* 335–354.

Ruigrok, W. and Van Tulder, R. (1996) *The Logic of International Restructuring.* Routledge, London.

Sabel, C. (1989) 'The re-emergence of regional economies.' In P. Hirst and J. Zeitlin (eds) *Reversing Industrial Decline?* Berg, Oxford.

Sapir, A. (1993) 'Regionalism and the new theory of international trade: do the bells toll for the GATT? A European outlook.' *The World Economy 16,* 423–438.

Saxenien, A. (1992) 'Contrasting patterns of business organisation in Silicon Valley.' *Environment and Planning D, Society & Space 10,* 377–392.

Sayer, A. (1982) 'Explanation in economic geography: abstraction versus generalisation.' *Progress in Human Geography 6,* 68–88.

Sayer, A. (1985) 'Industry and space a sympathetic critique of radical research.' *Enironment & Planning D, Society & Space 3,* 3–29.

Sayer, A. and Morgan, K. (1986) 'A modern industry in a declining region: links between method, theory and policy.' In D. Massey and R. Meegan (eds) *Politics and Method.* Methuen, London.

Scherer, F.M., Beckenstein, A., Kaufer, E., Murphy, R.D. and Bougeon-Masson, F. (1975) *The Economics of Multiplant Operations: an International Comparisons Study.* Harvard University Press, Cambridge, Mass.

Schoenberger, E. (1988) 'Thinking about flexibility: a response to Gertler.' *Transactions of the Institute of British Geographers NS 14,* 98–108.

Schoenberger, E. (1991) 'The corporate interview as a research method in economic geography.' *Professional Geographer 43,* 180–189.

Schott, M. (1991) 'Trading blocs and the world trading system.' *The World Economy 14*, 1–18.

Scott, A.J. (1983) 'Industrial organisation and the logic of intra-metropolitan location i: theoretical considerations.' *Economic Geography 59*, 233–250.

Scott, A.J. (1986) 'Industrial organisation and location: division of labour, the firm, and spatial process.' *Economic Geography 62*, 215–231.

Scott, A.J. (1988) 'Flexible production systems and regional development: the rise of new industrial spaces in North America and Western Europe.' *International Journal of Urban & Regional Research 12*, 171–186.

Scott, A.J. and Paul, A. (1990) 'Collective order and economic coordination in industrial agglomerations: the technopoles of southern California.' *Environment & Planning C, Government & Policy 8*, 179–193.

Simpson, D. (1987) *Manufacturing Industry in Wales: Prospects for Employment Growth.* Wales TUC, Cardiff.

De Smidt, M. (1992) 'International investments and the European Challenge.' *Environment & Planning A 24*, 83–94.

Smith, A. (1995) 'The principles and practice of regional economic integration.' In V. Cable and D. Henderson (eds) *Trade Blocs? The Future of Regional Integration.* RIA, London.

Smith, M. (1988) 'Pharmaceutical firm changes to cost jobs.' *Western Mail*, 2 July, p.5.

Stewart, J.C. (1976) 'Linkages and foreign investment.' *Regional Studies 10*, 245–258.

Stone, I. and Peck, F. (1996) 'The foreign-owned manufacturing sector in UK peripheral regions, 1978–1993: restructuring and comparative performance.' *Regional Studies 30*, 55–68.

Storper, M. (1992) 'The limits to globalisation: technology districts and international trade.' *Economic Geography 68*, 60–93.

Storper, M. (1995) 'The resurgence of regional economies, ten years later: the region as a nexus of untraded interdependencies.' *European Urban and Regional Studies 2*, 191–222.

Storper, M. and Harrison, B. (1991) 'Flexibility, hierarchy and regional development: The changing structure of industrial production systems and their forms of governance in the 1990s.' *Research Policy 20*, 407–422.

Storper, M. and Walker, R. (1989) *The Capitalist Imperative.* Blackwells, Oxford.

Streeten, P. (1992) 'Interdependence and integration of the world economy: the role of states and firms.' *Transnational Corporations 1*, 125–136.

Swyngedouw, E. (1992) 'The mammon quest. "Glocalisation", interspatial competition and the monetary order: the construction of new spatial scales.' In M. Dunford and G. Kafkalas (eds) *Cities and Regions in the New Europe: the Global-Local Interplay and Spatial Development Strategies.* Belhaven, London.

Taylor, M. (1986) 'The product cycle model: a critique.' *Environment & Planning A 18*, 751–761.

Taylor, J. (1993) 'An analysis of the factors determining the geographical distribution of Japanese manufacturing investment in the UK, 1984–91.' *Urban Studies 30*, 1209–1224.

Taylor, R. (1993a) 'Hoover outlines agreement to save Glasgow plant.' *Financial Times*, 26 January, p.6.

Taylor, R. (1993b) 'Nestlé job sweetener in Dijon is a bitter taste for Glasgow.' *Financial Times*, 5 February, p.14.

Teague, P. (1994) 'Governance structures and economic performance: the case of Northern Ireland.' *International Journal of Urban & Regional Research 18*, 275–292.

Thomas, D. (1991) 'The Welsh economy: current circumstances and future prospects.' In G. Day and G. Rees (eds) *Regions, Nations and European Integration: Remaking the Celtic Periphery.* University of Wales Press, Cardiff.

Thomas, D. (1992) 'Wales in 1990: an economic survey.' In G. Day and G. Rees (eds) *Contemporary Wales Vol. 5*, University of Wales Press, Cardiff.

Thomas, D. (1996) 'Winner or loser in the new Europe? Regional funding, inward investment and prospects for the Welsh economy.' *European Urban and Regional Studies* (forthcoming).

Thomsen, S. (1993) 'Japanese direct investment in the European Community: the product cycle revisited.' *The World Economy 16*, 301–315.

Thomsen, S. (1995) 'Regional integration and multinational production.' In V. Cable and D. Henderson (eds) *Trade Blocs? The Future of Regional Integration.* RIA, London.

Thomsen, S. and Woolcock, S. (1993) *Direct Investment and European Integration.* RIA/Pinter, London.

Thwaites, A.T. (1978) 'Technological change, mobile plants and regional development.' *Regional Studies 12*, 445–461.

Tomaney, J. (1995) 'Recent developments in Irish industrial policy.' *European Planning Studies 3*, 99–113.

Tsoukalis, L. (1994) *The New European Economy.* O.U.P., Oxford.

Turok, I. (1993) 'Inward investment and local linkages: How deeply embedded is "Silicon Glen".' *Regional Studies 27*, 401–417.

UNCTAD (1994) *World Investment Report 1994: Transnational Corporations, Employment and the Workplace.* United Nations, Geneva.

Vaessen, P. and Keeble, D. (1995) 'Growth oriented SMEs in unfavourable regional environments.' *Regional Studies 29*, 489–505.

Vernon, R. (1966) 'International investment and international trade and the product cycle.' *Quarterly Journal of Economics 80*, 190–207.

Vernon, R. (1979) 'the product cycle hypothesis in a new international environment.' *Oxford Bulletin of Economics & Statistics 41*, 255–268.

Wales TUC, (1989) *1992: The Economic Impact on Wales.* Wales TUC, Cardiff.

Wales TUC (1990) *Down and Out in the New Europe.* Wales TUC, Cardiff.

Walker, R. (1989) 'A requiem for corporate geography: new directions in industrial organisation, the production of place and the uneven development.' *Geografiska Annaler B 71*, 43–88.

Walsh, F. (1996) 'Enter the dragon: how Wales is stealing a march on Asia.' *Sunday Express*, 28 April, p.62.

Warner-Lambert (1991) *Annual Report and Accounts.* Warner-Lambert, Morris Plains, NJ, USA.

Warner-Lambert (1993) *Annual Report and Accounts.* Warner-Lambert, Morris Plains, NJ, USA.

Watts, H.D. (1980) 'The location of European direct investment in the United Kingdom.' *Tijdschrift voor Economische en Sociale Geografie 1*, 3–14.

Watts, H.D. (1991) 'Plant closures, multilocational firms, and the urban economy: Sheffield, U.K.' *Environment & Planning A 23*, 37–58.

Watts, H.D. and Stafford, H.A. (1986) 'Plant closure and the multiplant firm: some conceptual issues.' *Progress in Human Geography 10*, 206–227.

Weber, A. (1929), Friedrich, C.J. (Trans.) *Theory of the Location of Industries.* University of Chicago Press, London.

Wella, A.G. (1995) *The Business Year 1994.* Wella AG, Darmstadt, Germany.

Welsh Affairs Committee (1988) *Inward Investment into Wales and its Interaction with Regional and EEC Policies, Vol. 1.* HMSO, London.

Welsh Affairs Committee (1995) *Wales in Europe, Vol. 2.* HMSO, London.

Welsh Council (1971) *Wales and the Common Market.* Welsh Council, Cardiff.

Welsh Office (1967) *Wales: The Way Ahead.* Cmnd. 3334, HMSO.

Whitley, R. (1992a) 'Societies, firms and markets: the social structuring of business systems.' In R. Whitley (ed) *European Business Systems: Firms and Markets in Their National Contexts.* Sage, London.

Whitley, R. (1992b) 'The comparative study of business systems in Europe: issues and choices.' In R. Whitley (ed) *European Business Systems: Firms and Markets in Their National Contexts.* Sage, London.

Wijkman, P. (1990) 'Patterns of production and trade.' In W. Wallace (ed) *The Dynamics of European Integration.* RIA/Pinter, London.

Wilkinson, S. (1996) 'Lucky for Wales?' *Western Mail,* 13 May, p.10.

Williams, K., Haslam, C. Williams, J., Adcroft, A. and Sukhdev, J. (1991) *Factories or warehouses? Japanese manufacturing FDI in Britain and the US.* Occasional Papers on Business, Economy and Society No. 6, Polytechnic of East London.

Williams, K., Williams, J. and Haslam, C. (1991) 'The hollowing out of British manufacturing and its implications for policy.' *Economy and Society 19,* 456–490.

Williams, R.H. (1993) *Blue Bananas, Grapes and Golden Triangles: Spatial Planning for an Integrated Europe.* Working Paper 19, Department of Town and Country Planning, University of Newcastle-upon-Tyne.

Wood, A. (1993) 'Organising for local economic development: local economic development networks and prospecting for industry.' *Environment & Planning A 25,* 1649–1661.

Yannopoulos, G. (1990) 'Foreign direct investment and European integration: the evidence from the formative years of the European Community.' *Journal of Common Market Studies 28,* 235–260.

Young, S. and Hood, N. (1995) 'Attracting, managing and developing inward investment in the single market.' In A. Amin and J. Tamaney (eds) *Behind the Myth of European Union: Prospects for Cohesion.* London: Routledge. pp.282–304.

Young, S., Hood, N. and Peters, E. (1994) 'Multinational enterprises and regional economic development.' *Regional Studies 28,* 657–677.

Young, S. Hood, N. and Dunlop, S. (1988) 'Global strategies, multinational subsidiary roles and economic impact in Scotland.' *Regional Studies 22,* 487–498.

Zieburra, G. (1982) 'Internationalisation of capital, international division of labour and the role of the European Community.' *Journal of Common Market Studies 21,* 127–139.

Subject Index

References in italic indicate figures or tables.

Author Index